Authorship in Context

Authorship in Context

From the Theoretical to the Material

Edited by

Kyriaki Hadjiafxendi

and

Polina Mackay

First published 2007 by
PALGRAVE MACMILLAN
Houndmills, Basingstoke, Hampshire RG21 6XS and
175 Fifth Avenue, New York, N.Y. 10010
Companies and representatives throughout the world

PALGRAVE MACMILLAN is the global academic imprint of the Palgrave
Macmillan division of St. Martin's Press, LLC and of Palgrave Macmillan Ltd.
Macmillan® is a registered trademark in the United States, United Kingdom
and other countries. Palgrave is a registered trademark in the European
Union and other countries.

ISBN-13: 978–1–4039–4901–1
ISBN-10: 1–4039–4901–8

This book is printed on paper suitable for recycling and made from fully
managed and sustained forest sources.

A catalogue record for this book is available from the British Library.

Library of Congress Cataloging-in-Publication Data
Authorship in context:from the theoretical to the material/edited by
    Kyriaki Hadjiafxendi and Polina Mackay.
        p.   cm.
    Includes bibliographical references and index.
    ISBN 1–4039–4901–8 (cloth)
    1. Authorship. 2. Authorship—Marketing. 3. Literature,
    Modern—20th century—History and criticism. I. Hadjiafxendi, Kyriaki,
    1976– II. Mackay, Polina, 1975–
    PN137.A98 2006
    08′.02—dc28   2006047453

10   9   8   7   6   5   4   3   2   1
16 15 14 13 12 11 10 09 08 07

Printed and bound in Great Britain by
Antony Rowe Ltd, Chippenham and Eastbourne

To Emily and Haralambia

Contents

Part IV   Authorship and Criticism

Acknowledgements

Special thanks go to Isobel Armstrong, John Plunkett and James Mackay, whose insightful comments helped immensely in the development of this book. We also wish to thank Jon Cook, Denise Riley and Sue Wiseman who, through many discussions, aided the shaping of this project. Moreover, we have a collective debt to the School of Literature and Creative Writing at the University of East Anglia, especially to Helen Smith, for assisting in the organization of the 'New Visions: The Writer in Literature and Criticism' Conference (February 2002), which provided the conceptual seeds for this volume. In addition, we are grateful to the journal *Publishing History* for permission to reprint Helen Small's essay; the Estate of Flann O'Brien for permission to publish extracts from his writings for Joseph Brooker's essay; and the M. C. Escher Foundation for permission to use 'Drawing Hands' on the front cover. Finally, our thanks and gratitude go to all contributors who made this book possible.

KYRIAKI HADJIAFXENDI
POLINA MACKAY

Notes on the Contributors

Maria-Sabina Alexandru is Lecturer in Contemporary British and American Studies at the University of Bucharest, Romania. In addition to having articles and a book on postmodernism and postcolonialism published, she has recently completed a second PhD on contemporary Indian fiction in English at the University of East Anglia. She is currently co-editing a volume on post-communist women's literature in Eastern Europe.

Michael Bell is Professor in the Department of English and Comparative Literary Studies at the University of Warwick and a member of Warwick's Centre for Research in Philosophy and Literature. He teaches and writes on topics from Cervantes onwards. His most recent book was *Sentimentalism, Ethics and the Culture of Feeling* (2000) and he is currently completing a book on the study of education, authority and the novel as reflected in the form of the *Bildungsroman*.

Joseph Brooker is Lecturer in Modern and Contemporary Literature at Birkbeck College, London. His books *Joyce's Critics: Transitions in Reading and Culture* and *Flann O'Brien* were respectively published in 2004 and 2005. He co-edited, with Roger Luckhurst, Issue 50 of *New Formations* (2003) on 'Remembering the 1990s', and with Patrick Hanafin and Adam Gearey, a special issue of the *Journal of Law and Society* on 'Law & Literature' (2004). His other publications include essays on Joyce, Beckett, Flann O'Brien, Seamus Heaney, Roddy Doyle, Frank O'Hara and Geoff Dyer.

Terry Eagleton is Professor of Cultural Theory in the Department of English and American Studies at the University of Manchester. He is the author of nearly thirty books, of which the most recent are *After Theory* (2004) and *Myths of Power–Anniversary Edition: A Marxist Study of the Brontës* (2005), and numerous edited collections and articles on critical and cultural theory.

Kyriaki Hadjiafxendi is completing her PhD on George Eliot at the University of East Anglia. Her published work includes articles on nineteenth-century literature, philosophy and print and visual culture. She is the co-editor of three special issues (24.1–24.3) of the *European Journal of American Culture* (2005) on 'The American Culture-Industry of Image-Making'.

Polina Mackay has published work on William Burroughs, punk literature and art, and contemporary southern fiction. Her current project is a book on Burroughs' influence on women writers, artists and performers, entitled *William Burroughs, Women and the Beat Aesthetic*.

David Punter is Professor of English at the University of Bristol, where he is also Research Director for the Faculty of Arts. He has published extensively on Gothic and Romantic literature; on contemporary writing; and on literary theory, psychoanalysis and the postcolonial. His books include *The Literature of Terror* (1980); *The Hidden Script: Writing and the Unconscious* (1985); *The Romantic Unconscious: A Study in Narcissism and Patriarchy* (1989); *Gothic Pathologies: The Text, the Body and the Law* (1998); *Writing the Passions* (2000); and *Postcolonial Imaginings: Fictions of a New World Order* (2000), as well as four small volumes of poetry.

Tatiani G. Rapatzikou is Lecturer in the Department of American Literature and Culture in the School of English at the Aristotle University of Thessaloniki, Greece. She has recently published *Gothic Motifs in the Fiction of William Gibson* (2004) and articles on the technological uncanny and digital culture. She has collaborated with Penguin Classics for the 2003 edition of *Edgar Allan Poe: The Fall of the House of Usher and Other Writings*. With Kyriaki Hadjiafxendi she is co-editor of three special issues of the *European Journal of American Culture* on 'The American Culture-Industry of Image-Making'. Her current research interests focus on American print culture and electronic authorship.

Victor Sage is Professor of English Literature in the School of Literature and Creative Writing at the University of East Anglia. In addition to his book *Le Fanu's Gothic: The Rhetoric of Darkness* (2003), his recent publications include editions of Maturin's *Melmoth the Wanderer* and Sheridan Le Fanu's *Uncle Silas*; and *Good as Her Word: Selected Journalism* (2003), a collection of the critical writings and journalism of Lorna Sage, edited with Sharon Sage. He is currently working on a cultural history of European Gothic.

Helen Small is Fellow and University Lecturer in English Literature at Pembroke College, Oxford. Her books include *Love's Madness: Female Insanity in the Novel and Medicine, 1800–1865* (1996) and (ed.) *The Public Intellectual* (2002). She is currently writing on old age in philosophy and literature.

Introduction: Authorship and its Contexts

> 'And is the *Iliad* possible at all when the printing press and even printing machines exist? Is it not inevitable that with the emergence of the press bar the singing and the telling and the muse cease, that is the conditions necessary for epic poetry disappear?'
>
> — (Marx, 1996, p. 35)

The study of authorship is determined by two interconnected contexts. The first is the changing critical approaches to authorship as a scholarly field; the second is the way that different types of authorship are a product of a variety of literary, technological, cultural and historical conditions. By connecting these two contexts, this collection aims to offer a fresh perspective not only on the way literary scholarship over the past forty years has produced significant shifts in the conception of what it means to author a text, but also on the diversity of authorial practices across fields, ranging from the nineteenth-century literary market-place to postmodern culture. *Authorship in Context: From the Theoretical to the Material* examines the transforming relationship of criticism to the history of authorship in terms of changing theoretical models as well as the conditions behind its evolution. It comprises a series of essays that collectively aim to historicize the different modes of authorship and the principal factors that have fashioned them for the past two centuries.

There are many authorial types. Indeed, the business and practice of authorship almost always involves moving between the demands of different forms of writing, whether criticism, poetry, journalism or theory. What it means to be a critic, literary writer, a journalist or a theorist (among others) is constantly changing, as is the relationship between these literary genres. The central premise of this collection is that authors are fashioned by authorial practices, which are themselves shaped by a range of historical and discursive contexts.[1] Studying the cultural practices by which authors are constructed will help us to understand the principal ways that, over the last two centuries, authorial identities and reading communities have been shaped interactively by the conditions under which texts are produced, disseminated and consumed. *Authorship in Context* differs from other collections that attempt to demonstrate the ways in which authorship can be studied in different contexts. Its difference lies in that it does not treat authorship merely as a process of signification by which a text acquires its meaning through its relationship to its author and reader.[2]

The recent scholarly interest in book and print history has contributed to the redefinition of authorship as a site of material practices.[3] By shifting attention from what it means to author a text to what it means to be in print, such scholarship has pointed to the fact that authorship has many contexts. In addition to the familiar concerns with genre, language and style, context also includes processes of textual production, transmission and reception, varying from the author's act of composition and publishing policies to editorial and reading practices. Robert Darnton has argued that the author is part of a circular literary network that runs 'from the author to the publisher... the printer, the shipper, the bookseller, and the reader' (Darnton, 2002, p. 11). Darnton's system of cultural transmission is part of the scholarly shift from a theoretical to a more historicist appreciation of the conditions that form different types of authorship.

Authorship in Context argues that the conception of authorship diversifies according to the shifts and alterations in print media. We feel that there is a need for the theory of authorship to illustrate the ways in which the perspective it offers on notions such as the self, agency, ownership and authority is elaborated in individual examples, which are not always author-orientated or periodized. This collection provides a historical and conceptual map of the changes in the conception of authorship and its field of study, thereby provoking questions and further research into the contradictions as well as the overlaps that emerge from the crossovers between print culture and literary scholarship.

The role of print media in changing conceptions of authorship is signalled in the epigraph from Karl Marx's *Grundrisse* (1866), entitled 'Uneven Character of Historical Development and Questions of Art'. Marx suggests that the advent of printing technology in the fifteenth century gave birth to the modern author and reader at the cost of the death of an inspirational tradition of classical and medieval literature. The transition from the Middle Ages to modernity involved a violent and silencing process of transformation of voice into the graphic text, during which oral cultural forms lost their status within a growing media-saturated society. Marx's theory of the disappearance of the epic poet (as a performer) and his public (as spectators) exemplifies the role that changes in the material conditions of production play in the evolution of literary genres (for example, epic poetry) and their reception (from viewing to reading). Correspondingly, one notable aspect of this collection is to demonstrate the multiple forms of authorial practice that are produced by the growth of print culture. Authors' engagement with editors and publishers, and the diverse opportunities offered by new publishing forms, whether nineteenth-century periodicals or the internet, are a far cry from their reliance on the patronage of a wealthy nobleman.

The focus of this collection on authorial practices is itself a product of critical trends. One of the factors affecting the perception of authorship in relation to textuality is inevitably the practices of criticism and theory. The current focus on authorial practices rather than on the authors themselves could be said to have been precipitated in the late 1960s by two revolutionary articles: Roland Barthes' 'The Death of the Author' (1968) and Michel Foucault's 'What Is an Author?' (1969). These two works initiated the movement against the author through a theory of authorial absence, which signalled their disengagement from notions of origin and intention. Drawing on the Classical and Medieval views of the book, according to which the author of the Divine script had not the power to originate, Barthes, Foucault and many others like them (for example, Jacques Derrida) argued that the text derived from the creativity and authority of language. Seeking to separate authorial signature from the named individual, the conflation of which dominated criticism since the advent of signed publication, they all claimed that the text could no longer be considered as an expression of an author's unique personality. Rather, it is the product of a signifying process of difference and differentiation that make absolute truth and authority impossible.

In 'The Death of the Author', Barthes famously argued that 'we now know that a text is not a line of words releasing a single "theological" meaning (the "message" of the Author-God) but a multi-dimensional space in which a variety of writings, none of them original, blend and clash' (Barthes, 1977a, p. 146). This multi-layered text, which is constructed by the often conflicting and conflicted convergence of discourses, allows (or rather demands of) the author to enter 'into his own death [when] writing begins' (Barthes, 1977a, p. 142). Barthes' claim has had two effects: one, to give birth to the reader, which determines authorship as a reading strategy; and two, to locate the author in the text, which is a technique that specifically aims to challenge the Romantic myth of the artist as a solitary genius, looking instead to elevate the literary work over its author.

While Barthes put the idea of authorship as an intra-textual activity, Foucault treated it as an extra-textual field that was difficult to abolish because of its enduring social and aesthetic function. Challenging the idea of the author as the ultimate signified of the text, Foucault urged critics to 're-examine the empty space left by the author's disappearance' in order to understand how the individualization of authorship had taken place with the erosion of the publishing policy of anonymity in the nineteenth century (Foucault, 1988, p. 200). Foucault argued that the author functioned differently both across and within particular periods: 'An anonymous text posted on a wall probably has a writer – but not an author. The author-function is therefore characteristic of the mode of existence, circulation, and functioning of certain discourses within society' (Foucault, 1988, p. 202). The attention that Foucault drew to the diversity of the author-function, which involved the development of different types of authorship, encouraged its treatment as a site of material practices that reinvigorated and revitalized its field of study.

The shift from an ontological to an epistemological approach to literature in the late 1960s had an enormous impact on the study of authorship. In his seminal book *The Death and the Return of the Author: Criticism and Subjectivity in Barthes, Foucault and Derrida* (1992), and his introduction to his anthology *Authorship: From Plato to the Postmodern* (1995), Séan Burke suggested that the theoretical upheaval since the 1960s constituted a crucial historical change not so much in the conception of authorship but in its institution as a scholarly field. Reception theory, deconstruction and semiotics are all reading practices that developed from the attack against the author. Although they reduced authorship to a mere signification process, they raised questions about the authority of literary canons that gave rise to a variety of fresh approaches and fields – ranging from new historicism and cultural materialism to gender and postcolonial studies – that yoked it to more political concerns related to gender, class, and race. Moving away from questions of personality to the subject positions that the author occupies, critics took an interest in the possibilities offered to women, working-class writers and other racial and ethnic groups to assume an author-function within a predominantly white, male and bourgeois literary market-place.

It is important to note that this Introduction does not aim to offer an overview of all the different theories of authorship that emerged in the second half of the twentieth century (see, for example, Caughie, 1981; Love, 2002). The scope and limitations of the controversies around the aesthetics, ideologies and politics of authorship have undergone detailed analysis, particularly as they come under the rubric of literary history. What we try to do instead here is to outline some of the opportunities that such theoretical elaborations of authorial identity offered for addressing individual careers, as well as broader issues of national, ethnic and sexual politics. How do ethnic minority authors, for example, use literary genres or forms of writing to maintain or overcome their separate cultural status within a larger British national framework? How do women develop cultural, professional and authorial identities against their marginalization within the literary market-place? These questions exhibit the sensitivity of literary scholarship to difference as it has been shaped in various fields, ranging from cultural and communication studies to the sociology of the text. They draw attention to the importance of context and interdisciplinarity, which have offered new ways of thinking about authorship.

Authorship in Context is divided into four parts, each addressing a particular period and field of study. While the first three parts – 'Nineteenth-Century Literary Market-Place', 'Twentieth-Century Mythologies of Authorship' and

'Postmodern Culture' – explore the various conditions under which author-ship emerged and developed as an institution over the past two centuries, the fourth part 'Authorship and Criticism' concentrates on issues around the emergence of authorship as a scholarly field. Each part and the articles within them are structured chronologically in order to bring out different histor-ical modes of authorship and the contrasting critical concerns produced by these modes. In addition to offering insight into the formation of authors in relation to artistic trends such as realism, modernism and postmod-ernism, the collection both structurally and thematically produces a typo-logy of authorship on the basis of the different material forms it involves (graphic novels, newspapers, cinema, hypertext, periodicals) or the discursive demands of the forms of writing involved (criticism, journalism, theory, literature).

The first part, 'Nineteenth-Century Literary Market-Place', consists of three essays, by Victor Sage, Kyriaki Hadjiafxendi and Helen Small, which try to recover the complexities of a burgeoning print culture in relation to literary and journalistic authorship. The emphasis they all place on publishing patterns, opportunities, editorial censorship and authorial choice challenge received ideas about the figure of the author as a sole controller of the text. In demonstrating the collaborative process involved in the cultural construc-tion of authorship, they collectively show how the questioning of mono-lithic authorship that twentieth-century authors usually claim had already begun in the nineteenth century. While Victor Sage tries to eschew the dehis-toricizing tendencies of narratology through an exploitation of Foucault's insight into power and knowledge, Hadjiafxendi and Small examine the way in which authors and editors negotiate their position within an economy of power that defines how the nineteenth-century literary market-place, and more specifically particular periodicals, operated.

In 'The Author, the Editor and the Fissured Text: Scott, Maturin and Hogg', Sage engages critically with the role of the editor in the construction of novel-istic authorship. This teases out the political impact of narrative omniscience in Gothic Romance. In looking into the imaginative appeal of editorial and to a further extent translation practice, Sage shows how Scott, Maturin and Hogg use the figure of the editor-translator as a narrative device to mediate their authorial presence in discourse. The duplication of the narrator, Sage argues, creates a fissure in the text that is integral to the production of the Author-God.

Taking editing and translation as part of an Enlightenment rhetoric, Sage explores how its juxtaposition to superstition, and, to a further extent, the oral tradition, reflects political tension between regional (Scottish and Irish) and British national consciousness. Whereas in Scott, the textual fissure is conflated for narrative and for national unity, in Maturin and Hogg, the editing of folk tradition is parodied to produce rhetorical and polit-ical instability. Sage follows Maturin's and Hogg's discrediting of Scott's homogenizing authorial voice and the print culture of post-Enlightenment Edinburgh. He finds their Calvinistic ethics part of a radical attempt to allegorize rather than produce a framed representation of the state of Ireland. The re-appreciation of their work, Sage concludes, leads to the redefinition of modernity, for they parody the figure of the Author-God and its multicultural and political currency.

Sage's study of the impact of editorial practice on literary authorship in the first half of the nineteenth century is followed by Hadjiafxendi's particularized work on George Eliot's authorship. Drawing on the fresh scholarship on affect and the recent scholarly interest in nineteenth-century print media, Hadjiafxendi looks into Eliot's career choices (literary genres, types of periodicals and modes of publication) during 1856–59, in her transition from journalism to literature. Hadjiafxendi's essay ' "George Eliot", the Literary Market-Place and Sympathy' argues that Eliot's authorial formation as a promoter of sympathy was inseparable from the print culture in which she had to function as an author. It was keyed into her attempt to distinguish herself from other popular modes of female authorship that she criticized in her periodical reviews alongside the institution of criticism.

Focusing on the aesthetic, economic and moral constraints imposed on Eliot as a woman of the press, Hadjiafxendi suggests an interconnection between Eliot's attempt to embody an ideal of the 'cultured' woman author and her belief in the ineffectuality of translating and reviewing to arouse sympathetic feeling. Dealing with the paradoxes of Eliot's quest for a kind of art capable of extending sympathy without being intimate with its readers, Hadjiafxendi draws attention to the different meanings that 'George Eliot' acquired during the marketing of her authorial figure by George Henry Lewes and its reception by other female authors (for example, Margaret Oliphant) and readers (for example, Jane Carlyle). Hadjiafxendi concludes by emphasizing the centrality of Eliots male pseudonym to her realist authorship as it developed an aesthetic function out of her attempts to separate her life from work during her collaboration with the Blackwood firm.

Following from Hadjiafxendi's essay, Helen Small's 'Liberal Editing in the *Fortnightly Review* and the *Nineteenth Century*' explores the editorial practices of two major periodicals of the 1870s and 1880s: the *Fortnightly Review* and the *Nineteenth Century*. Focusing on the figure of the liberal editor, Small challenges the ways that contemporary scholarship has written about these periodicals. Moving discussion away from their publication of literature and science, she assesses the implication behind their self-defined 'scientific' approach to knowledge for journalistic authorship. Looking to bring all domains of thought within the purview of rationalism and of the new historical method, Small argues that these journals emphasized questions of authority. However, their belief in 'the natural emergence of truth by free expression and interplay of as many points of view as possible' came into conflict with the constraints of the publishing trade at the *fin-de-siècle*.

By re-examining the early editorial careers of John Morley and James Knowles, Small provides a more commercial and compromisedly social definition of what it meant to be a liberal editor. Their intellectual stances, she concludes, were the product of the commercial contexts of a spatial dimension: the editor's desk, the publisher's board room, the printing house, and the accountant's office. These material constraints on editorial power posed a greater problem for liberals such as George Eliot, George Henry Lewes and Matthew Arnold than it did for authors of other political persuasions. Together with the other two essays in this section, Small's essay points to the diversity of the author-function within a changing nineteenth-century literary market-place that the second part of this collection will take into the twentieth century.

The second part, 'Twentieth-Century Mythologies of Authorship', consists of three essays, by Michael Bell, Joseph Brooker and Polina Mackay, which examine the role that questions of personality played in the formation of literary genres in the transition from modernism to postmodernism. Drawing on late twentieth-century theoretical models of authorship (as, for example, by Roland Barthes and Jacques Derrida) that opened up textual notions of truth, authority and identity to postmodernist relativity, they explicate the ramifications of the divided authorial self by revisiting the modernist conception of authorial impersonality. Reassessing varied views on authorship in the twentieth century, all three essays illustrate in their own distinct ways how the dismissal of the text as an expression of authorial personality was mythologized in literature and film.

Michael Bell's essay 'F. R. Leavis: The Writer, Language, History' re-examines the literary and philosophical contexts in which F. R. Leavis' authorial personality as a critic was shaped, established and challenged from the 1930s to the 1970s. By placing Leavis out of the context of the theoretical debates surrounding authorial intention of this period in terms of which his literary canon has been dismissed, Bell offers an alternative Leavis disassociated from his stereotypical depiction as the propagator of what M. C. Beardsley and W. K. Wimsatt defined in 1954 as 'intentional fallacy'. In doing so, Bell challenges the mythology that Leavis helped to foster around the institutions of literary authorship and criticism with his 'Great Tradition'.

In examining Leavis' reinvention of modernist aesthetics, Bell shows how the Leavisite anti-theoretical conception of authorship involved a philosophical understanding of language as a problematic mode of personal presence that was coveted under anti-authorial theories in the second half of the twentieth century. According to Bell's analysis, the more Leavis tried to offer a discursive rationale for the ethical significance of separating literature and criticism from the personalities of literary author and critic, the less philosophical he appeared, which, as a result, damaged his reputation. Bell claims that Leavis' disavowal of criticism as authorship was nevertheless rooted in his interpretation of the modernist concept of impersonality, which post-structuralist critics subsequently re-appropriated in their abolishing of the humanist author. In effect it was interconnected to the critical mythology growing around Leavis' intuitive adherence to liberal humanist values as theoretical naïvete.

Following from Bell's concern with the modernist aesthetics of 'authorial impersonality', Joseph Brooker's essay 'Mind that Crowd: Flann O'Brien's Authors' examines the Irish-born Flann O'Brien's authorial figure as a pseudonymous journalist and impersonal fiction writer as part of his aesthetic formation as a modernist author. O'Brien, whose real name was Brian O'Nolan, not only used different pen names for his pseudonymous journalism but also regularly denied having authored any of his books. Focusing on O'Brien's attempts to obscure his writing identity, Brooker analyses his authorial signatures as repeatable, iterable and imitable forms. This testifies to the impossibility of their purity, which, according to Peggy Kamuf (1988), is one of the staples of deconstruction. These signatures, as Jacques Derrida pointed out in his article 'Signature, Event, Context' (1971), can still be legible without having to detach themselves from the singular intention of their production (Derrida, 1988, pp. 1–23).

In exploring the ways in which O'Brien's authorial personas manifest the regional and international character of modernism, Brooker reveals that context is determinable only by another context, a question by another question. Does the mask hide the author, Brooker asks, or allow him to show himself? Does he lose his identity amid the confusion of pen names – or does he rather find, or invent, himself in the very process of writing? O'Brien's use of different journalistic pen names and denial of his book authorship, Brooker suggests, does not signify the disappearance of the author but emphatically asserts his proliferation in a context of multiple personalities that are distinctly modernist because of their 'cosmopolitan' character. They are visible, not only on a regional but also on a national scale, in other modernist authors such as James Joyce and T. S. Eliot.

Polina Mackay's essay, 'Authorship in the Writings and Films of William S. Burroughs', examines authorship in the interrelated contexts of postmodernist literature and avant-garde writing and film. The author function in Burroughs is, on the one hand, emblematic of postmodernism: his use of the cut-up method, for example, which aims primarily to challenge the authority of the authorial voice, re-conceptualizing it as a 'third mind', is exactly analogous to Barthes' concept of 'third meaning . . . which open[s] the field of meaning totally' (Barthes, 1977b, p. 55). But this challenge to a unified and unique authorial signature is not primarily about questions of personality, impersonality or multiple authorial personalities that are placed exclusively within the context of the literary text. Rather, Mackay suggests, the abolition of the authorial subject is a result of the formation of an exclusively mediated reality, which in Burroughs is signified as a filmic reality.

Mackay explores Burroughs' claim that the author is 'a recording instrument' to argue that authorship is reconfigured as a technological artefact. While this is an example of how recent American writers respond to the increasing dominance of cinematic culture, it also introduces new possibilities for the study of authorship.

In this context, the death of the author is better understood as authorial suicide that exists exclusively not in the text but on the screen. Legitimizing the significance of this claim is the burgeoning of academic studies on cinematic authorship, which come to reclaim theoretical models of authorship for the history of film-making (see, for example, Gerstner and Staiger, 2003). In Burroughs' films, the death of the author appears as an ongoing process; as such it demands an approach that takes into account the past, present and future of the study of authorship. It is suggestive of the significance of this process, Mackay argues, that Burroughs' last full-length novel, *The Western Lands*, revisits a cultural history of authorship from the ancient Egyptian scribe to the postmodern *auteur*. Mackay's analysis reveals the equal significance of ancient, medieval and (post)modern views of the author-function in the shaping of contemporary authorship.

The theoretically-informed examination of mythological formations in all three essays in 'Twentieth-Century Mythologies of Authorship' reveals their uneasy relationship with the theoretical upheaval since the 1960s within a scholarly field that wonders what comes after theory. The final part of this collection, 'Postmodern Culture' tries to answer this question as its three contributors – David Punter, Tatiani Rapatzikou and Maria-Sabina Alexandru – examine the formal and linguistic diversity of contemporary print culture: the graphic novel, the internet and global literature. The thread that binds their examination of the postmodern as a cultural condition is their awareness of the heterogeneous approaches that the study of authorship involves as its different modes compete with one another across fields.

In 'Postmodernism, Criticism and the Graphic Novel', David Punter argues that the graphic novel is a feature of the postmodern. It is a multi-layered narrative that is suggestive not only of a new kind of textuality but also of a new type of authorial identity. Punter explores the work undertaken in the context of graphic writing, which involves a team of writers, artists, inkers, letterers and colourists, to argue that authorship in this context is unfixed. By examining such texts as *Witchcraft* (by a team headed by writer James Robinson), Punter asks: What is postmodern about this type of storytelling? Locating the postmodern in the ways in which the story 'becomes one of interplay between surfaces', Punter turns to more fragmented graphic narratives such as the series of texts written by Grant Morrison under the name of *The Invisibles* (1999).

In his reading of *The Invisibles*, Punter suggests that the author is invisible, as all the characters are predominantly part of somebody else's text (for example, Moorcock or Burroughs). On the one hand, the disappearance of the authorial figure replicates Barthes' definition of the text as 'tissue of quotations'. Barthes' assertion, however, implies that the resulting text is a celebratory endorsement of fragmentation, multiplicity and incompleteness. Moving away from such interpretations, Punter argues that the graphic novel is a product of several layers of 'fragmented ruins', as all texts articulate 'the impossibility of finding any authorial position outside the texts that have already been written'.

Following from Punter's discussion of the graphic novel as a collaborative form of production, Tatiani Rapatzikou's essay 'Authorial Identity in the Era of Electronic Technologies' examines the impact of technological developments such as the internet (and subsequently of hypertextual interactive communities (MUDs)) on the literary novel. Focusing on the symbiotic links between old and new media, Rapatzikou explores the ways in which they affect the circulation of formats, genres, texts and characters between different visual, print and electronic media. How can one create electronically-sustainable, interactive and reader-participatory environments through literature? Bringing together digital art and cyberpunk fiction, Rapatzikou's study of William Gibson's novels, in particular *Pattern Recognition* (2003), draws attention to the way digital publishing has created the need for a redefinition of the author-function.

Gibson's novel *Pattern Recognition*, Rapatzikou argues, deals with the cultural uncertainty concerning literary production in an era governed by brand names and huge online corporations such as eBay. For Gibson, it is never simply the case that electronic authorship is mediated. In our multimedia world, authorship is always remediated within a global network of intercultural and interracial communications.[4] His experimentation with novelistic form and narrative techniques respond to 'this newly-emergent tendency of viewing information or witnessing action taking place in intersecting or parallel environments in a non-linear fashion'. Gibson's contribution, Rapatzikou suggests, lies in his transformation of reading into a three-dimensional experience during which the readers, alongside the characters, can access parallel narrative places independently of space and time constraints.

While Rapatzikou's study of Gibson transports us to a virtual world, Maria-Sabina Alexandru's essay 'Towards a Politics of the Small Things: Arundhati Roy and the Decentralization of Authorship' deals with political aspects of the lack of cultural fixity and stability in a postcolonial world where geographical, linguistic and gender boundaries are constantly being challenged. Examining Roy's Booker prize authorship, Alexandru discusses how one of the few female winners negotiates her position as a literary woman between Western feminism and a male-dominated literary tradition of Indian fiction in English. She argues that Roy's novel *The God of Small Things* (1997), informed by her non-fictional work and political campaigns, problematizes her critical representation as a politically-driven postcolonial author, predominantly concerned with issues around caste and gender.

In contrast to other contemporary criticism on Roy, Alexandru reads her work in terms of identity politics, whereby Roy's authorship does not feed unequivocably into a postcolonial political agenda. Rather, Alexandru argues, Roy is in constant dialogue and in places in conflict with postcolonialism which, along similar lines to feminism in the 1980s, argued for the institutional recognition of the different types of postcolonial authorship (see Miller, 1988, p. 106). While postcolonial writers such as Salman Rushdie and feminists like Kate Millett worked for their inclusion in the literary canon, Roy, both as a woman and a postcolonial author, sees the need to work towards the decentralization of the authorial figure. The experience of exclusion, according to Roy, plays an integral role to the authorial formation of postcolonial women. One can take a political stance just by knowing how to attend to the 'small things' that dominate people's lives, often dismissed in grand narratives of centralized authority and canonicity.

Alexandru's essay is different in many respects in terms of its scope from Punter's and Rapatzikou's, in that it is concerned with authorship as a technique of the self. Yet, the questions it raises about the political function of authorship within a postmodern culture, with which postcolonialism as a field of study is seen to clash, invite an examination of the literary canon and academia. The fourth and final part 'Authorship and Criticism' consists only of an essay by Terry Eagleton, which examines the relationship between authorship and criticism that has become so troubling since the establishment of theory as a discipline. Reading the history of critical thought as a series of subversive strikes at the Cartesian *cogito*, Eagleton examines in 'The Decline of the Critic' the different ways in which criticism has been expressed in a public forum. He suggests that critical thought has not so far succeeded in engaging with or feeding into activism.

By locating the origins of critical practice in the interrogation of an ethically obligated authorial subject, Eagleton argues that criticism is a mode of authorship that has suffered a decline in public intellectual life akin to Roland Barthes' celebrated 'death of the author' in its development as a profession.[5] He hopes that its revaluation may help today's critics find a public role in national life again beyond the postmodernist aesthetics of writing. Eagleton, as a Marxist critic, takes authorship to be an ideological formation. By following the decline of what he calls the 'classical intellectual' within a consumerist and postmodern society that is growing less tolerant to the latter's claim to 'disinterestedness', he reasserts a central premise of Marxist theory; namely, the idea that the mode of authorship that criticism represents 'is part of our liberation from oppression' (Eagleton, 1976, p. 76). Taking intellectuals and academics to be different types of critics, Eagleton sees the need to re-examine their author-functions.

How different are their political allegiances and institutional affiliations, and how radical are their politics of change? The question Eagleton asks manifests his longstanding concern with political agency against the 'ominous face of global politics' in a post 9/11 world in which, as he puts it 'not even the most cloistered of academics will be able to ignore' (Eagleton, 2003, p. 1). Eagleton's assessment of the political impact of theory on criticism stands as a concluding address to the issues explored in all four parts of this collection. This is because it helps to recontextualize authorship in literary history, indicating how the shifting nature of context plays an integral role in the changing significance of the author-function. The attention he draws to the extent to which the meaning of the author changes through the self-reflective reassessment of critical practice gives rise to a set of questions that determine the scope of all the essays: What kinds of authors do we have today and how do authors of the past appear today in the light of new approaches to authorship?

All the parts in this collection – 'Nineteenth-Century Literary Market-Place', 'Twentieth-Century Mythologies of Authorship', 'Postmodern Culture' and 'Authorship and Criticism' – try to answer this question with regard to the field of study and period they cover. Their treatment of authorship as a shifting site of material practices testifies to the inclusiveness of print media in the changing significance of authorship as a concept and scholarly field as it is signalled by the image on the collection's cover. In M. C. Escher's lithograph *Drawing Hands* (1948), the hands, caught in the collaborative act of drawing one another – never quite sure where drawing ends and where being drawn begins – create a framework that shifts and alternates according to their movement, which is both creative and mechanistic. They are placed on a drawing board only to be placed within another frame as they exceed it with their three-dimensional existence, which is as physical and concretely real as their mechanical pencils, their means of production. It is precisely this material dimension of creativity that this collection tries to capture, with its stress on the study of authorship in open-ended contexts.

Part I

Nineteenth-Century Literary Market-Place

1
The Author, the Editor, and the Fissured Text: Scott, Maturin and Hogg

Victor Sage

To edit is to frame a text. To frame a text is to produce a hierarchy of discourses, in which other discourses can be framed; and essential to that act is to mark their edges in some way, by intratextual, intertextual or para-textual means, sometimes all three, and sometimes all together. The Editor is par excellence an Enlightenment figure, producing by writing an outward edge of reason, what Irving Goffmann calls a 'rim', along which the framing discourse operates, isolating and containing the framed material, or strip, in which the readers find themselves (Goffmann, 1975, pp. 81–2). This rim gives rise to the fissured text across a whole axis of genres, including fiction, where the notion of an Editor plays a crucial, but complex and ambiguous, role in the development of the novel. The Editor explicitly or implicitly claims Authority; and because of this, the Editor – a helpless substitute for the Author, who (after Quixote) has become mysteriously absent – is also often a butt, a clown, a fool figure. Miguel de Cervantes begins his novel by displacing the Author, as God the Father over the Universe of his text, into a kind of editorial scribe, a 'step-father', at two removes from the origin of the text. The parody of Spain's absolutism and religious autocracy is implicit in the self-conscious use of the Book in Cervantes (see Carlos Fuentes' argument in his preface to Cervantes, 2003). In the burgeoning print culture of the English eighteenth century, satirical and self-conscious writers, such as Alexander Pope, Jonathan Swift and Laurence Sterne, following Cervantes, choose the printed medium itself, and the hierarchical framing device of the Editor, as a locus of diabolical irony, parody or demonic inversion of meaning – often encoded in the oral ambiguities of the plain style – in which transgressively dark or absurd meanings are handed over to the reader with all the authority and innocent reasonableness of the Editor.

The notion of a lying or deceptive use of framing is contemplated by Goffmann, and his version of the reactions of an addressee, a person receiving or participating in such a structure (in which category we can think of a reader, or a Reader) is interesting for the way in which the process of discrediting is at the heart of the presentation of a narrative, which will have both a backward and a forward reach:

> It is here in regard to this reach that one can locate a basic concept: *suspicion*. It is what a person feels who begins, rightly or not, to think that the strip of activity he is involved in has been constructed beyond his ken, and that he has not been allowed a sustainable view of what frames him. Suspicion must be distinguished from another important feeling, *doubt*, this being generated not by concern about being contained but concern about the framework or key that applies, these being elements that ordinarily function innocently in activity. Suspicion and doubt, then, are two very central affects generated by the way experience is framed. Insofar as it is hard to imagine a citizenry without suspicion or doubt, it is hard to imagine experience that is not organized in terms of framing. (Goffmann, 1975, pp. 121–2)

This relationship is a universal for Goffmann. The reader is a part of his citizenry of experience, whether he is thinking of the American or French Revolutions as an index of a modernity or not. I want to retain this idea of a position of doubt for the reader, extending backwards, for the purposes of this discussion, the age of suspicion. The fissured text is not necessarily Gothic – Satire's darkness is not that of the Gothic Romance – but Gothic, in the sense in which Michel Foucault (1980) thinks of it, as the photographic negative of Enlightenment discourse, certainly thrives on the doubt and suspicion produced by a parade of framing devices that were standard pieces of Enlightenment textual equipment. There is an important caveat one needs to make here. Foucault's metaphor allows for a complication in the image of the Editor as an Enlightenment stereotype. Enlightenment authors themselves, classically trained in irony, take to this particular form of rhetorical indirection with enthusiasm. Denis Diderot, for example, uses a comic framing device in his source-text for the Gothic, *La Religieuse* (1760). The straight and parodic forms of the Editor are born (or reborn) at the same time, in this example, and both are equally Enlightenment.

Having said that, the fissured text is peculiarly visible in the opposition between the rational drive of Enlightenment rhetoric and the question of its structural opposite: Superstition. The later eighteenth century gives us plenty of indications of the way in which folk materials are framed as they are represented by editorial activity, so that the beliefs of the past are brought, apparently in the spirit of anthropological enquiry, into the progressive present, for the modern reader's contemplation. In the later eighteenth century, this textual manoeuvre was also associated with the rhetoric of nationhood, as recent writers have shown (Trumpener, 1993, pp. 685–731; Ferris, 1991; Ferris, 2002, pp. 102–27). Johann Herder and his discussion of the *Volksgeist*, the Ossian controversy (1773), Bishop Percy's collection of ballads (1765), Charles Perrault's tales (1697), Antoine Galland's first French translation of the *Arabian Nights* (1717), and Sir Walter Scott's 'Minstrelsy of the Scottish Border' (1803), Johann-Karl Musaeus's, Ludwig Tieck's, and the Grimm's *Maerchen* (1782–1812); all of these involve a form of framing, in which the (often oral, superstitious) materials of the past are boxed and presented for a contemporary reader, whether Irish, Scottish, English, French or German.

This particular range of material, and the necessity of framing it, has a strong but as yet undefined relationship to both the laminated textuality and the crabwise development of the Gothic tale and novel. Superstition is one of the great themes of the Gothic: as the Marquis de Sade put it, in 'The Fruit of Revolutionary Tremors' from *Idée sur les romans* (1800): 'universally he [man] must pray, universally he must love' (Sade, 1990, p. 48). Religion and Love he identifies as the twin subjects (narrative pre-texts) of this type of dark romance. The Gothic Romance begins with an editorial fiction: Horace Walpole's vanishing act, as the author of *The Castle of Otranto* (1764) is a form of counterfeiting, a slip into the role of (fictive) Editor and Translator, creating a recessive set of documentary frames for a text that exposes to the gaze of rational, post-1688 antiquarian Britons, Southern European superstition of the medieval period. The political reflex of this particular case and the genre in general is to act out a drama in the text between the bourgeois and the feudal, which even puts the apogee of the frame itself – the apparently originary label, 'A Gothic Tale' – into semantic contention, as many commentators have shown. What the term 'Gothic' means depends notoriously on who you are.[1] The first readers were taken in; but as the novel achieved its readership, so the deceptive nature of the frames became evident, and suspicion and doubt crept in as part of that reading experience.

The straightforward Enlightenment effect, on the other hand – the one that gives rise to the Editor as a butt in the first place – is to make an opposition between past and present, and oral and written, often at the same time. The Editor is everywhere, mediating potentially unintelligible, divergent, or unsettling meanings, and translating them for the benefit of his contemporary readership, into a form that makes sense to them. Editors, although not always the Author of the text in which they play a role, possess Authority.

Another agenda that attaches to this process in the later eighteenth and early nineteenth century is to convert the national languages, and much of the consciousness, of the inhabitants of Ireland and Scotland, into English form. The Editor becomes a kind of God of the text, operating from beyond the limits of the reader's known universe. Here is Scott in *Waverley* (1814), for example, restoring the power of the Godlike editor by the use of multiple frames. His hero, Edward Waverley, has been wounded on the stag-hunt in the Highlands, and is being treated by an old 'smoke-dried Highlander', who refuses to perform any operation to alleviate Edward's pain until he has 'perambulated his couch three times from east to west', which we are informed is called 'making the *deasil*', an item of Gaelic that demands a footnote in Scott's edition of 1829, remaining in its italic form a written sign of both the foreign and the spoken, even after we have read the note:

> After this ceremony was duly performed, the old Esculapius let his patient's blood with a cupping-glass with great dexterity, and proceeded, muttering all the while to himself in Gaelic, to boil upon the fire certain herbs, with which he compounded an embrocation. He then fomented the parts which had sustained injury, never failing to murmur prayers or spells, which of the two Waverley could not distinguish, as his ear only caught the words *Gaspar-Melchior-Balthazar-max-prax-fax*, and similar gibberish. The fomentation had a speedy effect in alleviating the pain and swelling, which our hero imputed to the action of the herbs, or the effect of the chafing, but which was by the bystanders unanimously ascribed to the spells with which the operation had been accomplished. Edward was given to understand that not one of the ingredients had been gathered except during the full moon, and that the herbalist had, while collecting them, uniformly recited a charm, which, in English, run thus:
>
> > Hail to thee, thou holy herb,
> > That sprung on holy ground!
> > All in the Mount Olivet
> > First wert thou found:
> > Thou art boon for many a bruise,
> > And healest many a wound;
> > In our Lady's blessed name,
> > I take thee from the ground.
>
> Edward observed, with some surprise, that even Fergus, notwithstanding his knowledge and education, seemed to fall in with the superstitious ideas of his countrymen, either because he deemed it impolitic to affect scepticism on a matter of general belief, or more probably because, like most men who do not think deeply or accurately on such subjects, he had in his mind a reserve of superstition which balanced the freedom of his expressions and practice upon other occasions. (Scott, 1986, p. 118)

The effect of this rhetorical procedure is to bring into play the terms of a binary split:

Spoken [framed as superstition] Past
Written [the frame of reason] Present

Of course, not all past language is spoken; and not all language belonging to the present of the text is written only. 'Esculapius', for example, is a polite misnomer which is shared perhaps by narrator and character, Edward, a mock-heroic joke, an inflated title which recalls inappropriately the classical tradition and a written culture of past authority, by which to compare, unfavourably, the spoken world of this 'smoke-dried' creature. So, not all the past is spoken. The spell, which recalls the comic technique of Ben Jonson in *The Alchemist* (1610), invokes the italic sign of spoken and foreign language but deliberately empties it of its content. Or not quite, for some of the gibberish is made up of the names of minor exotic devils and Shakespeare characters. So the suspicion of juggling is lightly suggested. But then the Narrator/Editor himself cheats, having purloined the spoken rhyme from a written English source and passed it off as another piece of Gaelic, which he has had to translate for the benefit of the reader: Reginald Scott's *Discoverie of Witchcraft* (1585). Written language is theatrically framed and masked as the speech of the past. In the meantime, these effects are immersed in a solution of drawing-room politeness, which fixes a variable, but firmly inscribed, distance between the reader, the character, Waverley's mind, and the question of superstition. We are even offered a shrewd thrust about how Fergus McIvor, the Highland Chieftain, might (probably) have come to accept these absurdities – that his mind had a sort of blank space, a residue where thought might be in other minds (the reader must judge at this point which category he or she belongs to), in which superstition still resided and qualified his apparent freedom of thought. The implication is that part of Fergus' mind – the part that doesn't think – discernible in his reaction to the values enshrined in this spoken language, was living in the past, even 'Sixty years since'.

Scott is an expert at using what Mikhail Bakhtin calls 'images of language', first to symbolize, and then to efface, difference, by embedding them in the amber of his narrative prose (Bakhtin, 1988, pp. 124–56). The result is, first, to draw attention to the double layer of representation, and then to collapse it by a conflation – by equal foregrounding – of the Narrator (that is, 'the Author of Waverley') and Editor. This double-headed figure (also known, familiarly, as 'the antiquarian narrator') is also an expert at translation: quotation is usually, we are shown, translatable into modern English. The very lamination of the text, its absorption of the tricks of Miguel de Cervantes and Laurence Sterne, creates rhetorical stability of effect through knowingness – so the appeal to probability belongs to Scott's realism here.[2] Rational judging minds are all at the same distance from the problem, provided they can have access to the evidence. The distance between reader and text needs to be stable. One of Scott's favourite metaphors for this rhetorical process is that of the money-contract, and one of his favourite puns the notion of credit (that is, belief and debt – trust falls somewhere in between). In *Waverley* he refers to the relationship between reader and text as a tax.[3] He repeatedly tells Maturin in his letters not to draw too strongly upon the credit of the reader: the hyperbolic Gothic effects that Maturin himself, on his own admission, lusts after, will empty his bank account. Scott's advice, which was commercially sound – leading to the only real financial success that Maturin ever had – led also to acts of self-censorship on Maturin's part, as he struggled with these friendly prescriptions.

Maturin, from the tone of his Prefaces, tried heroically to internalize this advice.[4] But when he came to write *Melmoth the Wanderer* (1820), he seems to have broken out into nervously open rebellion against Scott's conflation of Narrator and Editor in that text and parodied it in a most outrageous way. The opening of the novel is visibly Scott-like: young John Melmoth goes out to visit his uncle in County Wicklow in 1816. There, at his uncle's house, he meets the housekeeper, a 'withered Sybil' (a piece of detached classical sarcasm he has appropriated from *Waverley*), who is an expert at telling the fortunes of young girls. Again, the theme is superstition. We have the same framing effects, the same translation of spoken Gaelic into written English, but here the effect is unstable. The tone is not amused, but fierce and contemptuous:

> No one was more skilful or active removing every iron implement from the kitchen where these ceremonies were usually performed by the credulous and terrified dupes of her wizardry, lest, instead of the form of a comely youth exhibiting a ring on his white finger, a headless figure should stalk to the rack (*Anglice*, dresser), take down a long spit, or, in default of that, snatch a poker from the fireside, and mercilessly take measure with its iron length of the sleeper for a coffin. No one, in short, knew better how to torment or terrify her victims into a belief of that power which may and has reduced the strongest minds to the level of the weakest; and under the influence of which the cultivated sceptic Lord Lyttleton, yelled and gnashed and writhed in his last hours, like the poor girl who, in the belief of the horrible visitation of the vampire, shrieked aloud that her grandfather was sucking her vital blood while she slept, and expired, under the influence of imaginary horror. Such was the being to whom old Melmoth had committed his life, half from credulity, and (*Hibernice*, speaking) *more than half* from avarice. (Maturin, 2000, pp. 13–14; see also pp. 11–12)

The technique is a pastiche of Scott's rhetorical method: the Narrator takes it upon himself to mediate to his English reader the native, spoken vocabulary: 'rack (*Anglice*, dresser) . . .' and he pedantically distances us from the illogic of the Irish idiom in the spoken phrase: 'more than half' by using the same technique, this time the flourish suggesting that he himself might be culturally outside Ireland: '*Hibernice*, speaking'. The Italian gesture gives the Narrator's voice an Editorial Authority (via music, where Italian has become the lingua franca of the Editor) and detachment from the hyphenated position of the Author, as Irish-English. But the allusion to the historical figure of the sceptical Lord Lyttleton, who correctly prophesied his own death three days before the event, which, though luridly presented, is still a framing comment on the power of superstition over weak minds, metamorphoses into a passionate Gothic hyperbole about an unknown girl, who might well have come from Byron's 'The Giaour' (1813) and the whole figurative base of the analogy has spilled over and exceeded its rhetorical function of mediation. The effect is not Scott-like at all, because the energy of the passage overrides the frame-effect, reproducing the conflict between superstition and rationality and the victory of the former at a higher level, in the mediating discourse itself. The presence of such pervasive and powerful superstition in 1816, far from producing Scott's continuous, relativizing, distancing effect, brings it into the virtual historical present of the text, and gives its fierceness a wholly different (political and psychological) point.

The grotesquely barbaric nature of this opening scene is a consequence of post-Union neglect and ruination in Ireland. Commentators have drawn attention in recent years to the way in which the early romances of Maturin and his friend Lady Morgan before Scott's *Waverley* in 1814 already write cultural division into their representation of the national culture and the national story of Ireland.[5] Scott's achievement, through his reviewing project as well as his editing of folk tradition, is to produce a rhetorical stability that makes fiction and history seem a natural analogy, a shared territory, and which therefore gives fiction an Authority, borrowed from the impersonal analysis of History. This is done by framing the oral culture of the past in the writing of the present, and by mediating the witnesses, reproducing their speech as a self-consciously embedded form.[6] Even in the courtroom scene in *Waverley*, when Evan Maccombich tries to redeem his chief, Fergus McIvor, with his life, and, laughed at for his pains, is allowed a touching moment of proud rebuke to the courtroom, the sympathetic judge goes on to contrast the clan loyalty, which this 'poor, ignorant man' displays in his personal word, and the contractual loyalty to king and state that he should have exhibited, we sense the difference between the feudal notion of a bond and the contract on which the modern British state, post-1688, is built. This is a distinction, according to Ian Duncan, between the spoken and the written (Duncan, 1994, p. 29ff).

But in Maturin, Old Melmoth's house of avarice and ruin is an allegory about the state of Ireland, not a framed representation of historical process: it takes Young Melmoth some time to work out why his miserly old uncle, who is transcendently mean – too materialistic to be superstitious himself – should be haunted and driven mad on his deathbed by the Wanderer, and here again we see the vertical layering of the text breaking down into a divided consciousness and a divided culture. Young Melmoth, the framing device, recalling the old woman's testimony, whose way of speaking has already been reproduced expertly at much too great and confusing a length for decorum, is not a means of containing contradiction and managing it, but of revealing it, forensically, in the present:

> He recapitulated the Sybil's story word by word, with the air of a man who is cross-examining an evidence, and trying to make him contradict himself.
>
> The first of the Melmoths, she says, who settled in Ireland, was an officer in Cromwell's army, who obtained a grant of lands, the confiscated property of an Irish family attached to the royalist cause. The elder brother of this man was one who had travelled abroad, and resided so long on the Continent, that his family had lost all recollection of him. Their memory was not stimulated by their affection, for there were strange reports concerning the traveller. He was said to be (like the 'damned magician, great Glendower,') 'a gentleman profited in strange concealments'. (Maturin, 2000, p. 29)

The Melmoths are probably English settlers in Ireland from the Cromwellian invasion, the eldest of whom is a witness to that appropriation of property, whose wanderings on the Continent suggest that he was on 'the other side' and fought for the Royalist cause. Maturin uses the two brothers' plot elsewhere as a romance device that intersects with the National story, as for example, in *The Milesian Chief* (1812) (for recent commentary, see Miles, 2002, pp. 98–101; and Ferris, 2002). Here the textual fissure, which repeats itself in the plot motif of the brothers, represents the inherited guilt about appropriated land which by 1816 has not been used or developed – the desolate miser's garden – to which the wandering elder brother was a living witness. The Scott-like Shakespearian references, which can scarcely be part of the old woman's testimony, brings back the theme of magic and superstition into the frame and leaves it there, spilling untidily out of its parentheses, to enhance the mystery of the Wanderer, recalling the defeated Northern and Celtic rebellion from *Henry IV* (1597), and the realpolitik (or treachery) that defeated it, mapping that on to the later Civil War period, as a family memory.

The two Gothic conventions – the manuscript that is read by the hero and the portrait dated 1646, which comes alive – are thus set in the context of a ruined and divided Ireland, starved of all modern improvements and progress, revealing the suppressed guilt of the Melmoths to the fresh eyes of the young man:

> As he [the attorney] spoke he shewed the lines to Melmoth, who immediately recognized his uncle's hand (that perpendicular and penurious hand, that seems determined to make the most of the very paper, thriftily

abridging every word, and leaving scarce an atom of margin), and read, not without some emotion, the following words: 'I enjoin my nephew and heir, John Melmoth, to remove, destroy, or cause to be destroyed, the portrait inscribed J. Melmoth, 1646, hanging in my closet. I also enjoin him to search for a manuscript, which I think he will find in the third and lowest left-hand drawer of the mahogany chest standing under that portrait – it is among some papers of no value, such as manuscript sermons, and pamphlets on the improvement of Ireland, and such stuff . . . ' (Maturin, 2000, p. 24)

He goes on to adjure him – holding him under oath to a dying man, under penalty of a dying man's curse – to burn it, preferably without reading it. The readerly tease is complete here: the fairytale prohibition that drives the character, and therefore the reader, to transgress as soon as possible, is fully established at this point. But the bitter joke about the improvement of Ireland is also explicit, though a passing glance, breaking the frame momentarily. This passage is a mockery of the legal written medium, which might look like (and be meant to look like) Scott's comfortable jokes about legal pedants, but which portrays the contractual world of the Hanoverian modern state in Ireland as a medium of penury. This is precisely the point at which Old Melmoth's handwriting bleeds into his voice ('such stuff . . . '). Its other contract, quite a different one, is Faustian: the Wanderer is the ghostly witness to this historical process of violent political expropriation and Imperial neglect.

The rhetorical law of Maturin's text is that framing is a paradoxical act, because, at every point on the vertical axis where a fissure (a 'rim') is required, the framed will escape into the frame and appear higher up.[7] We see this in the evident embarrassment about the role of the Editor, which is one of the messy instabilities of the text. At times, the Editor will jump tactlessly into the frame whose stability he guarantees, and will playfully assert 'Fact – teste me ipso' ('A fact that I witnessed myself'), but also fact is a legal term for testimony, as if God the Author needed to demonstrate his presence to suspicious mortal readers by employing a kind of lexical Angel to shout corroboration of his words in footnotes. Another notorious example, picked out destructively by an early English reviewer to score a point, sees him asserting the truth of a story about the Author's Grandfather *suo periculo*, (that is, 'on the peril of his own soul'), a legal phrase which suggests that he was an eyewitness to something that happened several generations before he was born. As the reviewer comments:

The *author of the tale* either fables, or does not understand, the Latin words he uses. He *might* have repeated the story on the authority of his mother, or, what would have been better still, his grandmother, but to tell it *suo periculo* is to say that he, the reverend author, was present when his

> grandfather hired the turbot-abjuring servants; which, as that must have taken place a century ago, can hardly be true, unless indeed Mr Maturin be Mr Melmoth himself. (Maturin, 2000, p. 308)

The reviewer's last point is perfect, because it is precisely what is envisaged here as an impossibility, and a breakdown of the conventions of fictional authority established by Scott, which is the rule of this text. The space between Editor and Text, framer and framed, is always too close or too far away for the comfort and confidence of Scott's middle-distance effects. *Melmoth the Wanderer* is set up as the vanishing object of the tales about him, but in the later stages of Immalee's Tale, he appears – impossibly – and tells his own story to her father in the third person. Again, in the middle of 'The Lover's Tale', at a most pathetic juncture when Elinor Mortimer, realizing that she has been abandoned for ever by her lover, hears a peasant boy playing a pastoral tune on his flute, the Editor, ruining the pathos of the moment, foists a couple of lines of score into the text and comments absurdly in a footnote: '*As this whole scene is taken from fact, I subjoin the notes whose modulation is so simple and whose effect was so profound' (Maturin, 2000, p. 545). Maturin was married to a singer: this joke for full effect demands even more than the spoken voice – it asks the reader to sing or play the score, in the interests of fact. The parody of Scott could not be more pointed. Maturin is re-appropriating the sceptical jokes of Swift and Sterne about the authority of print culture, and grafting them on to a tale of Calvinistic Puritanism of which Scott indeed might well have approved.

Similarly, the elaborately foregrounded process of transmission, in which oral and written levels of the text are brought into a supporting relationship to one another, is layered to the vanishing point in *Melmoth the Wanderer*, one layer of representation leaking inconveniently into the next. Take for example, the following narrative incident in 'The Tale of the Spaniard'. Melmoth is the Audience for the oral tale. We approach a moment of titillating horror, as the young man, imprisoned in the convent, is surrounded by whispers like auditory hallucinations:

> 'It is better to be mad at once, than to believe that all the world is sworn to think and *make* you be so, in spite of your own consciousness of your sanity. The whispers this night were so horrible, so full of ineffable abominations, of – I cannot think of them – that they *maddened my very ear*. My senses seemed deranged along with my intellect. I will give you an instance, it is but a slight one, of the horrors which – Here the Spaniard whispered Melmoth.*' (Maturin, 2000, p. 176)

The Sternian joke about the limits of representation in speech by the printed medium is perfect – there is no narrative convention that allows a reader to hear what was not audible to the Narrator in a printed text. Orators can use aposiopesis, as Sterne himself showed, but mimetic Narrators cannot. The expectations of the linear reader are tormented, as the hearer-in-the-text shudders; but, by the rules of the real – here perversely obeyed – he is already the perfect witness, and has no need to tell us.

But the Editor rushes in at this point with a shouting footnote and gives the whole game away:

> '*We do not venture to guess at the horrors of this whisper, but every one conversant with ecclesiastical history knows, that *Tetzel* offered indulgences in Germany, even on the condition that the sinner had been guilty of the *impossible* crime of violating the mother of God'. (Maturin, 2000, p. 176)

So this is what they are whispering. The impossibility of the crime is emphasized because this is the point at which we return, via the Protestant appropriation of the Enlightenment, to sceptical mode; at the same time, this is one of those blasphemous Satanic hyperboles which the early reviewers complained of, the italics in the self-contradictory footnote rendering a spoken yell of derision and disgusted fascination. The frame-effect has collapsed in confusion, or rather has induced doubt and suspicion in the Reader about the transmission of this text and the Authority of its Author.

This rebellion of the text against its own elaborately set-up conventions is part of Maturin's uncomfortable rebellion against Scott's historical romance; and it is of a piece with the diabolism, the Gothic drive of his text to blaspheme, to speak in the voice of the Devil, whose logic of representation is rather like Blake's printing house in Hell. This text opens out from its Irish beginning into a comparative study of the theatre of imperial power in sixteenth-century Spain and India, in which its Faustian hero stands outside History looking in and seeing the same patterns recurring in different cultures and times, like a member of a theatre audience roaming the seats of a vast auditorium in discontent both at the spectacle, and the angle from which it is viewed. The most embarrassing examples of this frame-breaking activity are those Editorial footnotes that concern the Irish rebellion of Robert Emmett, mob rule and murders in the streets, all directly and inconveniently asserted as witnessed, which curve away steeply into the horrific.

Scott was clearly a very difficult friend for less successful writers to have. His personal kindness is obvious in his correspondence. But his very obliging manner, his connections, his powerful sense of where the market was going, we can see, puts the other writer under pressure. When Maturin got the script of his tragedy, *Bertram* (1816), back from Drury Lane, he cried out in an anguished letter to Scott: 'they have *un-Maturined* it completely' (Scott, 1980, p. 59). They had cut out the figure of the Black Knight, partly at Scott's own instigation. Scott's own influence was not neutral, however kind he was, and however complex his behind-the-scenes role in that particular affair. Scott acted as creditor, agent, informal editor, but also as censor, and Sir Walter disliked certain things – in particular, the grotesque, the morbid, and the indecorous. Maturin was a gentleman, which gave him a certain *cachet*. Hogg was not, and his relations with Scott are, even more uncomfortably, made up of bursts of personal gratitude and writerly rebellion. Their correspondence reveals that their relationship had a mock-feudal aspect that was not entirely humorous.[8] Both Hogg and Maturin were closer to Calvinist thought than Scott; they were anarchistic Tories who, for different reasons, did not want to make an accommodation with the Hanoverian British state, and whose work rebelliously disrupts the linear progression that leads to the textual space of an approved present moment (Hasler's introduction to Hogg, 2003, p. xliii, fn. 57).[9]

There are similarities between Hogg's and Maturin's relationship with Scott. Both writers belong to what has been referred to as, according to Garside's phraseology, the 'second wave of intellectual Gothic' of the 1820s. It is the relation between textual self-consciousness, the representation of self-division, and the frame-breaking of their Gothic excess, focused in the fissured text, that I want to concentrate on here. Hogg's own masterpiece, *The Private Memoirs and Confessions of a Justified Sinner* (1824), like Maturin's, re-appropriates through parody the framing devices used by Scott to assimilate the writing of fiction to the writing of history.[10]

Criticism of Hogg's *Confessions* has undergone a revolution since the start of the 1990s. One of the results of this expansion of critical interest is the steady discrediting of the figure of the Editor, and the authority of the novel's narrative frame, both in the opening section, and in the final account of the suicide's grave at Eltrive, based on an original letter of Hogg's to *Blackwood's*, which serves as a pre-text, in which the author appears in his own text and refuses to ride with the Editor and his party to visit the suicide's grave.[11] The text of *Confessions* has nowadays become a battleground that resembles Milton's War in Heaven. The Editor's narrative, with its opening appeal to tradition, is now seen as a parody of Scott, and of the print culture of post-Enlightenment Edinburgh, at whose hands Hogg himself finally received such a bruising (see Garside's introduction to Hogg, 2001, p. lvff). The demonic is present in his vocabulary: in letters, Hogg refers to his former colleagues, Wilson and Lockhart, as 'master spirits'. Professor Garside, in his critical Introduction to the Edinburgh edition, gives plenty of evidence of how cruelly Hogg was treated. This included censorship and the interventionist role of the printer, Ballantyne – against which Hogg rebelled by succeeding in getting *Confessions* printed, not by Ballantyne, as was specified in the contract, but by James Clarke. Hogg drank with printers, preferring the company of the honest ones to the Oxford-educated literati of the 'Athens of the North'. This rebellion is itself parodied in the incident in the printing house, in which Robert Wringhim almost succeeds in getting printed the memoir that we are reading, but is violently ejected with only a single copy in his pocket, an incident which, as Garside points out, gives a new meaning to the phrase 'printer's devil'.

It is worth adding, as other commentators have revealed, that Hogg himself, as a founding member of the *Blackwood's* fraternity and co-author of the infamous 'Chaldee M/S', which already parodied Scott, had been educated in that very self-conscious and aggressive Tory anarchist print culture. It is no use our appealing to oral speech in Hogg as a level of authenticity or nature, without our acknowledging that he knew perfectly well that he himself was bound to the bodiless, voiceless world of print (Murphy, 1992, pp. 625–49). The difference between written and oral language in what has been called (by Hasler) Hogg's 'deeply disjunctive style' is notoriously unstable (Hasler, 1993, p. 65). Here, for example, the Editor puts in a comment in parentheses whose irony, instead of establishing the stability of the frame's 'rim', opens it to the scepticism of the reader:

> The day arrived – the party of young noblemen and gentlemen met, and were as happy and jovial as men could be. George was never seen so brilliant, or so full of spirits; and exulting to see so many gallant young chiefs and gentlemen about him, who all gloried in the same principles of loyalty, (perhaps this word should have been written *disloyalty*), he made speeches, gave toasts, and sung songs, all leaning slyly to the same side, until a very late hour. (Hogg, 2001, p. 36)

The comment on disloyalty in the notes alerts us to the presence of double irony here: 'i.e. disloyal to the established monarch: a reference to the Jacobitism of George and friends, as filtered through the Editor's new establishment Toryism' (Hogg, 2001, p. 223). Like Maturin's *'impossible* crime', the italics here are the sign of an indeterminacy between speech and writing, which occurs just at the point where irony backfires: the Editor wittily calls into question the transparency of his own reportage of their speech, in order to contrast the slipperiness of spoken treason with the determinacy of a written contract, only to have to rely on the written convention for a spoken emphasis. (Let the reader try reading it aloud to confirm this point.) The textual fissure between frame and framed, instead of establishing the authority of the written over the spoken as a symbolic *fait accompli*, provokes suspicion and doubt in the reader, and this is clearly tied to the question of ongoing political divisions in the culture. Dalcastle, like Scottish culture, is a divided house, an allegory of what is referred to in the text as party, and the opening part of the Editor's narrative establishes the range of this metaphor, when he reports, for example, that the laird had his first son 'christened by his own name and nursed in his own premises'. Does 'premises' here refer to the Great House of the Laird, or the Episcopalian Church? The possibility of a pun forces the reader to make the uneasy journey between mind and environment, and back.[12] The Editor is a parody of Scott. He seeks to retain control and authority over the text, in order to lead us through a documentary narrative to a present moment, which in Hogg's text is constantly escaping his grasp. It is not so much the bias of the Editor as a person, as the textual treatment of voice, a sensory aspect of reading, which is at stake here. The dramatic irony is in the reader's position. It is true, as Hogg's modern Editor urges, that the gaps in the text of *Confessions* are produced by acts of oral rebellion (Mack, 1999, p. 13ff). Hogg indeed finds a way of bringing on the witnesses and making the discomfort of their speech a focal point of suspicion and readerly doubt about the reporting of events. Here is Arabella Calvert, to her counterpart, Arabella Logan, when the latter visits her in jail:

> 'I am deeply indebted to you for this timely visit, Mrs Logan,' said she. 'It is not that I value life, or because I fear death, that I have sent for you so expressly. But the manner of the death that awaits me, has something peculiarly revolting in it to a female mind. Good God! when I think of being hung up, a spectacle to a gazing, gaping multitude, with numbers of which I have had intimacies and connections, that would render the moment of parting so hideous, that, believe me it rends to flinders a soul born for another sphere than that in which it has moved, had not the vile selfishness of a lordly fiend ruined all my prospects and all my hopes. Hear me then; for I do not ask your pity: I only ask of you to look to yourself and behave with womanly prudence. If you deny this day, that these goods are yours, there is no other evidence whatever against my life, and it is safe for the present. For as the word of the wretch that has betrayed me, it is of no avail; he has prevaricated so notoriously to save himself. If you deny them, you shall have them all again to the value of a mite, and more to the bargain. If you swear to the identity of them, the process will, one way and another, cost you the half of what they are worth.'
>
> 'And what security have I for that?,' said Mrs Logan.
>
> 'You have *my word*,' said the other proudly, 'and that never yet was violated'. (Hogg, 2001, p. 42)

The bond offered at the point of italics here is the bond of a spoken promise, made on the life of the speaker and rendered into print by an Editor who was not present. Arabella Logan almost misses her chance here, and when she, morally speaking, wakes up, it is effectively too late: the disgusted whore, Bell Calvert, is about to take her secret, the thing that Arabella Logan longs for most in the world – nothing less than her eyewitness account of the murder of George Dalcastle – to the next world. The key lies in the representation of Bell's speech, and the pride that drives her; we see that she really would have preferred not to save herself than to give in.

The problem for the Enlightenment reader is that Bell has seen the devil, and that is superstitious; but she has also seen how Gil-Martin, his opponent, swung George Colman round on the 'bleaching green', so that Wringhim could dart out of the shadows and stab him in the back. The eyewitness even reports his words, an overheard cue. Lee is quite right about this, I think:

> Therefore, when Simpson argues that the actual presence of the devil is proved by the reports of certain people who saw him, one must answer that Hogg is being more artful than that. Caught up in the immediate context, we too see that Gil-Martin at the moment that Miss Logan, the ancient mistress of the senior George Colwan, and Mrs Calvert, the woman who has witnessed Robert stab his brother in the back, observe Gil-Martin and Robert walking together. We do indeed see the man, then, that Wringhim's memoirs will by indirection tell us is the Demon. But we are *seeing* at a number of removes: the editor may accept tradition as fact, but Hogg has reminded us that the tale is based on a tradition, a notoriously inaccurate reporter of factual truth. (Lee, 1966, p. 231; see also pp. 230–9)

This is an important caveat: we do not see anything. In this parody of Scott's invention of tradition, the facts are not discernible. But the power of the legalistic frame still insists on its own epistemological force. We are placed in a corroborative position by the arrangement of the text: we wait to measure the account of Wringhim himself against what Bell has said, since it is clear the narratives will converge on this central incident. The Editor has already discredited Wringhim's memoir as fanaticism, and we try to find a way, as we read on, of reconciling our discounting of this judgement – since, as we have already seen, the Editorial frame is unstable – with our discounting of Wringhim's account as deluded.[13] Wringhim's own eyewitness account dissolves before our eyes into layers of imputation, as he reveals that he is even aware that he was witnessed, and seeks to refute charges of unfairness made at the time:

> They fought round the green to the very water, and so round, till they came close up to the covert where I stood. There being no more room to shift ground, my brother then forced him to come to close quarters, on which, the former still having the decided advantage, my friend quitted his sword, and called out. I could resist no longer; so, springing from my concealment, I rushed between them with my sword drawn, and parted them as if they had been two schoollboys: then turning to my brother, I addressed him as follows: – 'Wretch! miscreant! knowest thou what thou art attempting? Wouldst thou lay thy hand on the Lord's anointed, or

> shed thy wickedness, and not for the many injuries thou hast done to
> me!' To it we went, with full thirst of vengeance on every side. The duel
> was fierce; but the might of heaven prevailed, and not my might. The
> ungodly and reprobate young man fell, covered with wounds, and with
> curses and blasphemy in his mouth, while I escaped uninjured. Thereto
> his power extended not.
>
> I will not deny that my own immediate impressions of the affair in
> some degree differed from this statement. (Hogg, 2001, p. 118)

The reader, aware of Bell's account which flagrantly contradicts this, is
dragged into the fruitless and impossible task of trying to separate one type
of delusion, one degree of superstition, from another: Wringhim goes on to
make it clear that Gil-Martin (whose name is the equivalent in Gaelic of 'Old
Foxy') has persuaded him of what really happened.[14] The disturbing thing
is that disbelief does not protect the reader at all, since the incident of the
murder has already compelled our imaginative consent to it as an event. The
most powerful example of this paradox about the representation of seeing
belongs to Wringhim's narrative, when the devil finally shows himself in
his real form to his deluded disciple:

> 'If you will not pity yourself, have pity on me,' added he; 'turn your eyes
> on me, and behold to what I am reduced.'
>
> Involuntarily did I turn round at the request, and caught a half glance
> of his features. May no eye destined to reflect the beauties of the New
> Jerusalem inward upon the beatific soul, behold such a sight as mine then
> beheld! My immortal spirit, blood and bones, were all withered at such a
> sight; and I arose and withdrew, with groanings which the pangs of death
> shall never wring from me. (Hogg, 2001, p. 162)

The reader's position is subject to contradiction here. Wringhim, as the
groaning play on his name in the last line of this passage suggests, turns
his eyes ultimately upon himself; this is surely, in the theological frame, the
moment of despair that leads directly to his suicide, the maximum point at
which his 'friend' (that is, his own immortal soul) becomes repulsive to him.
The text teases the reader with looking at something we cannot see, just as
Maturin's text teases us with listening to something we cannot hear. The
expression 'Turn round', for example, has to be read either as delusion on the
part of the speaker, or metaphor on the part of the text. The phrase 'a half
glance' is finely calculated to get our naturalistic expectations goggling and
straining for the image which is not there. In the psychoanalytic frame, at
this point, we are made complicit with the mechanism of repression, the gaze
that does not see. One commentator, anxious to combat the reductiveness
of the theological frame, makes an interesting point here about the position
we are put in:

Wringhim disturbs us because we the community are the authors of his madness. A cultural or anthropological frame is, at least to me, morally superior to a religious puritan frame. And this, as it turns out, is simply another way of saying that I prefer dealing with a criminal to dealing with a sinner. (Petrie, 1992, p. 66)

I sympathize with this reaction; but unfortunately the reader cannot exercise such choices because the frames are unstable and liable to collapse all the time, and that includes the post-Enlightenment distance of the anthropological. This is the point about the double-edged nature of Hogg's relationship to print culture, that he was the victim of it, but he also grew up in it, and is an adept as manipulating the contradictions of textuality. His early tales, in the Gothic tradition, foreground explanation, different registers of which he allows to lie next to one another in his texts. This form of irony has direct and inescapable consequences for a reader, as Jill Rubinstein explains:

The tales confront head on the unresolved dilemma of Lockean epistemology: if knowledge is the representation of reality formulated through the senses, how can we be sure of an accurate correspondence between the objective order of things and their subjective representation when human perception is so demonstrably unreliable. (Rubinstein, 1993, p. 1)

Here, it might be worth remembering Swift's point about the relationship between the text of a satire and its audience, that satire is a glass in which the Reader sees everyone's face but his own. The mutual discrediting of narrative frames brings about neither a secure position nor a preferred set of values for the reader: two negatives do not make a positive. The satire of the epistemology of the Enlightenment, which filters through to the *Blackwood's* writers and to Maturin from English eighteenth-century satire, is by nature neither pure nor stable. It thrives precisely on the edges between registers, as Rubinstein goes on to argue convincingly about Hogg's earlier and shorter work, offering the choice of final explanation and then denying it (Rubinstein, 1993, pp. 2–11). Clearly, then, there is much at stake in Maturin's and Hogg's parody of Scott; the discomfort of these writers is not just a biographical matter. Their use of the vertical aspects of the text, their attack on the Editor, disrupts Scott's horizontal privileging of linearity and teleology, and disturbs the analogy between Fiction and History which Scott makes so much a part of the reading process in his earlier fiction.[15] Hogg appears as a sulky version of the Author in the Editor's final section of *Confessions*, someone who refuses to accompany the Editor and his friends to exhume the suicide's grave, an encounter that turns characteristically on the difference between spoken and written language, and which leaves the Editor hopelessly stranded. Hogg has, deviously, made a superstitious mistake in describing, in his original letter to *Blackwood's*, the document on which this section is based – the unmarked grave as sited at the borders (equivalent to the crossroads) between three estates, as Ian Duncan explains:

> The 'romantic and now classical country' through which the literati ride (p. 246) is Sir Walter Scott's, not least because Scott's writings have made it 'classical', ie the property of an official literary tradition. The hilltop grave of the 'lost sinner' is located on land owned by the Duke of Buccleuch – and not, as Hogg's letter misleadingly claimed, at a point where different estates meet (pp. 243, 258). These names of landlords, genealogies of Scott, efface that of James Hogg, whose neighbourhood in fact this is: Fall Law is one of the stark hills behind St Mary's Loch and Altrive Farm in the Vale of Ettrick. In short, the ancestral ground of the Scotts, the heritage claimed in *The Lay of the Last Minstrel*, is now the desolate site of Hogg's self-cancelling – an accursed and nameless grave which yields a baffling confessional fragment. Such is the author's testament, such is his estate. (Duncan, 1993, p. 21; see also p. 31)

Interestingly, it took French interventions to turn the tide for the appreciation of both these authors. In Britain, during the nineteenth century, they fell rapidly into obscurity, while Scott's reputation grew higher and higher. They were thought to be both provincial and incoherent (wild, in both senses). In the case of Maturin, it was Honoré de Balzac, but more particularly Charles Baudelaire who saw the modernity of what Maturin had achieved in *Melmoth the Wanderer*. In Hogg's case, it was André Gide's 'Preface' to the Cresset edition in 1946 (Gide himself being a past master of the fissured text) that began the critical revolution.

2
'George Eliot', the Literary Market-Place and Sympathy

Kyriaki Hadjiafxendi

> 'Creation is the superadded life of the intellect: sympathy, all-embracing love, the superadded moral life.'
>
> — (Eliot, 1885, vol. 1, p. 176)

George Eliot's fiction is well known for the way in which it experiments with the sleights and shifts of emotive language (see Hardy, 1985, pp. 131–57). This essay argues that her conception of art as an extension of solidarity played a formative role in her literary authorship. Marian Evans Lewes, the anonymous yet well-known 'writer of the articles of the *Westminster Review*', shifted from translating and periodical reviewing to writing fiction on 23 September 1856 (Eliot, 1954–78, vol. 2, p. 287). By 1858, after the anonymous serialization of her short stories *Scenes of Clerical Life* (1857) in *Blackwood's Edinburgh Magazine*, and their pseudonymous book publication followed by that of her novel *Adam Bede* (1859) with the Blackwood firm, she came to be known as the literary author 'George Eliot'. An examination of her career choices (literary genres, types of periodicals and modes of publications) during 1856–59 in her transition from journalism to literature will help to explicate her authorial formation as a promoter of sympathy.

In recent years there has been increasing interest in the importance of affect to aesthetic discourse, which has resulted in a number of studies on Eliot's experimentation with feeling. Shifting attention away from her rhetorical representation of affective experience, literary scholars such as Michael Bell and Forest Pyle have attempted to historicize her engagement with emotion by revealing its philosophical bearings (Pyle, 1995, pp. 147–71; Bell, 2000, pp. 119–49).[1] Their contribution to the field of George Eliot studies is notable for inscribing her fiction within an ever-changing history of sentiment, shifting and alternating in its development from eighteenth-century sentimentalism to its Romantic re-appropriation. They have recognized that her aesthetic of feeling has a history that overlaps with but is also separate from that of the Enlightenment and its aftermath. Thus, they have opened up new ways of thinking about her literary work, not only in terms of ideas but also in terms of an accumulated culture of feeling through which it also worked.[2]

Despite the historical acuity of their scholarly work, Bell and Pyle, have not considered the continuities of Eliot's periodical reviews and fiction, which illustrate the centrality of affect to her authorship. They have thus been unable to recognize how her authorial formation as a promoter of sympathy was keyed into her anxiety about her position in the literary market-place. In the last essay she wrote as a periodical reviewer – 'Silly Novels by Lady Novelists' (October 1856) – Eliot argued that female authorship was a genus with many species exhibiting either 'the subtle penetration of feeling' or 'feminine silliness' (Eliot, 1963c, p. 316). Sympathetic feeling was the critical standard behind her typology of authorial types that separated 'cultured women' (for example, Harriet Martineau and Elizabeth Gaskell) from 'lady novelists' (for example, Lady Chatterton and Lady Scott).

Eliot's perception of her authorial role as a 'woman of true culture' was inextricably linked to the adoption of sympathy as a principle of aesthetic judgement (Eliot, 1963c, p. 316). This chapter locates itself in relation to the fresh scholarship on affect as well as to the current scholarly interest in print media. Exploring the complex relationship between periodical reviewing and literature, nineteenth-century scholars such as Hilary Fraser (2003) and Barbara Onslow (2000) have provided models for studying female presence in a male-dominated institution such as the periodical press. How did 'women of the press' gain access to the publishing industry? What were their motives? How did they overcome the difficulties they faced in their roles as editors, reviewers or fiction writers? What choices did they make in terms of periodical publications, publishing modes and policies as part of their career planning? Such practical exploration of nineteenth-century female authorship offers new ways of thinking about Eliot's professional development from journalism to literature.

Taking her career change as part of the increasing professionalization of authorship in the first half of the nineteenth century, this chapter focuses on the aesthetic, economic and moral constraints imposed on Eliot as a woman of the press as well as the way in which she attempted to subvert them through her aesthetic of sympathy. It will examine the way that the change in her perception of reviewing and literature as emotive discourses led to her shift from one literary genre to the other and the periodical publications (Review/Magazine) to which they were related.[3] An examination of her career plans includes a macro-analysis of the market conditions that influenced the above self-conscious choices and the resolution of her indecision between serial and book publication. However, it also has a micro dimension in that it argues that her exploitation of the capacity of fiction to extend sympathy was a continuation of her periodical reviews.

This chapter consists of four connected sections that aim to identify some of the obstacles that, according to Eliot, female authors needed to overcome in order to be accepted by the critical establishment. The first section examines how Eliot's argument for a more cultured model of female authorship developed conceptually from her belief about the constant battle between literary women and the institution of criticism. The second section explores the connection between her attempt to realize her ideal of the woman author through her authorial figure, and her belief in the ineffectuality of translating and reviewing to arouse sympathetic feeling among the reading public in the here and now of the reading experience. The third section deals with the paradoxes of Eliot's quest for a kind of art capable of extending solidarity without being intimate with its readers in relation to her adoption of a male pseudonym. Finally, the fourth section looks into the centrality of affect to her authorship as it was newly-fledged within the Blackwood firm.

This chapter in its entirety aims to demonstrate how inseparable Eliot's authorial formation as a promoter of sympathy was from the print culture in which she had to function as an author. Growing out of her awareness of the bias of reviews against female authors, Eliot's concern with affect permeated her writing and her relationship with readers and critics, as well as her affairs with editors and publishers. Eliot's plea for sympathy as a true criterion of feeling in her periodical reviews was a condemnation of sentimentality as a false emotive discourse. The presence of sympathetic understanding as an aesthetic principle was needed to condition literary excellence; its absence as a critical standard was synonymous, from her point of view, with gender discrimination. Within the literary market-place, sympathy involved for her psychological support from the publishing house with which she collaborated by showing approval of her ideas; practical assistance by defending her against unsympathetic criticism; and finally economic provision for her material needs. It is the diverse fields that such aesthetic discourse formed – as part of Eliot's developing conception of authorship in her transition from translation and periodical reviewing to literature – that this chapter will be examining in all its sections.

Defining female authorship in 'Silly Novels by Lady Novelists'

Eliot's experimentation with different writing practices – translating, reviewing and fiction – was part of a practical exploration of the extent to which affect could permeate the literary market-place. This section intends to examine how the ideal of the woman author that 'George Eliot' came to embody emerged from her redefinition of female authorship in her periodical reviews, and more specifically, from 'Silly Novels by Lady Novelists'. Throughout her reviewing career, which overlapped in part with her professional engagement with translation, Eliot complained about the abundance of incompetent women writers in contrast to the scarcity of female literary excellence (ratio 3:1) (Eliot, 1963c, p. 324).[4] She saw it as her duty to compensate for their incompetence through her aesthetic of sympathy. The capacity of reviews and fiction to extend solidarity was, in her view, more than a distinguishing criterion between 'cultured women' and 'lady novelists'. It was also what distinguished her journalistic and literary authorship from the mass of contemporary feminine literature and their laudatory reviews.

Eliot's knowledge of a potentially mass publishing industry played an integral role to the self-perception of her authorial function as a 'woman of true culture'. The latter is an elitist term that Eliot defined in juxtaposition to 'lady novelists' in order to distinguish highbrow from lowbrow women authors.[5] The 'woman of true culture' embodied Eliot's vision of a new kind of female authorship organized around the values of 'patient diligence', 'sense of responsibility involved in publication' and 'appreciation of the sacredness of the writer's art' (Eliot, 1963c, p. 323). Eliot considered the application of the term 'lady novelists' to all female authors to be derogatory, because of the implication that writing for women was a habit rather than a vocation or a profession. In 'Silly Novels by Lady Novelists', she found the term applicable to popular fiction writers whose mediocrity resided in their lack of conscientiousness rather than in their wanting intellectual powers (Eliot, 1963c, pp. 320, 323).

Eliot saw the need for nineteenth-century women authors to find their purpose in truthfully representing and being truly representative of the feminine intellect (Eliot, 1963c, p. 316). In 'Silly Novels by Lady Novelists', Eliot argued that women were incapable of critically judging their own competence in writing fiction because of their foolish vanity of wishing to appear in print. By being false to themselves, they were untruthful in their delineation of feeling and character which, in her view, was the sacred task of every writer (Eliot, 1954–78, vol. 2, p. 397). Eliot claimed that the purpose of authorship, as an instrument of true moral and intellectual culture, was not to give information on life but to offer instead the possibility for emotive experience:

> A really cultured woman, like a cultured man, is all the simpler and the less obtrusive for her knowledge; it has made her see herself and her opinions in something like just proportions; she does not make it a pedestal from which she flatters herself that she commands a complete view of men and things, but makes it a point of observation from which to form a right estimate of herself... In conversation she is the least formidable of women, because she understands you, without wanting to make you aware that you *can't* understand her. She does not give you information, which is the raw material of culture, – she gives you sympathy, which is the subtlest essence. (Eliot, 1963c, p. 317)

Eliot's quest for a kind of art capable of extending solidarity was in fact a quest for sympathetic readership. Her double search for an aesthetic of feeling and an affective reader links her concern with the purposelessness of female authorship to the lack of high standards in criticism. As she put it in her review of the third volume of John Ruskin's *Modern Painters* (April 1856), where she first defined realism as the goal of art, learning how to appreciate a work of art within the culture in which it was produced was a principal means of widening sympathy (Eliot, 1990a, p. 368).

In Eliot's opinion, 'lady novelists' contributed to the prejudice against women's education by misrepresenting their gender irresponsibly as intellectually shallow and feeble (Eliot, 1963c, p. 316). Instead of faithfully depicting the everyday as 'cultured women' did, their fiction was the product of a fanciful imagination, which was untruthful to commonplace life. In addition to being remote from the working class, their abstract depiction of high society was equally unfaithful to its object of representation (Eliot, 1963c, p. 304; see also p. 303).

Significantly, Eliot turned her critique of the lack of realism of 'silly novels by lady novelists' in her homonymous essay into an attack on the nineteenth-century institution of criticism (Eliot, 1963c, pp. 316, 301). She demanded that reviewers assume responsibility for their incompetence by acknowledging their share of blame in the discrimination against 'really cultured women'. Eliot argued that literary puffery played an important role in cultivating female readers' vanity to appear in print to the extent that all of them were potential 'lady novelists' (Eliot, 1963c, p. 324). Her concern with the negative construction of stereotypes of the female author and reader in periodical reviews was complicit with contemporary patriarchal ideologies associating high art with masculinity and commercial art with femininity. Her partner, George Henry Lewes, for example, argued that there was no writer who was not haunted by the terror of the 'lady reader' and what she could exclaim. In his letter of 3 May 1857 to John Blackwood, he characteristically described the reader of 'silly novels' as a wet blanket on a writer's shoulders (Eliot, 1954–78, vol. 2, p. 325).

Despite the ideological limitations of her critique, Eliot tried to address the critical double standard that defined female authors and readers as lesser and inferior than men. She blamed the institution of criticism for encouraging female readers to see themselves as part of a 'common novel reading class' public as contrasted to that of 'the most cultured sort' (Eliot, 1954–78, vol. 2, pp. 325, 411). Eliot proposed the necessity of re-educating the female reader within a culture where knowledge did not circulate freely. Such re-education involved equal access to the stores of knowledge that men had without which 'a truly womanly culture' could not emerge (Eliot, 1954–78, vol. 5, p. 58; 1963a, p. 80):

> Let no woman rush into print who is not prepared for the consequences. We are aware that our remarks are in a very different tone from that of the reviewers who . . . tell one lady novelist after another that they 'hail' their

productions 'with delight'... No sooner does a woman show that she has genius or effective talent, than she receives the tribute of being moderately praised and severely criticized. By a peculiar thermometric adjustment, when a woman's talent is at zero, journalist approbation is at the boiling pitch; when she attains mediocrity, it is already at no more than summer heat; and if ever she reaches excellence, critical enthusiasm drops to the freezing point... In the majority of women's books you see that kind of facility which springs from the absence of high standard... The foolish vanity of wishing to appear in print, instead of being counter balanced by any consciousness of the intellectual or moral derogation implied in futile authorship, seems to be encouraged by the extremely false impression that to write *at all* is a proof of superiority in a woman. On this ground, we believe that the average intellect of women is unfairly represented by the mass of feminine literature, and that while the few women who write well are very far above the ordinary intellectual level of their sex, the many women who write ill are very far below it. So that, after all, the severer critics are fulfilling a chivalrous duty in depriving the mere fact of feminine authorship of any false prestige which may give a delusive attraction, and in recommending women of mediocre faculties – as at least a negative service they can render their sex – to abstain from writing. (Eliot, 1963c, pp. 322–3)

According to Eliot, nineteenth-century reviewers had to answer for not treating female authorship as a profession and/or vocation. The images they constructed around 'lady novelists' as 'destitute women turned novelists' in their laudatory reviews helped to promote the works of female authors as products of 'busy idleness' (Eliot, 1963c, pp. 323, 324). Feeding into the melo-dramatic rhetoric of 'silly novels', their sentimentalist portrayal of female writers of popular fiction echoed in their untruthfulness the latter's self-sacrificial heroines. It put forward the idea that authorship was as an unfavour-able option from the point of view of these women as that of the profession of the governess, so well known for its hardships and low social status.

The parallel drawn between female authors and governesses in their reviews established a connection between the stereotypes of the lonely and oppressed woman. By placing weight primarily on women's roles as daughters, mothers and wives rather than as authors, the reviewers' representations defined femininity in relation to social position within an oppressive community; and hence stood as an apology for accessing the publishing industry in the first place. They gave rise to a kind of female authorship organized around an 'ideal of womanliness', which primarily defined itself in terms of self-sacrifice (to family and children) in juxtaposition to the generally accepted 'manly' virtue of self-assertion:

We had imagined that destitute women turned novelists, as they turned governesses, because they had no other 'lady-like' means of getting their bread . . . We felt the commodity to be a nuisance, but we were glad to think that the money went to relieve the necessitous, and we pictured to ourselves lonely women struggling for a maintenance, or wives and daughters devoting themselves to the production of a 'copy' out of pure heroism, – perhaps to pay their husband's debts, or to purchase luxuries for a sick father. Under these impressions, we shrank from criticizing a lady's novel: her English might be faulty, but, we said to ourselves, her motives are irreproachable; her imagination may be uninventive, but her patience is untiring. Empty writing was excused for by an empty stomach, and twaddle was consecrated by tears. (Eliot, 1963c, p. 303)

This extract relies on the detection of irony in Eliot's interpretation of the misplaced chivalry of reviewers. Eliot opposed the myth of the impoverishment of 'lady novelists' by constructing the latter as upper-class women of an aristocratic background. The truth that she allegedly uncovered was that 'lady novelists' became authors out of vanity rather than economic necessity. Eliot believed that money was never an issue for popular women novelists, who were, to her great horror, intellectually rather than financially impoverished (Eliot, 1963c, p. 304). The destitution upon which their reviewers based their laudations was part of an attempt to mislead the middle-class reading public about the real motives behind popular female authorship.

Eliot argued that women should not have to justify their right to employment through masquerade. On the contrary, 'true women of culture', like men, had to make a living as periodical reviewers, editors or literary authors, with or without the benefits of university education or family financial support. They deserved to be given equal attention to men as professionals in the same way that 'lady novelists' ought to have had opportunities for different occupations where they could excel (Eliot, 1963c, p. 323). In contrast to reviewing, fiction allowed her, as we shall see in the next section, to explore emotive experience because of its capacity to flood both men and women alike with the same conflicting emotions as the surrounding world with its 'mystery and beauty and pain and ugliness' (Eliot, 1954–78, vol. 2, p. 341).

From reviewing to fiction-writing – from profession to vocation

This section argues that Eliot's embarkation on fiction writing stemmed from her professional dissatisfaction with the inability of periodical reviewing to advance a sympathy-based ethic under which literary authorship could develop as its instrument. Eliot's major change of feeling towards essay-writing preceded a change of mind that formed part of her critique of Enlightenment sentiment and its aftermath (see Pyle, 1995, pp. 147–71; Bell, 2000, pp. 119–49). During her employment as a periodical editor between

1851 and 1854, and as a reviewer up to 1856 at the *Westminster Review*, Eliot criticized in her contemporaries what she perceived to be a pretentious belief in their self-ordained roles as cultural teachers and guides. She was in search of an aesthetic language organized around the combination of affect and intellectual argument rather than around the propagation of instruction.

In her essay 'The Morality of Wilhelm Meister' (July 1855), Eliot argued that overt moralizing was not a guarantor of the moral influence of authorship because of its disengagement of the sympathy of the reader (Eliot, 1963b, p. 145). Eliot's opposition to the separation of feeling and reason is the thread that binds together her reviews and fiction, distinguishing her authorial function from that of popular fiction writers. Although it was not immediately evident to her contemporary readers and critics, Eliot tried to redefine the purpose of literary authorship, including that of 'lady novelists', through her realist redefinition of literature as a truthful representation of commonplace life.

Eliot defined realism in her review of the third volume of Ruskin's *Modern Painters* as 'truth to nature'. She argued that the duty of the author was not 'simply to teach truth' but to 'compel men's attention and sympathy' (Eliot, 1990a, pp. 368–9). By July 1856 she differentiated in her essay 'The Natural History of German Life' her aesthetic of sympathy from the moralizing and melodramatic imagination characterizing, among others, popular fiction writers such as 'lady novelists':

> Art is the nearest thing to life; it is a mode of amplifying experience and extending our contact with our fellow-men beyond the bounds of our personal lot. All the more sacred is the task of the artist when he undertakes to paint the life of the People. Falsification here is far more pernicious than in the more artificial aspects of life. It is not very serious that we should have false ideas about evanescent fashions – about the manners and conversation of beaux and duchesses; but it is serious that our sympathy with the perennial joys and struggles, the toil, the tragedy, and the humour in the life of our more heavily-laden fellow-men, should be perverted, and turned towards a false object instead of the true one. (Eliot, 1990b, pp. 110–11)

Eliot's rejection of didactic and sentimentalist fiction in 'The Natural History of German Life' involved the development of sympathy as a criterion of true feeling, which defined itself in opposition to sentimentality. It concerned, as Michael Bell has noted for her philosophical predecessor David Hume, the sources of the ethical (Bell, 2000, pp. 2, 17). In her letter of 5 July 1859 to Charles Bray, Eliot drew attention to the moral basis of affective experience: '[I]f Art does not enlarge men's sympathies, it does nothing morally' (Eliot, 1954–78, vol. 3, p. 111; see also 1990c, p. 206). For Eliot, the moral function of aesthetic discourse did not reside in the prescription of rules. Rather, it could only be understood in relation to a feeling that was never as natural and intuitive as sentimentalism had presented it.

In 'The Natural History of German Life', Eliot recognized how much more powerful was fiction than reviews, since it could actively arouse moral feeling in the reader through its characters' stories. However, for her, sympathy involved more than the capacity to have imaginative access into another's situation through reading. It also entailed an imaginative consideration of other people's circumstances through writing. Her turn to fiction was thus a way of explaining what Michael Bell has called the 'emotional dynamic of temporality' which was applicable to all forms of art and life because of their ephemeral nature (Bell, 2000, p. 9). It was inseparable from, and yet incommensurable with, the literary market-place in which it took place in that it embodied an anxiety about the transient nature of printed matter ranging from various modes of periodical production to book publication.

In 'Silly Novels by Lady Novelists', Eliot warned her readers as potential producers of 'silly novels' about the intellectual and moral degradation involved in futile authorship (Eliot, 1963c, p. 323). Marking the end of her journalistic career, this essay was written during a period when she also had to ask herself whether she was running the risk of adding herself to the number of 'lady novelists'. Eliot embarked on her literary career only after she was persuaded by Lewes, that she had sufficient dramatic power (Eliot, 1954–78, vol. 2, p. 407). Motivated by a high sense of responsibility towards femininity, Eliot's condemnation of the reduction of female authorship to 'busy idleness' entailed a self-perceived progression from periodical reviewing as a professional livelihood to fiction writing as a vocational calling.

For Eliot, periodical production was no more than a temporary means by which the vast majority of professional authors, writing out of necessity rather than vanity, earned their bread. In contrast, literary authorship for Eliot implied a life-time commitment because of its vocational motivation. Vocation imbued fiction with a more permanent value than what she perceived as a short-term occupation writing reviews. An examination of Eliot's conceptual shift from trade to vocation in terms of her authorship requires an excursus into the publishing conditions under which it was formed. Eliot's conception of literary authorship as a lasting vocation is evident from her rejection, on the instruction (in her own words) of her 'domestic critic' Lewes, of all commissioned reviews between 1857–58 (Eliot, 1954–78, vol. 4, pp. 396–7; vol. 2, p. 289). These included John Chapman's request for her to review Newman's 'The Religious Weakness of Protestantism' (January 1858); and Bessie Rayner Parkes' £1,000 fee offer for a contribution to *English Woman's Journal* that was newly-founded to serve the purposes of working women (Eliot, 1954–78, vol. 2, pp. 420–1, 426–7, 430).

Eliot's rejection of reviewing was not because of the doctrinal function that the Tractarian Newman attached to periodical production, or because of the *English Woman's Journal*'s campaign for the education of women.[6] Rather it was, as she explained in her letter of 3 February 1858 to Parkes, because she could not 'shilly-shally' about her new commitment, the writing of books:

> My negative about the writing has no special relation to the 'English-woman's Journal' but includes that and all other Reviews. I dare say you have not seen Mr. Chapman lately, or have not made any allusions to me in conversation with him, or he would have told you that I have not written for the *Westminster* since the last Christmas but one ['Worldliness and Otherworldliness: The Poet Young'] – that is, just a year ago – and that I have been obliged to say 'No' to all his requests for contributions. I have given up writing 'articles', having discovered that my vocation lies in other paths. In fact, *entre nous*, I expect to be writing *books* for some time to come. Don't speak of that at all; but I tell it to you that you may not in the least misapprehend my negatives. If it were a mere question of a little more or less of effort, I should have contrived to write an article for Mr. Chapman for old friendship's sake. But it is not that. It is a question whether I shall give up building my own house to go and help in the building of my neighbour's garden wall. (Eliot, 1954–78, vol. 2, p. 431)

Eliot's excessive play about writing books for sometime to come suggests that she considered book authorship of a higher status than the writing of articles for the periodical press. Although Lewes agreed that a longer genre of writing, like fiction (and more specifically the novel in contrast to the short story), would be more appropriate for affecting the reading public as if the characters were before them, he did not share her viewpoint (Eliot, 1954–78, vol. 2, p. 378). He insisted on the importance of ranking essay and fiction at the same level. In his essay 'The Condition of Authors in England, Germany, and France' (1847), Lewes recognized the rarity of literary men and women capable of producing 'serious' work (here 'serious' means extended, as opposed to the brevity of periodical reviews) that would eventually come to constitute an *oeuvre*. None the less, he argued that short works such as essays should not be looked down upon because of their length, since they could be complete conceptually:

> Those who talk so magniloquently about serious works, who despise the essay-like and fragmentary nature of periodical literature, forget that while there are many men who can produce a good essay, there has at all times been a scarcity of those who can produce good works. A brilliant essay, or a thoughtful fragment, is not the less brilliant, is not the less thoughtful, because it is brief, because it does not exhaust the subject. (Lewes, 1847, p. 289)

In contrast to Eliot, Lewes earned his living by writing for the periodical press. Their disagreement about journalistic and literary authorship was based on the different weight they placed on authorial agency. Lewes had given up his acting career in 1852 in order to dedicate himself to writing (reviews and essays) as part of his everyday quest, in his own words, for the 'obscurity of nobodies' (Eliot, 1954–78, vol. 4, p. 346). In contrast, Eliot shifted from reviewing to literature (in the same way that she gave up translating), in order to develop an identity of her own as a writer. As a translator, Eliot silenced her own voice to communicate faithfully another author's voice in a different language. Similarly as a reviewer, she wrote anonymously as the corporate voice of the *Westminster Review*. However, as a book author, she would publish anonymously or pseudonymously, as an individual with a voice of her own.[7]

Despite her different views from Lewes on authorship, Eliot agreed with him that any kind of professional writing should not be a mere trade (Lewes, 1847, p. 285). Notably, Lewes distinguished between trade, vocation and profession. Professionalism was a necessary condition for answering one's vocational calling, which, in Eliot's fiction, stands directly for giving voice. It safeguarded against the reduction of authorship to a series of business transactions. With these distinctions in mind, Lewes helped Eliot to establish her literary reputation with his advice to first serialize short stories in monthlies, then publish novels in book form, and finally plays and poetry when once known.

Eliot recognized her indebtedness to Lewes by dedicating, on 23 March 1859, the manuscript of her first novel, *Adam Bede*. Her recognition of Lewes' help was coupled with her admission of 18 October 1859 to D'Albert Durade, the Swiss painter and translator of her novels *Adam Bede* and later of *Mill on the Floss* (1860), *Silas Marner* (1861), *Romola* (1863) and collection of short stories, *Scenes of Clerical Life*, that she had discovered her true vocation in fiction. Eliot told D'Albert Durade that she was able to respond to her vocational calling because of the 'moral and intellectual sympathy' that she shared with Lewes in their 'married life' (Eliot, 1954–78, vol. 3, p. 186; see also vol. 2, pp. 343, 344). Eliot's statement to Durade reveals how her definition of the ethical function of art in terms of a cognitive aesthetic of feeling originated from her personal life, which she paradoxically tried to keep apart from her fiction through her pseudonym.[8]

Eliot's anxiety about the conflation of her life and work originated, independently of her ambition, from her lack of confidence in her ability to do well as a fiction-writer. Whereas her publishers kept congratulating her on being a popular and a great author, she was still haunted by the dread of a reading public that had no mind or little to give apart from intimacy (Eliot, 1954–78, vol. 3, p. 33). 'George Eliot' was born out of her vacillation between doubt and belief in her capacity to manipulate reader sympathies that only Lewes could moderate. The following quotation from Lewes' letter of 8 March 1859 to William Blackwood testifies to the plasticity of Eliot's authorial figure while being marketed and publicly received:

> G. E. has been made very happy by your [William Blackwood's] news; but like 'Oliver Twist' he is for ever 'asking for more'. He seems to be a sort of obverse of the Roman Emperor who had a slave at his elbow to whisper constantly to him 'Remember you are mortal'. He wants a friend at his elbow to whisper 'You see, George, you really are not a confounded Noodle, and the public *doesn't* think so.' (Eliot, 1954–78, vol. 3, p. 31)

Whether she was a character out of Dickens' novel (Oliver Twist) or a figure from classical mythology (Roman Emperor), these images demonstrate that 'George Eliot' was nothing more than a screen on to which both its bearer (Marian Evans Lewes) and admirers (literary agents, publishers, readers and critics) projected their desire to bring the unknown closer to them through its imaginative reinvention. Eliot imagined herself at the receiving end of sympathy as a deaf person who, being unconscious of her popularity, was unable to hear her readers' compliments (Eliot, 1954–78, vol. 3, p. 34). The name 'George Eliot' acquired its significance out of this perceptual gap between the exhibition and reception of sympathetic feeling as it grew bigger in the history of her authorship. It came to embody, as we shall see in the next section, a missed encounter between author and reader that made possible the sympathetic identification she craved only within the boundaries of her fiction.

'George Eliot': meanings and discontents

Eliot's literary career differed from other female authors writing out of necessity, such as Margaret Oliphant, Mary Elizabeth Braddon and Mrs Henry Wood, who either kept reviewing for the periodical press (Oliphant, *Blackwood's*), or were elevated to the position of periodical editors (Braddon, *Belgravia*; Wood, *The Argosy*). Eliot felt competitive towards non-Blackwood best-selling authors such as Braddon and Wood, who sold their novels relatively cheaply to maximize their readership. The following quote from Lewes' letter of May 1877 to John Blackwood indicates how Eliot's rivalry with other writers varied over time across magazines: 'While Mrs Henry Wood, Miss [Mary Elizabeth] Braddon, Wilkie Collins etc. sell their novels at 6/- [six shillings] surely G.E. may expect a public?' (Eliot, 1954–78, vol. 6, p. 345). Eliot established her reputation by promoting herself as being in a different league from popular fiction novelists. No matter how tempting it was for her to sell as cheaply as six shillings, the key to success for her was to balance the aesthetic and economic currency of her work.

Eliot's literary and economic success led prolific Blackwood authors such as Oliphant, whom Eliot admired for her capacity to do 'a perfectly stupendous amount of work of all sorts' (98 novels, 50 short stories, 25 non-fiction, 300 periodical articles), to challenge retrospectively their own career choices (Eliot, 1954–78, vol. 4, pp. 25–6). Although Eliot happily shared the firm's readership with other Blackwood authors, she did not fit the type of 'general utility woman' – to use Elisabeth Jay's term for Oliphant – who depended on her publishers for patronage and never received the security of editorial tenure that she deserved (Jay, 1995, p. 248). The following question from Oliphant's autobiography is more than rhetorical: 'Should I [Oliphant] have done better if I had been kept, like her [Eliot], in a mental greenhouse and taken care of?' – looked after by 'a caretaker and worshipper unrivalled – little nasty body though he [Lewes] looked' (Oliphant, 1990, p. 15; see also Oliphant, 1885, p. 540).[9]

In this extract Oliphant compares her authorial dependence on the House of Blackwood to Eliot's protective partnership with Lewes that so many of her female acquaintances criticized (for example, Eliza Lynn Linton, Mrs Humphrey Ward). Oliphant involuntarily invites here a problematic comparison between herself as a 'general utility woman' and Eliot as a woman of sensibility. Lewes was notorious for overprotecting Eliot by keeping any unsympathetic criticism secret from her, with the collaboration of her publishers. The image that Lewes created around Eliot's authorial figure raises questions about gender divisions in relation to nineteenth-century authorship. As part of an early attempt to moderate John Blackwood's sharp editorial criticism of her work, Lewes presented the anonymous author of 'The Sad Fortunes of the Reverend Amos Barton' from *Scenes of Clerical Life* as somebody writing out of vocation rather than vanity: 'my friend [George Eliot] . . . unlike most writers is anxious about excellence than about appearing in print' (Eliot, 1954–78, vol. 2, p. 276). By marketing Eliot primarily as a writer independently of being either a man or a woman, Lewes implicitly challenged social expectations of the woman writer in the literary market-place.

In his fictional narrative, 'George Eliot' ended up contributing to the erosion of orthodox gender hierarchies despite the apparent and much criticized limitations of her cross-gender pseudonym. The journalist and novelist Eliza Lynn Linton, whom Eliot had met through John Chapman in 1850, was one of the most severe critics of the myth that Lewes helped to built around 'George Eliot'. Finding Eliot too self-conscious and reflective, Linton argued that the female writer who, like Eliot, put her authorial function above her '*metier* as woman' only 'ape[d] the manliness she could never possess'(Linton, 1979, p. 20). For her, Eliot's stress on her aesthetic rather than gender formation as an author was a sign of conformity to established patriarchal/masculine standards (Linton, 1897, p. 88).

Lewes' portrayal of Eliot as a woman of intellectual and emotional capacities, however, was very different from 'the image of the ideal George Eliot' that J. W. Cross tried to embalm posthumously (quoted in Anderson, 1987,

p. 181). Cross' manipulation of Eliot's letters and journals to play down her partnership with Lewes, which resulted in the discounting of his biography, is well known. His 'George Eliot' was a sibylline figure who became with success 'artificial, *posée*, pretentious, unreal' (Linton, 1899, p. 97).[10] The question that arises from Lewes' and Cross' contradictory portrayals is, 'What does it mean to be "George Eliot" '?

The burden of feminist criticism has been to reassess misinterpretations of Eliot's political disengagement as lacking sympathy with nineteenth-century feminism (Showalter, 1977, p. 107). One of the goals of her authorship, as of her fiction, was to endlessly show the need for sympathy with the fate of women. In this light, 'George Eliot' captures more than the irresolution she felt for the woman question. In fact, it embodies the likelihood of being sympathetic with the feminist cause without necessarily being a political activist. As Virginia Woolf asserted controversially on 20 November 1919 in the *Times Literary Supplement*, Eliot did not renounce her inheritance as a woman despite her masculine appearance. While looking past 'the burden and complexity of womanhood', Eliot incorporated in her writing 'the difference of view, the difference of standard' that she inherited as a female author (Woolf, 1971, p. 204).

The controversy that arose around the gender of Eliot's authorial identity coincided with the erosion of the policy of anonymous/pseudonymous publication in 1859 (see Hirsch, 2001, pp. 78–97; Easley, 2004, pp. 117–52). The debate over signed publication intensified the controversy around the discrimination against literary women in the periodical press. In her review of *Adam Bede* for *Bentley's Quarterly Review* (July 1859), Anne Mozley, expressing the suspicion that 'George Eliot' was a woman, argued that the novel should continue to receive credit for being ably done in its reviews, independent of its author's gender. She hinted that Eliot's secrecy was the product of the conditions under which women had to write (Mozley, 1971, pp. 86–103). This is a thread that twentieth-century feminist critics such as Penny Boumelha and Gillian Beer have developed in interpreting 'George Eliot' as a manifestation of her ambivalent and anxious relationship with patriarchal authority as a woman writer at the time (Boumelha, 1987, p. 16; Beer, 1986, p. 25).

In this light it is important to reconsider Eliot's cross-gender pen name as a safeguard against the manufacture of female authorship as 'an unwholesome commodity' (Eliot, 1963c, p. 316). Of particular relevance here is Barbara Onslow's claim that Eliot's pseudonym was more than a protective shield against her union with Lewes. Although anonymous/pseudonymous publication was not the norm, it was a common policy in the 1850s, which was justified by both men's and women's anxiety about the vulnerability of their authorial position in the literary market-place. In his article 'The Condition of Authors in England, Germany, and France', Lewes raised the necessity of showing sympathy towards the hardships of authorship, since it was a profession haunted by poverty beyond and above gender differences. Full-time authors had to struggle against unprofessional writers who were willing to and able to work for lower wages, since they practised writing as a supplement to their main occupation (Lewes, 1847, p. 294).

Eliot did not fit either the man or the woman of feeling whose combination of emotion with moral principle collapsed into reifying reason or sensibility, respectively. Whereas Mozley, for example, detected her femininity in her ability for sympathetic understanding, Oliphant was convinced that she was male (Eliot, 1954–78, vol. 2, p. 436). Her cross-gender image as a (wo)man of sensibility, which helped her to escape classification, was keyed into her aesthetic of sympathy through which she attempted to reconcile the affective and the ethical. This is a connection that has been ignored by some feminist critics, who tried to reveal how Eliot was partially defined by the gender beliefs that she interrogated. As Eliot wrote to Emily Davies, the most effective way of promoting female education was by pointing out that 'complete union and sympathy' between men and women 'can only come by women having opened to them the same store of acquired truths and beliefs as men have' (Eliot, 1954–78, vol. 4, p. 468).

In this light, Eliot's pseudonym was so much more than a transcendental terrain, as suggested by Sandra Gilbert and Susan Gubar, or a neutral space emptied of the contextuality of her name, as Gillian Beer has claimed (Beer, 1986, p. 25; Gilbert and Gubar, 1979, p. 53). At least in her eyes, 'George Eliot' carried out her quest for a kind of art capable of extending sympathy, without inviting intimacy, with the reading public. It is due to her questioning of her readers' demand for participation in her life that her pen name developed an inextricable link with her realism. In addition to being a safeguard against unnecessary exposure in the literary market-place, Eliot used her pen name to challenge the biographical approach to literature by separating her life from work. Unpublished anonymous tributes in verse, archived at Beinecke Library of Yale University, testify to the public desire to hear her voice and see her picture unmediated by her fiction. It is out of her strong desire to monitor the sympathetic feelings that she tried to arouse in her readership – through the realist depiction of character – that her authorial signature developed an aesthetic function.

In her biographical entry for *Oxford Dictionary of National Biography* (2004), Rosemary Ashton has argued that Eliot needed her pseudonym to separate herself from the 'strong-minded woman' of the *Westminster Review* (Eliot, 1954–78, vol. 2, p. 176n.). According to Ashton, 'George Eliot' testifies to the plasticity of her authorial figure which was an extension of her private life. (Mary Anne Evans (from birth) was also known as Mary Ann Evans (from 1837), Marian Evans (from 1851), Marian Evans Lewes (from 1854), and Mary Ann Cross (1880).) Although Ashton takes Eliot's moniker as a manifestation of her 'anomalous' social position, her claim invites a reconsideration of 'George Eliot' as a distinguishing mark of her authorship. Eliot's uncommon choice to maintain her pseudonym after its revelation in 1859 was connected to her belief that the advent of signed publication would only reinforce rather than eradicate prejudice against literary women. Her decision to serialize *Romola* with the signed illustrated periodical *Cornhill Magazine* in 1862 played an integral role to her self-invention as a signed, yet pseudonymous, realist author from the 1860s onward.

Eliot's distaste for biography, alongside her dismissal of other visual and scientific genres of portraiture (such as phrenology and painting) that she had used in her early fiction, was due to her conviction of the impossibility of having immediate knowledge. Just like her efforts for narrative control through the use of free indirect discourse, which became synonymous to her realist mode of address, her male moniker manifested her anxiety over reading practices in what she saw as a discriminatory print culture governed by the spectacle of personality. It is obvious from her comments on the nature of interpretation that a book, for her, stood for the author's mind rather than his/her life (Eliot, 1954–78, vol. 2, p. 342). By keeping her pseudonym, whose adoption had paradoxically led to the lionization of her figure as the author of *Scenes of Clerical Life* and *Adam Bede* in the first place, she tried to place even more weight on the Book rather than on the Author.

Eliot's implied reader was someone who would find, as Jane Carlyle did in January 1858, the most sympathetic and helpful friend in her fiction rather than in her as the author (Eliot, 1954–78, vol. 2, p. 425). It is quite uncanny how Jane Carlyle picks up on the way Lewes presented Eliot as someone with intellectual and emotional capabilities. Jane Carlyle imagined the author of *Scenes of Clerical Life* and subsequently of *Adam Bede* as someone who combined the feminine and masculine, the heart with the brain. It is precisely in this marriage of femininity with masculinity that she locates the power of the Book to befriend the reader, its power to extend sympathy:

> You will believe that . . . it needed to be the one sort of Book [*Scenes of Clerical Life*], however named, that still takes hold of me, and that grows rarer every year – a *human* book – written out of the heart of a live man, not merely out of the brain of an author – full of tenderness and pathos without a scrap of sentimentality, of sense without dogmatism, of earnestness without twaddle – a book that makes one *feel friends*, at once and for always, with the man or woman who wrote it!
>
> I hope to know someday if the person I am addressing bears any resemblance, in external things to the Idea I have conceived of him in my mind – a man of middle age, with a wife from whom he has got those beautiful *feminine* touches in his book, a good many children, and a dog that he has as much fondness for as I have for my little Nero! for the rest, not just a clergyman, but Brother or first cousin to a clergy-man!—How ridiculous all this *may* read, beside the reality! (Eliot, 1954–78, vol. 2, pp. 425–6)

Jane Carlyle as a reader is a product of her own times in the sense that she places the author of *Scenes of Clerical Life* in a heterosexual domestic situation that in many ways resembles her own marital relationship to Thomas Carlyle. However, unlike many of her contemporaries, she is conscious of the fact that her portrait of 'George Eliot' as a middle-aged married man with children and a dog is a figment of her own imagination; a projection of her personal agenda on to the authorial figure. The character of the author is nothing but a construct, just like that of the narrator or of the other characters in the novel. Eliot the family man is another fiction, adding to those of other readers who imagined her as a clergyman, a scientist or even as the son of a prosperous Nuneaton baker. 'George Eliot' found in Jane Carlyle a reader capable of exhibiting sympathy with her desire for a non-biographical approach to literature.

Eliot's pen name, which helped her to dissociate her life from her work, came to embody a self-perceived difference from other women writing out of vanity as well as from those writing out of necessity. Despite her eagerness to answer her vocational calling, Eliot agreed with Lewes that literature was a more profitable profession than periodical reviewing. With the exception of her translations, it is evident from her advice to Sara Hennell, on 2 January 1857, that she never published anything without commission (Eliot, 1954–78, vol. 2, p. 287). Eliot tried to combine genius with industry by taking into consideration, in addition to genres of writing, as we will see in the next section, periodical publication and modes of publishing to maximize the profitability of her authorship.

Changing periodicals: from the *Westminster Review* to *Blackwood's Magazine*

Eliot's careful career planning involved, in her transition from *Westminster* to *Blackwood's*, a choice between two competing genres of periodical publication: the quarterly Review and the monthly Magazine. This section argues that such a transition says as much about her anxiety about the future of the periodical press as about her position within it. Eliot's attachment of an ethical and an aesthetic function to her authorship was inseparable from the periodical publications in which her reviews and fiction were sold and marketed. Of particular relevance here is Benedict Anderson's conception of print as a form through which imagined communities construct identities. Anderson's concept will help us to examine the role that the quarterly *Westminster* and the monthly *Blackwood's* played in the individuality of her authorial role within their imaginary communities of reviewers, literary authors and readers.

Eliot took her journalism and literature as continuations of one another. An examination of the parallel, yet overlapping, history of the quarterlies and monthlies in which they were published will offer a further insight into the dual nature of her identity as an author-critic within the House of Blackwood. The Review originated from the foundation of Archibald Constable's Whig *Edinburgh Review* in 1802, which established the superiority of periodical reviewing as an analytical mode of writing over more creative forms such as the Magazine. Since their respective foundations in 1817 and 1824, *Blackwood's Edinburgh Magazine* and *Westminster Review* had challenged the image that the *Edinburgh* had created for monthlies as frivolous forms of entertainment and quarterlies as instruments of moral instruction.

The *Westminster* tried to revitalize the Review by working under the same format as the *Edinburgh*. Yet, it struggled, under the sequential editorships of John Stuart Mill, George Eliot and John Chapman, to change opinions currently in vogue about its role as a Review; as, for example, the idea that reviews must be didactic and exaggerated in order to make a striking impact as responsible organs of public opinion. According to Eliot, recent contributions to the *Westminster* by George Meredith, J. R. Wise and W. M. W. Call were neither informed nor judicious (Eliot, 1954–78, vol. 2, pp. 188, 389). In fact, they were repugnant, read at first glance, as she told Sara Hennell on 17 January 1858, because of their far-fetched associations:

> The article on Shelley [by J. R. Wise] is a perfect puddle for an unfortunate editor [Chapman] to have fallen into. Can anything be more feebly foolish or foolishly feeble than that stuff about the 'blood-red hand of the baronet *covering up* atheism' and that false sarcasm on the same page about mesalliance? I have not, of course, read the article – I have only dipped in here and there, but a mere taste of an undone cake made with rancid butter is enough. (Eliot, 1954–78, vol. 2, pp. 421–2)

Eliot distrusted John Chapman as a reviewer to the extent that she steered him away from the idea of contributing articles himself. She advised him that it was a wiser editorial policy to hire writers with conservative ideas but whose writing was coherent and argumentative rather than hiring bad writers with liberal ideas (Eliot, 1954–78, vol. 2, p. 427). Her suggestion revealed more than a concern about his ability as an editor to maintain the corporate voice of the *Westminster* as a periodical. Rather, it suggests once more her interest in preserving quality rather than the politics of a quarterly with the radical history of the *Westminster*. The 'flippant' tone of the new contributions in the *Westminster*, as she repeated in their correspondence during 1856–58, did not suit the literary tone of the quarterly (Eliot, 1954–78, vol. 2, pp. 420–1; see also pp. 487, 489). Rather, its 'journalistic' mode of address reduced quarterlies like the *Westminster* to the level of oracular weeklies like the *Athenaeum*, whose short laudatory reviews, especially of popular female fiction, lacked the necessary knowledge to make criticism and suggestion valuable (Eliot, 1954–78, vol. 2, p. 389).

According to Eliot, laudations in the newspaper press 'rarely give any idea of the character of the book', most often dismissed in three lines (Eliot, 1954–78, vol. 2, p. 318). Their only function is to 'help the sale; but otherwise it is hardly worth while to trouble one's self about newspaper reviews unless they point out some error, or present that very rare phenomenon, a true appreciation, which is the most delicious form in which *sympathy* can reach one' (Eliot, 1954–78, vol. 2, p. 400). In her letter of 9 November 1857, Eliot argued that sympathetic criticism conditioned literary excellence. However, the discrimination against literary women made it evident that it was a very rare phenomenon in the literary market-place (Eliot, 1954–78, vol. 2, p. 400). She claimed that quarterlies fell to the level of journalistic newspapers and periodical weeklies, they so discredited, by failing in extending solidarity.

Eliot found it necessary to set the standards of criticism through her fiction as part of her attempt to regenerate the aesthetics of authorship, especially for women. The commercial success of the Blackwood firm and its monthly periodical with and in which she published most of her fiction throughout her literary career, with the exception of her novel *Romola* and short story *Brother Jacob* (1864), made it obvious that literature was more popular, and hence more influential, than criticism. Despite the successful republications of essays, periodical reviewing was still a short-lived mode of publication that was intended as an easy means of dissemination of information.

Being anxious about her literary reputation, Eliot found the House of Blackwood attractive because of its promise to give her work a more permanent value. Its monthly periodical made the Magazine format accessible. It proved to be a strong competitor that no quarterly editor, including herself, could afford to ignore. By 1857, when she joined the Blackwood community of authors, the magazine was no longer considered to be a 'species of degradation', as T. F. Ellis conceived it in his letter of November 1837 to the *Edinburgh* editor Macvey Napier (quoted in Shattock, 1989, p. 89). However, for Eliot, authorship was defined by modes of publication. Publishing innovations were a determining characteristic of Eliot's collaboration with John and William Blackwood (Eliot, 1954–78, vol. 4, p. 353). Significantly, the Blackwood firm diverged from other publishing houses in terms of its publication strategies. It pioneered the republishing of serialized fiction in book form before Henry Colburn's and Richard Bentley's use of such marketing strategies for Charles Dickens in the late 1830s in *Bentley's Miscellany*. Its publishing patterns, prices and book forms guaranteed that 'good' literature would sell well (Sutherland, 1978, pp. 13–40).

At this early stage in her literary career, Eliot acknowledged the role that the issue of fiction in different forms played in maximizing the aesthetic, moral and economic currency of her authorship. She took Lewes' advice to serialize *Scenes of Clerical Life* from January to November 1857 in *Blackwood's*, with a two-volume republication (1,050 copies) following in 1858. Serialization afforded her time to fix, as John Blackwood told her in his letter of

28 October 1857, 'your reputation more firmly and *familiarly* in the public mind and given the reprint a better change of a start at first' (Eliot, 1954–78, vol. 2, p. 393). However, when it came to the publication of her first novel, *Adam Bede*, Eliot rejected his proposition for serialization (Eliot, 1954–78, vol. 3, p. 202).

Eliot challenged John Blackwood's assumption that the publisher was more appropriate than the author in determining the value, price and form of a work of art for consumption in the literary market-place. Despite his initial insistence, John Blackwood finally consented because of the sensitive material of *Adam Bede*'s subject matter: the fallen woman and matricide. As her bestseller novel was being translated into Dutch, French, German, Hungarian and Russian because of its rigorous analysis of character and motive, Lewes was not exaggerating when he stated that they were 'becoming quite European celebrities' (Eliot, 1954–78, vol. 3, p. 274).

Eliot's clash with her publisher in the case of *Adam Bede* was related to her concern about the commercial success of *Scenes of Clerical Life*. Although the publishing industry aimed at producing profitable commodities, Eliot aimed at producing high-quality literature that was meant both to educate and to entertain. Her letter of 14 December 1857 to John Blackwood suggests that, for her, book authorship, as opposed to serial publication, did not rely on the applause of the moment, as did the 'class of silly novels of lady novelists'. It signified success because of its combination of literary excellence and popularity:

> I hear a great many favourable opinions of the Scenes and, what is more to the purpose, I know that they are *good*, but I see that you understand the difference between a general and a literary reputation and it is impossible to say whether that general buzz which is the precursor of a large sale has arisen about the book. (Eliot, 1954–78, vol. 2, p. 413)

It is important to stress Eliot's perception of the book as a serious and high-brow mode of publication. Serialization was redolent of popular literature and mass readership because of the success of penny journals carrying serial fiction. It was seen as an ephemeral commodity because of the need to create narrative suspense at the end of each instalment and the pressure to write to strict journalistic deadlines. But Eliot saw books as more solid objects because of the coherence and wholeness of their narratives. They helped to internalize emotional response from both characters and readers in a process that involved recollection and reflection.

On the basis of these assumptions, the book publication of *Adam Bede* as a triple-decker novel (2,101 copies; price 31*s*.6*d*. per copy) helped Eliot to maintain the novel as an organic whole, while reinforcing its emotive and ethical functions. It did not clash with the preceding serialization of *Scenes of Clerical Life*, whose eleven instalments consisted of three complete narratives as part of a greater whole: a collection of short stories. The difference in their mode of publication was, in effect, a result of the different genres in which they were written.

Eliot's book authorship was linked both to her critique of female literature and the critical practice of reviewing that supported its popularity. The publication of a novel in volume form was often accompanied by the author's preface explaining his/her motives for writing the book. Eliot's initial refusal to write a preface to *Adam Bede* can be taken as a manifestation of her well-known critique of the biographical approach to literature. In this context, chapter 17, by means of which Eliot suspended narration, acquires further importance.[11] Its significance resides in the place of the preface that she eventually wrote but never published because of her critique of passive reading (Eliot, 1954–78, vol. 2, pp. 509–10). Eliot suspended her narration in order to compel her readers to become speculative and sceptical while reading fiction. Whereas a preface would be an extrinsic element drawing more attention to the figure of the author, chapter 17 allowed her to combine literary and critical rhetoric intrinsically in such a way as to place weight on the Book itself.

After agreeing with her publishers, John and William Blackwood, to withdraw her unpublished preface to *Adam Bede*, Eliot was persuaded by Lewes to write an advertisement asking her reviewers not to reveal the plot in their reviews (Eliot, 1954–78, vol. 2, 512). Yet her advertisement was still an attack against contemporary art and literary criticism, which John Blackwood found equally 'dangerous', since its publication would subject Eliot to personal revenge on the part of contemporary reviewers (Eliot, 1954–78, vol. 2, pp. 510, 513). However, Eliot's letter of 22 December 1858 to John Blackwood suggests that there was more to its withdrawal than her castigation of reviewers for dismissing individual authors:

> At Mr Lewes's suggestion, I have written the enclosed 'Remonstrance' which he recommends me to prefix to 'Adam Bede'. I confess, I have written it rather against the grain – although the evil in question is one that used to excite some indignation in me long before I became a novelist myself... Still, I should feel (metaphorically) flayed alive, if the story of 'Adam' were to be told in all the variety of bad journalistic styles. (Eliot, 1954–78, vol. 2, p. 509)

Eliot's unpublished remonstrance established continuities between her periodical reviews and fiction that Blackwood found disturbing. Her efforts to maintain the quality of analytic thinking that reviewing entailed in the creative act of fiction-writing was integral to her coterminous creation, as she herself put it in her letter of 4 February 1857 to William Blackwood 'as a man of science and a writer of fiction' (Eliot, 1954–78, vol. 2, p. 292). They form part of her attempt to impose an overarching identity on her entire work (reviews/fiction) independently of the 'holistic' house imprint under which her authorial figure was sold and marketed.

Eliot formed her cognitive aesthetic of feeling on the basis of the double meaning of theory as literary artifice and a mode of perception. For her, gender discrimination in the literary market-place was partly a result of the dependent relationship between literature and criticism. It was only through reconciliation between cognition and creativity that equality could be achieved. Such formation was keyed into her self-perception of her dual role as an author-critic. It reveals her capacity to espouse change by working within the Blackwood firm, while yet escaping the aesthetic boundaries assigned to her as one of its authors.

The House of Blackwood took pride in affirming its dedication to establishing personal relationship with its collaborators (Finkelstein, 2002, p. 25). Eliot's and Lewes' correspondence with John and William Blackwood testify to the part that her need for a sympathetic editor played in her choice to publish her early fiction with an old periodical like *Blackwood's*, regardless of the economic benefits (Eliot, 1954–78, vol. 2, pp. 295, 335, 353, 395, 405–6). 'Confidence' and 'Friendship' were terms that John Blackwood used to describe the firm's relationship with its male and female authors throughout his career. In addition to his emphasis on personal contact, however, Eliot's and Lewes' demand for a publisher capable of sympathy entailed an economic imperative that the self-image of the House of Blackwood seemed to fulfil.

In his article 'The Condition of Authors in England, Germany, and France', Lewes argued that the publishing industry needed sympathetic editors who could also anticipate 'by prospective benevolence' and 'anticipative charity' the financial miseries of authorship. His joint attempt with Eliot to combine, under John and William Blackwood's tenure, moral seriousness with commercial success reflects the power of their self-fostered image as agents of a unique intellectual community. It exemplifies a type of authorial identity contained within the frame of Blackwood's publishing activity different from that of Oliphant, whose authorship was not the most profitable of literary property.

Despite John Blackwood's estimation that their ability was of the same rank, 'George Eliot' represented tangible capital with enormous profitability that Oliphant would never achieve (quoted in Finkelstein, 2002, p. 33). The House of Blackwood was run on paternalistic lines with a family-based approach to publishing typical of a nineteenth-century bourgeois household (Finkelstein, 2002, p. 17). What made it unusual, though, was the fact that it owned both the editorial and the printing sites, whose physical spaces revealed much about their symbolic positioning within the firm. Whereas in the cramped printing office of Thistle Street Lane, literary works were treated as mechanized production processes, in the sumptuous quarters of the editorial office on George Street they were disseminated as individualized aesthetic products.

Eliot was caught between these two spaces that were symbolic of the firm's self-perceived reliance on an aesthetic judgement and new market forces which evaluated texts on how quickly they could be turned into commodities. The following extract from her letter of 4 January 1857 to William Blackwood is illustrative of the state of flux in which the Blackwood firm found itself: 'I am very sensitive to the merits of cheques for fifty guineas, but I am still more sensitive to that cordial appreciation which is a guarantee to me that my work was worth doing for its own sake' (Eliot, 1954–78, vol. 2, p. 288). Eliot's attempt to balance the literary and economic value of her work was integral to her promotion of sympathy as a Blackwood author.

3
Liberal Editing in the *Fortnightly Review* and the *Nineteenth Century*

Helen Small[1]

The *Fortnightly Review* and the *Nineteenth Century* have strong claims to be considered the two journals which did most to provide the late Victorian intelligentsia with open forums for debate on science, literature, politics and religion. The *Fortnightly* enshrined independence from party affiliation and church doctrine in its 1865 prospectus, though almost all of those writing for it shared a commitment to the new historical method and to Millian rationalism. By the early 1870s, however, the journal had come to be seen as the unofficial organ of radical liberal thought and, somewhat to its editor John Morley's frustration, of Comtean Positivism. The *Nineteenth Century*, founded in 1877 by James Thomas Knowles after a provocative editorship of the *Contemporary Review*, quickly challenged the *Fortnightly*'s claim to be the most intellectually progressive organ of the day. Like its rival, the *Nineteenth Century* espoused 'the natural emergence of truth by free expression and interplay of as many points of view as possible' (Hamer, 1968, pp. 73–4), but, while clearly Liberal on party political matters, it carefully avoided the other journal's increasingly pervasive party bias and soon secured a much wider audience.

The literary pages of the two periodicals were of a strikingly different complexion: to the limited extent that the *Nineteenth Century* was literary at all, Tennyson and Arnold were in the forefront, whereas the *Fortnightly* favoured the younger and more risqué voices of the new 'aesthetes' – Swinburne, Meredith, Rossetti, Morris and Pater. At first glance, their treatment of science seems to have been much more like-minded. Both journals supported the advancement of science against conservative pressures from the religious establishment. Several leading scientific writers wrote for Knowles as well as for Morley (Huxley and Tyndall, most notably), but the *Fortnightly* and the *Nineteenth Century* are of interest for historians of science not just because they drew such names to their pages but because they made one of their central concerns the definition of a 'scientific' approach to knowledge. Seeking to bring all domains of thought within the purview of rationalism, articles in every field characteristically placed questions of evidence, logic, belief and authority to the forefront. The journals split, however, on the extent of the remit they were willing to claim for 'Science'. The *Fortnightly Review* welcomed articles such as Francis Palgrave's 'On the Scientific Study of Poetry' (1869, pp. 163–78) and Lionel A. Tollemache's 'Historical Prediction' (an enquiry into whether historical phenomena admit of scientific treatment) (1868, pp. 295–310). Here 'scientific' betokened the application of inductive and historical methods of analysis to the cultural domain, putting literary, historical and art criticism on a par with the scientists' examination of the natural world. The *Nineteenth Century* was wary of treating the word so elastically. Like Morley, Knowles encouraged debate about the impact of science on contemporary culture, but articles in the *Nineteenth Century* were often more specialized than those in the *Fortnightly*. W. B. Carpenter, for example, wrote on 'The Radiometer and its Lessons' in the second issue; Thomas Watson on 'The Abolition of Zymotic Disease' in the next (Carpenter, 1877, pp. 242–56; Watson, 1877, pp. 380–96). There was also a fairly regular column devoted to 'Recent Science', in which contemporary discoveries were reviewed in short summary, but still in more detail than a reader would find in Morley's journal.

The description provided thus far represents, albeit in compacted form, an immediately recognizable intellectual-cum-historical approach to the *Fortnightly Review* and the *Nineteenth Century*. Although the account of their treatment of science goes further than existing sources, it is in all other respects an entirely standard account of their aims and achievements. It is the purpose of this chapter, however, to suggest that intellectual history has, to date, given us only a very limited conception of the aims and achievements of late nineteenth-century periodical editors, and in the process has been too quick to reinforce Victorian liberal ideals of what periodical publication was about. By re-examining the first ten years of John Morley's and James Knowles' tenure of their respective journals I want to suggest a more complicated, more grubbily commercial, more laborious, and above all a more compromisedly social definition of what it meant to be a liberal editor in 1870s and 1880s London than has prevailed so far. In the process, I shall argue that what have to date been construed as two competing versions of liberal politics and of scientific rationalism were not simply or purely that at all. Rather, the political and intellectual stances of these two journals were to a significant degree the product of the markedly different publishing contexts from which they emerged – contexts which strongly influenced, and sometimes dictated, the kinds of decision an editor could make, and which might mean that the material forms and content of a periodical were not in fact 'editorial' choices at all.

* * *

In the mid-to-late Victorian period, editorial practice, of course, varied widely (see Wiener, 1985). Some editors took a very close hand in the running of their journals, while others were content to be little more than advertising fronts for their proprietors. The possibility of a less than committed man taking over the intellectual direction of the *Fortnightly Review* was a source of serious concern to Anthony Trollope when he wrote to G. H. Lewes in November 1866, reluctantly accepting the latter's resignation as editor on health grounds, and asking for Lewes' opinion of his proposed successor:

> Do you think that Mr. Morley is competent for the work? And do you believe that his opinions as to politics and literature are of a nature to support those views which we have endeavoured to maintain? If I found that the Review had drifted into the hands of a literary hack who simply followed out his task without any honesty of purpose, I should wash my hands of it. (Trollope, 1983, vol. 1, pp. 353–4)

Behind Trollope's intellectual anxieties was an unhappy awareness that the journal was not well placed to secure the kind of dedication he was looking for. Intellectually, it had been a much-trumpeted success during its first eighteen months, but financially, the *Fortnightly* was in trouble.

The authors of the *Wellesley Index* locate the explanation for this predominately in its audience: the British public was simply not accustomed to politically non-partisan journals, and the *Fortnightly*'s vaunted freedom from editorial directiveness was in danger of making it seem merely eclectic and flavourless (Houghton *et al.*, 1966–89, vol. 2, p. 175). But there were also structural reasons for the journal's failure to thrive in the marketplace. George Eliot noted, not quite accurately, at the time of the journal's inauguration, that the company of proprietors was 'unconnected with the publishing trade' (she overlooked Frederic Chapman the owner-director of Chapman & Hall) (quoted in Houghton *et al.*, 1966–89, vol. 2, p. 174). In her eyes this was all to the good – it protected the 'seriousness' of the journal from the commercial pressures likely to be exerted if a publishing house were in direct control. But it was very nearly ruinous. By November 1866 almost nothing of the original fund of £8,000 remained and, at a meeting that month to decide not just the editorship but the future financial direction of the *Fortnightly*, the proprietors agreed to the inevitable, relinquishing the journal to Chapman & Hall for a few hundred pounds.[2] Almost the last act of the outgoing company of directors was to agree a shift from fortnightly to monthly publication – a change which probably rescued the *Fortnightly* in the immediate term but which saddled it for the rest of its publishing history with an absurd misnomer.[3]

The new proprietors promised a far more prudent approach to the running of the journal. The incoming editor John Morley, a young man of 29, where Lewes had been a seasoned editor in his mid-50s, was given notionally the same freedom as his predecessor, but in reality considerably less power. From the surviving evidence – letters between Morley and his contributors (mainly in the British Library), the minutes of the board meetings of Chapman & Hall from 1880 when it became a limited company (now in Reading University archive), and the textual evidence of the *Fortnightly* itself – it quickly becomes clear that the periodical numbers that emerged each month were not simply the product of an editor's commitment to the advancement of scientific rationalism and to an increasingly radical form of liberalism, but the result of an ongoing and difficult process of compromise between editorial aspiration and managerial cost-cutting.

Chapman & Hall had no hesitation in using the most obvious means of control over Morley in their command: the editorial salary. Like Lewes before him, Morley was paid an annual sum of £600, and had the assistance of a sub-editor and a clerk, but ephemeral editorial expenses had to be paid by the editor and, at least in the first years, he was responsible for advancing payment to contributors out of his own bank account (Meredith to Swinburne, 27 January 1868, in Meredith, 1970, vol. 1, pp. 366–7). Just how significant a strain was placed on the editor's pocket by this mode of handling the finances is apparent from the correspondence of George Meredith, who took temporary charge of the editor's desk during Morley's absence on a visit to America in November and December 1867. Never financially in easy circumstances, Meredith had expected to be well remunerated, but he soon found himself hard pressed to pay the journal's contributors let alone have anything left over for himself. 'My dear Fred', he wrote to Chapman, in December 1867,

> Please send the remaining £40 for the monthly expenditure of *Fortnightly* to my bank, L[ondon] & Westminster, St. James's branch, by *Monday*'s post, so that I may hear of no complaints, and work in ease of mind. . . .
>
> From what I see of the *Fortnightly* there is a chance of its making a permanent stand. But contributors must feel that what money they are to get is sure to be paid punctually to the day. This is the case with *Fraser*, with *Blackwood*, and the *Cornhill*. (Meredith, 1970, vol. 1, p. 365)

When Swinburne wrote to complain about the drop in payment from what he had been receiving under Lewes, Meredith was frank about the new regime in his reply:

> The *Fortnightly* is no longer in the hands of a company, but of a publisher, who tries to diminish the expenses as much as he can; the editor being the chief sufferer. I had to pay for the two poems . . . When I see Morley I will state your complaints to him; but from the sum he gets it's scarcely possible to pay more, without doing so out of his own pocket. (Meredith to Swinburne, 27 January 1868, in Meredith, 1970, vol. 1, pp. 366–7)

Morley was also under pressure to reduce costs throughout the late 1860s and early 1870s by cutting back on the number of articles and lowering the overall length of each monthly issue from 128 pages to 104. In December 1867, Meredith, again, had to explain defensively to Chapman & Hall, on Morley's behalf, that such demands could not immediately be met. Until March 1868, when G. Whyte Melville's novel *The White Rose* would have run its course, the page count would have to remain 124. Thereafter, Morley would undertake to keep it at 104 (Meredith, 1970, vol. 1, pp. 365–6).[4] The fact that from 1875 until 1881 (the last year of Morley's editorship) the *Fortnightly* published no fiction at all has always been interpreted exclusively as a mark of the journal's high intellectual seriousness – its refusal to pander to popular taste, and its Positivist antipathy to the romance genre. In reality it was as much a consequence of the editor's inability to afford the £250 to £1, 000 that a novelist of any stature would expect to command.

Morley did his best to keep his publishers at arm's length. Within a month of his taking over the editorship there are signs that he was seeking to extricate himself from their day-to-day scrutiny by getting rid of the sub-editorial post – and in that he seems to have been, eventually, successful (Trollope to John Dennis, 1 January 1867, in Trollope, 1983, vol. 1, pp. 364–5). But he could do little to counter incursions on his authority from other members of the board – particularly from Trollope, who seems to have found it difficult to relinquish a proprietorial interest in the magazine. Relations between the two men became badly strained in early 1871 over Trollope's insistence that Morley not be permitted to make cuts in a novel by Trollope's sister-in-law, Fanny. Two-thirds of the way through its run Morley wrote to Trollope's son Harry, a partner in Chapman & Hall, to complain that the novel was plagued by redundancies and would need extensive pruning in order to complete serialization in the time required. Failing that, Trollope's own *Phineas Finn* would have to be delayed. Trollope senior fired off a savage letter on 1 April 1871, not to Morley but over his head, to Frederic Chapman insisting that any redundancy was 'entirely due to [editorial] carelessness in not having seen that a proper proposition was inserted in each number of the Review. I do not know how to ask her to leave out 100 pages, which would I imagine utterly destroy her narrative' (Trollope, 1983, vol. 2, p. 543). The Trollopes had their way, and the size of each instalment, which had been reduced from 30 to 25 pages for the past seven months, suddenly doubled to 40 pages for the remaining four months of its run. The May 1871 issue, as a whole, was raised to 136 pages. Trollope was also able to demand that Morley be overruled on the question of whether or not *The Eustace Diamonds* could begin serialization in two months' time, overlapping Fanny Trollope's work for two issues and putting Morley in the unenviable position of having two works of fiction by close relatives running concurrently. 'I must insist,' Trollope wrote: 'Should it not be done my indignation would be very great . . . If necessary you could allow him an extra sheet' (Trollope,

1983, vol. 2, p. 544). Once again, editorial principles – though, in this case, also the publisher's budget – had been overruled.

There was a further complicating factor in Morley's struggle for greater freedom of decision-making – namely, the influence on the editorial board of the printer James Sprent Virtue, manager of one of London's largest printing firms. Virtue and Co. handled almost all of Chapman & Hall's book and periodical production.[5] Although Virtue's name is mentioned neither in Trollope's *Autobiography* (1883) nor in Edwin Everett's history of the *Fortnightly Review, The Party of Humanity* (1939), it is clear from Trollope's correspondence that Virtue attended meetings of the *Fortnightly* editorial board at least as an adviser and perhaps as a full member (Bodleian MS Don.c.10*, ff. 7–10).[6] Virtue was no 'mere' sub-contractor. He was a wealthy man who moved in the same social circles as the *Fortnightly*'s editor and its publishers. He was also one of the principal creditors of the maverick publisher Alexander Strahan. Saddled with £10, 000 worth of Strahan's debts in the mid-1860s, Virtue had sought to recoup his losses by starting a new periodical, the *St. Paul's Magazine*, under Trollope's editorship. Though generously funded, it had lost money steadily.

Morley is therefore likely to have found Virtue an increasingly cautious member of the board. Their personal relationship was complicated. Morley's Oxford tutor and mentor, James Cotter Morison, had married James Virtue's sister Frances in 1861. Meredith, a reader for Chapman & Hall as well as a contributor to and sometime editor of the journal, was a close friend of both Virtue and Morley, and would certainly have encouraged support for the young editor. On the other hand, Morley was briefly engaged to another of Virtue's sisters during late 1864 and, according to Meredith, the liaison had not met with fraternal approval. Meredith gossiped exuberantly that 'James (grown dyspeptic and savage) is, it is expected, the *bête noire* of the sweet dream', and it was soon over (Meredith to William Hardman, 7 December 1864, in Meredith, 1970, vol. 1, p. 298).[7]

What effect did the hierarchical and socially complex management structures of the *Fortnightly* have on Morley's ability to shape the role of the editor? Obviously, they limited his ability to purchase work by those who were unwilling to write for less than the usual rate of pay, but to a considerable extent they also determined the material form of the journal. The monthly numbers of the *Fortnightly* cut a sober appearance in the publishing world. Printed on inexpensive paper (which has yellowed badly with time), the articles were prefaced by advertisements and sewn into a plain beige wrapper, the undecorated front cover of which simply listed the price (raised by Chapman & Hall from 2*s*. to 2*s.*6*d*. from 1867), the date, editor's name, contents list, publisher's address, and the reservation of the right of translation.[8] On the back cover, in the usual manner, were printed further advertisements. This much remained constant, but there were other signs, from issue to issue, of commercial pressures shaping editorial decisions.

The constraint on word length was evident. Although Morley never achieved Chapman & Hall's hoped-for 104 pages, he did get the *Fortnightly* intermittently to as low as 112. The number of articles was also subject to sudden drops, notably in the second half of 1867, when it fell from the usual eight or nine to seven, and even, in August, to six. In 1869, when James Virtue was feeling the burden of Strahan's debts most acutely, and trying hard to persuade Chapman & Hall to assist, the September issue was suddenly reduced to 113 pages and only seven articles, and remained in that region until the following January.

More difficult to assess is the degree to which the board's policies affected Morley's ability to intervene substantially in the content of the journal. In principle, he was inclined to take a light hand. In April 1878 he reviewed for the *Fortnightly* the recently published letters of Macvey Napier, editor of the *Edinburgh Review* between 1829 and 1847, and the article provides his most explicit account of how he had come to view the editorial role. These papers, he wrote, shed welcome light on 'the man of letters and . . . that more singular being, the Editor, the impresario of men of letters, the *entrepreneur* of spiritual power' (Morley, 1878, p. 596). The self-conscious flourish of the phrase hovers somewhere between fanfare and irony, and, as the article continues, it becomes clear that the faintly dubious conflation of principle, profit and power that Morley discerned in Napier's editorial career had by now all but passed from the British periodical scene. The source of that change was to be found immediately to hand in the waning of the principle of anonymity in journalism:

> a man in such a position as Jeffreys . . . had [in Lord Cockburn's words] 'to discover, and to train authors; to discern what truth and the public mind required; to suggest subjects; to reject, and more offensive still, to improve, contributions'. (Morley, 1878, p. 601)

The modern editor was, by comparison, happily free from such labours. His function was no longer directive but suggestive; he was not answerable for every word or phrase printed, because the writer's views and language were plainly his or her own; he was, in short, no longer an impresario but a facilitator.

Morley's practice seems to have borne out this understanding of the editor's function. No proof sheets of the *Fortnightly* appear to have survived. There is, however, quite a lot of evidence to suggest that Morley restricted his interventions largely to the commissioning stage and the first response to manuscript drafts. In a letter of 27 April 1869 to his close friend and regular contributor, Henry Crompton, he explicitly stated,

> I don't consider that an editor has the right to alter a phrase – but [given the pressure on space] that he sh^{d}. have the right to omit is seriously

> indispensable . . . As the Review has to go into exactly 128 pp. [tighter
> restrictions were about to be imposed], it constantly happens that three
> or four writers have to lose a page each. Who those writers must be,
> and what the page shall be – are points that surely must be left to my
> discretion. (BL Add. MS 71701, f. 5)

Admittedly, where he strongly disagreed with a contributor's views, his role
as editor could come into conflict with his belief in the free exchange of
ideas. On one occasion he declined to interfere with the text of an article by
Frederic Harrison on the German church laws, only to append an editorial
note criticizing the 'doctrinaire' manner of his argument (Morley, 1874,
pp. 293–4, quoted in Hamer, 1968, p. 66; see Everett, 1939, pp. 298–300).
More commonly, Morley exercised his editorial influence before articles went
to press and, if possible, before first drafts reached his desk. Regular and
trusted contributors like Thomas Henry Huxley seem to have been given a
free hand. Letters to less proven or to prospective contributors were regularly
directed towards pre-empting problems with submitted material. They gave
detailed guidance not only on word length and subject matter but also
on style.[9] Strikingly, he used the pages of the journal on more than one
occasion to rebuke potential, and existing, contributors for shoddy or, in his
politically suggestive term, 'disorderly' manuscripts:

> 'I fear my manuscript is rather disorderly', says [an author] 'but I will
> correct carefully in print.' Just so. Because he is too heedless to do his
> work in a workmanlike way, he first, inflicts fatigue and vexation on the
> editor whom he expects to read his paper; second, he inflicts considerable
> and quite needless expense on the publisher; and thirdly, he inflicts a
> great deal of tedious and thankless labour on the printers, who are for the
> most part far more meritorious persons than fifth-rate authors. (Morley,
> 1878, p. 597)

It has to be conceded, however, that principle chimed conveniently with
circumstance in this regard. Given their other attempts at bringing the
budget of the *Review* under control, it is highly unlikely that the editorial board would have countenanced large bills from Virtue & Co. for
compositors' labour and additional paper costs. Indeed, the Minute Books for
Chapman & Hall show that in 1884 they moved to fix an £8 monthly cover
charge for all printers' corrections and a £5 limit for re-imposing, correcting
for press, night work and postage.[10]

As the *Fortnightly*'s position in the market-place became more secure, the
potential for strain between the ideal of minimal editorial intervention and
the actual power exercised by the editor became more of an issue. By 1872
circulation had risen from its 1867 low of 1,400 to 2,500 (Hirst, 1927,
vol. 1, p. 84), and with that success behind him Morley began to chafe for a

greater degree of freedom. In his 1968 study of Morley's intellectual career, D. A. Hamer notes that Morley held the classic Millian liberal belief that 'natural order can and does evolve out of the free play of forces, whether in the intellectual, the economic, the social, or the political sphere'. That assumption was, however, 'under mounting attack from many thinkers [Matthew Arnold, most famously] who were maintaining that "liberty" produced "anarchy", not order, and that the regime of "liberty" was bringing about a great crisis in which principles of authority were urgently needed' (Hamer, 1968, pp. 86–7). It is against this context that Hamer identifies in Morley an intensifying anxiety about the 'unsystematic nature' of editorial work, made explicit in 1875 when Morley contributed an article on Diderot to the *Fortnightly*:

> A man engaged in an enterprise such as [Diderot's] Encyclopaedia – or the *Fortnightly Review* – lacks an organic doctrine, an effective discipline, a definitive, comprehensive aim. His activity is characterized by 'dispersiveness.' He popularises 'detached ideas' by dressing them up 'in varied forms of the literary act', and guides men 'by judging, empirically and unconnectedly, each case of conduct, of policy, or of new opinion as it arises.' (Hamer, 1968, p. 119; quoting Morley, 1875, pp. 160–1)

It was in response to this concern, Hamer argues, that Morley began, from around 1873, to exert what power he had accrued from the rise in the *Fortnightly*'s circulation, to lend a greater appearance of system to the periodical by structuring debate around large issues – the education cause, the reform of the land laws, the campaign for Church disestablishment, and the reining in of Britain's imperial ambitions in India.[11] From 1876 he also started to encourage Joseph Chamberlain to use the journal as a platform for his political views. The primary casualty of that shift in editorial policy (not explored by Hamer) was science. In Morley's view, one of an editor's primary obligations was to ensure that contributors did not lose sight of general principles in their pursuit of detailed analysis. He viewed the 'scientific specialist' with particular distrust as 'the most likely of all men to lose "the social and humane point of view" and to forget "care for Freedom and Humanity" because he suffered from the narrowness or minuteness of the specialist's conception of Truth' (Hamer, 1968, pp. 89–90). The impact of this reasoning on the *Fortnightly*'s handling of science is plainly visible. From the start of Morley's tenure as editor, scientific specialization was eschewed in favour of large historical overviews of the progress of knowledge, and provocative but generalist pieces, such as Huxley's 'On the Physical Basis of Life' (February 1869) or Tyndall's 'Climbing in Search of the Sky' (June 1870) (Huxley, 1869, pp. 129–45; Tyndall, 1870, pp. 1–15). As Morley's concern to avoid the narrowly specific grew, the pressure to expand the term 'Science' into the search for general historical and social laws became more obvious.

By the later 1870s 'science proper' was in danger of being squeezed out of the *Fortnightly* altogether in favour of articles on 'larger' topics, such as national and international politics. From December 1876 to March 1877 not a single scientific article appeared – this despite the centrality of the subject to the journal's success so far (see Morley, 1917, vol. 1, p. 90, on the impact of Huxley's February 1869 article).

Claims that liberal intellectual anxieties shaped Morley's actions as editor are persuasive, but they become much more so when the social and commercial context of his work on the *Fortnightly Review* is taken into account. The conditions under which he was labouring as editor must have greatly exacerbated his concerns about the possibility, first, of the free and open exchange of ideas, and, secondly, of a progressive synthesis emerging from the interplay of those ideas. Worries about the systematic nature of intellectual labour to which he was already prone by virtue of his philosophical background in Millian liberal thought, can only have been enhanced by the experience of having the content, scope and arrangement of the *Fortnightly Review* not fully within his control, and of seeing them subject not only to the usual hazards of the printing press, but to the more wilful sabotage (as it could sometimes seem) by the editorial board and its individual members.

One of the best-kept secrets of the *Fortnightly Review*'s editorial history is, indeed, the manner of Morley's leaving. According to all the published sources, he resigned in 1882 primarily because he was finding it too difficult to juggle responsibility for the *Fortnightly* with his new editorship of the *Pall Mall Gazette*, and felt that the latter role offered him better prospects for making a practical contribution to British politics.[12] In fact, the Minute Books of Chapman & Hall Ltd reveal that he had had an irreparable falling out with the board of directors over the extent of his editorial authority. At its meeting on 4 May 1882 the board received two letters from a rival publisher, Kegan Paul & Co., defending their republication in book form of a series of *Fortnightly Review* articles on 'The Future of Islam' and citing a letter from Morley stating that Chapman & Hall had been informed and had given their permission. A letter from Morley to the board maintained his right to give such permissions to contributors, on the grounds that a refusal to afford him such discretionary power would place the *Fortnightly* at a serious disadvantage in the competition for articles. The board resolved, 'That Messrs Kegan Paul & Co. be informed that the permission of the proprietors of the *Fortnightly Review* had neither been given nor asked . . . and that they be requested to withdraw the book from sale at once or this Co. would apply for an injunction to restrain its publication' (RULA, Chapman & Hall Min., Bk. 2, p. 33). Morley's letter of resignation was in their hands the next day (RULA, Chapman & Hall Min., Bk.2, p. 36). For the remainder of his tenure relations with the board were very bad indeed. He removed all of his own books (except for one, which he was contractually unable to retrieve) from Chapman & Hall, who then tried to force him to pay not just for the copyrights but for the stock in hand, the stereotype plates, and the interest accrued by the firm in keeping them. The matter was only resolved through lawyers (RULA, Chapman & Hall Min. Bk 2, pp. 41–54). Though Chapman & Hall finally mustered a letter of thanks to Morley for all his years of work on the journal, and received a briefer but polite letter of reply, feelings remained bad enough for Morley to agree to write for his successor, T. H. S. Escott, only on condition that his authorship was kept 'a secret, especially from the lowminded brigands in Henrietta St' (Morley to Escott, 16 April 1884, in BL Add. MS 58787, Escott Papers 1079C, f. 40). There could be no more telling symptom of the degree to which the constraints on the periodical's production had overtaken its liberal idealism than that Morley's editorship should have ended in his maintaining a connection with the *Fortnightly* only at the cost of betraying its most cherished principle, the signing of articles.

*   *   *

When the *Nineteenth Century* began publication in March 1877, its editor, James Knowles, was determined that he would not be hamstrung by a publishing house or editorial board. Knowles was acquainted with Morley and probably knew something of the constraints under which the *Fortnightly Review* was produced, but he had also had direct and hard experience of how little freedom or security even a highly successful editor could possess when saddled with an interfering or, worse, an incompetent directorship. Knowles had had high-profile success as the editor of Strahan & Co.'s *Contemporary Review*, launched in 1866, in direct competition with Chapman & Hall, to be 'the Fortnightly of the Established Church' (Houghton *et al.*, 1966–89, vol. 1, p. 210). But when Strahan's business failed, the *Contemporary* became the property of new owners, who were less than happy with the fact that Knowles had taken the journal so far from its original old-style liberalism towards open-platform, progressive liberalism of the Morleyan sort, which might countenance scientific articles attacking cherished tenets of Anglican theology. In December 1876 the *Contemporary* changed hands again, Knowles' contract was terminated, and he indignantly refused to sign a new agreement which would bind him to working under the direction of Strahan and his creditors – with the result that Strahan privately published and distributed a series of defamatory articles denying that Knowles had ever legally been the editor of the *Contemporary*. (Knowles sued successfully for damages of £1,500.)[13] The decision to go it alone was in part financial (he had had enough of seeing the profits of his labour swallowed up by Strahan's debts), but it was also one of journalistic principle: 'I should have no care to edit any Review [he wrote to Gladstone] which was not *utterly impartial* – believing as I do, that full and fair and free discussion is the best way for arriving at and disseminating Truth' (2 November 1876, quoted in Metcalf, 1980, p. 273).

Thus far Knowles sounds remarkably akin to Morley, and to a significant degree he was. Indeed, Morley was an occasional contributor to the *Nineteenth Century*, though Knowles does not appear to have written for the *Fortnightly*. Their intellectual like-mindedness can be seen at a glance in the number of contributors who wrote for both journals and who gave each a flavour of advanced rationalism – Huxley, Tyndall and Harrison the chief among them. However, Knowles differed from Morley in being comparatively free from anxiety about 'systematization'. Far from seeking to encourage conformity of intellectual style, Knowles relished diversity and dispute in his pages, using Huxley as his scientific bulldog and goading more theologically conservative figures like Gladstone into the fray with him. His model for these 'free and frank exchanges of ideas' was the Metaphysical Society. So much has been written about Knowles' incorporation of its aims into the format of the *Nineteenth Century* that it is necessary only to sketch the principal points here. Knowles sought to replicate the range of views and interests represented by the Society in the content of his journal; but he also made effective efforts to manage the debate in ways that would avoid the lack of coherence that so troubled Morley without subordinating rational argument to a preconceived system. Hence his introduction, in April 1877 (the second issue of the *Nineteenth Century*), of the 'Modern "Symposium"', described in his prefatory note as follows:

> A certain number of gentlemen have consented to discuss from time to time, under this title, questions of interest and importance. Each writer will have seen all that has been written before his own remarks, but (except the first writer) nothing that follows them. The first writer, as proposer of the subject, will have the right of reply or summing-up at the end. (Knowles, 1877, p. 331)

Even outside the formal confines of these 'Symposia', Knowles tended to follow the same principle of 'organized controversy' in the structuring of periodical numbers. Articles of interest to him were regularly sent out to potential respondents with the aim of provoking a response for publication in the same issue, or letters would urge the necessity of X's views (enclosed) being 'set right' by Y. As his correspondence with Huxley (in the Imperial College, London archive) and Gladstone (in the British Library) demonstrates, Knowles was not averse to allowing each participant to believe that his sympathies lay with them, though direct comparison makes it clear that his real convictions were for Huxley and the scientific rationalists.

Knowles' ability to draw such contradictory talents into the pages of his magazine rested on several factors. Even more than Morley he was expert not only at letters of solicitation but at effulgent thanks, and he had the tact to make his writers feel that his own – surprisingly candid – ambitions for wealth and influence were entirely dependent on their good offices.

Privately, Morley had his doubts about Knowles' literary standing, as he indicated in a letter to Escott on 29 January 1884, advising him on the best method of securing election to Morley's London club: 'The Sec^y informs me (privately) that Knowles was refused last year. But you are in quite a different case, as being a real man of letters and a successful author, which is not our friend's position' (BL Add. MS 58787, f. 32). Whether or not Knowles quite passed muster in the highest liberal intellectual circles, it undoubtedly eased his way that, as sole proprietor, he was able to pay well. Writers who had delivered work to Morley for little, or sometimes no, fee found themselves able to command substantial figures from Knowles. Huxley was regularly paid £2 per page, Gladstone £4, and Tennyson £150 for the five-page 'De Profundis' (all figures from Metcalf, 1980, pp. 284–5).

Knowles established the *Nineteenth Century* as his own property by drawing on the capital he had accrued as a successful architect. His father provided £2,000 security for the venture but, as Priscilla Metcalf records, 'It was a matter of pride not to have to touch it' (Metcalf, 1980, p. 275). From the start, he took a wager that a more expensive-looking product would attract a wider audience than that of the *Contemporary* or the *Fortnightly*, warrant a higher cover price, and generate correspondingly larger margins of profit. The monthly numbers of the *Nineteenth Century* were published between distinctive, pale- green wrappers on high-quality paper. Though priced equivalently at 2*s*.6*d*., the first issue was visibly a far more substantial product than the *Fortnightly*, and at 176 pages it was half as long again. The *Fortnightly* made a gestural attempt at competition over the next few months, but quickly gave up.

The *Nineteenth Century*'s first issue had as its preface a poem by Tennyson, the Poet Laureate, and boasted an opening article by Gladstone and supporting pieces by Matthew Arnold, Cardinal Manning and Huxley (the latter in the capacity of 'aider and adviser' to the editor on the 'Recent Science' column). The journal sold brilliantly from the start; before long over 10,000 copies per issue had to be printed. The resulting profits to Knowles put him in an entirely different position from Morley's, and enabled a dramatically more authoritative style of editorship: one much closer to the image of the late eighteenth-century impresario, even as he responded to the newer principle of open debate between named contributors. The most telling signs of that style are to be seen in his dealings with his publishers, authors and – most especially – printers.

When it came to publishers, Knowles was adamant: whomever he chose would be in his employ, not a sharer in the profits or the management. After deliberation, he declined an offer from Longmans, who had been his first choice (Knowles to Tennyson, 6 January 1877, Tennyson Research Centre, Lincoln Central Library), and opted instead to give his business to Henry S. King with whom he had worked amicably during their temporary take-over of the *Contemporary Review* from Strahan & Co. in 1872–73. Strahan accused Knowles of exploiting King & Co.'s command of the machinery of publication and distribution of the *Contemporary*, using it 'in modes familiar to anyone acquainted with the trade . . . to promote the sale of the *Nineteenth Century* and at the same time destroy that of the *Contemporary Review*' ('Last Words from Alexander Strahan about "The Contemporary Review" and Mr. J. T. Knowles', p. 1, in BL Add MS 44453, f. 204, discussed in Srebrnik, 1986, pp. 165–6). It was probably as a direct consequence of the choice of publisher that Spottiswoode & Co., of New Street Square, East London, became Knowles' printers. His relationship with the partners, G. A. Spottiswoode and Cholmeley Austen-Leigh, was crucially different from that of Morley with James Virtue. The surviving Knowles letters in the Tennyson Research Centre at Lincoln and carbon-copy records of outgoing letters from Spottiswoode & Co. at the Essex Record Office indicate dealings that were entirely professional, though sometimes combative and, on occasion, even rebarbative.

Knowles used his printers with something approaching the casualness that a modern editor would take to a photocopier. He routinely sent the work of familiar contributors like Huxley straight to New Street Square without reading it himself, with the result that he occasionally found himself alarmed, at proof stage, by an excessive severity of style. In planning the 'Symposia' he necessarily adopted the practice of having each contribution printed up for distribution to all the participants (except the originator), and appears to have allowed extensive revision and occasionally numerous sets of proofs. Most of the evidence for this is in letters (especially those of Huxley and Spencer), but one – admittedly exceptional – set of proofs from the *Nineteenth Century* does remain in the Lincoln Tennyson Research Centre collection: a manuscript, first proof, and no fewer than four heavily marked-up revises for Knowles' elegy on Tennyson after the Laureate's death in 1892. Proofs for poems by others, including Huxley and Palgrave, also survive, some with little or no correction; others significantly revised, though none approaches the extent of Knowles' rewritings.

As John Bush Jones has demonstrated, the near standardization of the practice of proofing in gallery slips by the mid-1870s made it feasible for printers to handle far more extensive revisions in proof than had been readily admissible before (see Hargreaves, 1971, pp. 295–311; Jones, 1976, pp. 105–17). A financially constrained managing board like the *Fortnightly Review*'s might still seek to limit the practice as far as possible (and, as we have seen, John Morley had objections in principle to making unnecessary demands on the printer's 'tedious and thankless labour') but, when an editor was willing to pay for the cost of compositors' work, the only limit on the number of revises was the monthly deadline for going to press – and one of the advantages that Knowles purchased from his printers was a measure of flexibility over the printing schedule, so that individual issues could sometimes be timed for the greatest political impact (Metcalf, 1980, p. 285).

How much his proof changes cost Knowles would have depended on the nature of his contract with Spottiswoode and, potentially, on whether the company was putting the work out to fixed-salary or piece-rate workers. He certainly kept close tabs on Spottiswoode's internal costs – a role performed, less effectively, for the *Fortnightly* not by Morley but by Frederic Chapman. In September 1879, for example, George Spottiswoode had to counter sceptical inquiries about whether the paper used in the *Nineteenth Century* was the best value available. Spottiswoode was working with Messrs Grosvenor, to their mutual satisfaction, but Knowles had apparently been in receipt of, or had requested, a sample from another manufacturer. Spottiswoode took some pains on this occasion to explain to Knowles that the market was currently flooded with paper 'offered at almost any price', the vast majority of which was not as durable, heavy or reliable for printing as it claimed to be (Essex Record Office MS D/F 182/4/1/1, Out-Letters Bk of Spottiswoode & Co., 28 December 1867–May 1897, p. 444). Knowles also put repeated pressure on his printer (perhaps surprisingly, not his publisher) to increase the revenue raised from advertisements (Essex Record Office MS D/F 182/4/1/1, Out-Letters Bk of Spottiswoode & Co., 28 December 1867–May 1897, pp. 388, 434, 485, 487). Spottiswoode and Co.'s wage books do not list the *Nineteenth Century*'s print costs separately but, whatever the figure, Knowles was unlikely to have been able to better it elsewhere. The history of the London Society of Compositors records that Spottiswoode's was closed to members of the union between 1836 and 1917, and judged guilty of 'unfair' practices – bluntly, systematically underpaying its workers (Howe, 1947, pp. 54, 366–71).

In short, by excluding the publisher and printer from any share in the direction of his journal, and by being willing to spend comparatively heavily on the production of each issue in the knowledge that he would recoup the costs handsomely from sales, Knowles had managed to re-establish an editorial role which John Morley, only a few years earlier, had described as a thing of the past: the editor as impresario.

* * *

John Morley's increasingly pessimistic view of whether the liberal editor could be the facilitator of a debate which would, by the very nature of scientific rationalism, tend toward synthesis and moral and social progress, was thus founded on his own experience of the very divided powers and resources of an editor answerable to a financially restrictive publication board which included the printer as a social equal. If Morley's editorial style in the early years was in keeping with the liberal idea of unconstrained rational debate, it was partly so because he was himself constrained, having no power to coerce opinion, and only limited power to direct content and form. As he gained a greater, though never a full, measure of authority in the mid-1870s, the principle of contributors' liberty was to a significant degree compromised by his desire to guard against an anarchy of specialisms. Ironically, the confining of the editor's powers was, therefore, both a threat to liberalism in the *Fortnightly Review* in the early years of Morley's editorship and yet the best defence it had. James Knowles' editorship of the *Nineteenth Century*, by contrast, encouraged a more structured diversity of views from the start. Less anxious about the intellectual coherence of late nineteenth-century liberalism, Knowles was unembarrassed about defining himself as both editor and proprietor, conducting his business somewhat in the manner of a gentlemen's debating society, and treating his printer and publisher not as equal members of that society but as its subordinate employees. The irony in this case works in reverse: Knowles' consolidation of a larger measure of power meant that his journal was able to offer greater freedom to contributors – even if those contributors were too predominantly 'lions' to satisfy a strict definition of 'open' debate (quoted in Metcalf, 1980, p. 289). It was also able to be more responsive to the manner in which contemporary science was progressing – through scientific and piecemeal advances in the laboratory and the lecture hall.

Many of the claims this chapter has made would, of course, hold true for any periodical or journal. Any editor's intellectual freedom will always be constrained by the presence of those others who have an interest in, and a degree of influence over, the way a periodical takes shape: not just its authors, but its publisher, printers, paper, type and ink suppliers, and the holders of the purse-strings. But such constraints were peculiarly over-determined in the context of late Victorian liberalism, where interference in the content and form of a periodical represented a threat to the ideal of free and open debate and, therefore, to the very mechanism of scientific rationalism and social progress. The editor's function was itself a form of interference, though a necessary one. Non-editorial interventions were not so readily defensible on intellectual grounds. In short, it mattered more for liberals like Morley and Knowles, and of course for the contributors who wrote for them, that textual production should be so complexly social and commercial an affair. For an embattled liberal, anxiety about the dangers of unconstrained liberty could only be amplified when one of the most important arenas in which the remedy for social ills was held to lie – the periodical press – revealed itself as fundamentally compromised.

Part II
Twentieth-Century Mythologies of Authorship

4
F. R. Leavis: The Writer, Language, History

Michael Bell

F. R. Leavis (1895–1978) had a strong conception of authorship in which a post-Romantic view of the artist was crystallized by modernism. For him, the author was an indispensable focus of moral responsibility and cultural insight while also manifesting a version of that dissolution of the 'old stable ego' that D. H. Lawrence noted as a radical feature of modernity (Lawrence, 1981, vol. 2, p. 183). Although Leavis represents an important position in the spectrum of modernist possibilities, by the late twentieth century he was widely misunderstood, both in his opposition and partial anticipation of later theoretical models. Moreover, his thought is enmeshed in a fraught personal and institutional history, since questions of personality are of the essence in his criticism. But if his principled conception has been obscured by reactions, admiring or hostile, to his personality, personality has a peculiar force for him in relation to the notion of the major literary artist.

In placing Leavis' view of authorship within the context of modernism, it is also important to note that the understanding of modernism itself has shifted significantly. A feature that almost all the modernists shared was a detestation of sentimentality, whether in literature or in personal and public life. They saw the Victorian age as having been corrupted with cheap and false emotionalism, of which the publicly induced patriotism of the 1914–18 war was a continuing manifestation. The seismic, and generally positive, shift in Western sensibility associated with eighteenth-century sentimentalism had its weak and indulgent aspects, for which we use the word 'sentimentality'. The cult of sentiment, or sensibility, in both good and bad senses, was associated with the female and, as its positive impact became mainstream, the softer and weaker side became especially so. The modernist generation therefore used a masculinist rhetoric of disciplining and controlling feeling, the gender bias of which has become more evident in retrospect. Leavis was not exempt from this epochal form but was to some extent gender-blind in a benign as well as damaging sense. The notion of an historical 'dissociation of sensibility' popularized for a time by T. S. Eliot struck a chord with Leavis, in whom personal and cultural wholeness was a criterion as vital as it was difficult. For Leavis, the felt need to impose artistic will on supposedly inchoate feeling – T. S. Eliot's 'undisciplined squads of emotion' – was itself a symptom of the problem, and hence his radical rejection of Joycean modernism and his high regard for George Eliot. The one contemporary writer of now generally acknowledged stature who arguably suffered from this modernist bias was Virginia Woolf, though Leavis' critique of her was based on other criteria, which will become evident in the course of this chapter.

As a younger contemporary of T. S. Eliot, James Joyce, D. H. Lawrence and Ezra Pound, Leavis was the critical spokesman of the modernist turn in so far as this may be considered collectively. He endorsed the historical critique and cultural renewal variously promoted by these writers, who between them largely formed the modern academic study of English. But he also exercised an internal critique of modernism, and developed from its partly opposed principles and practices a coherent view of literary significance and the critical function. The importance he attached to teaching, and to critical revaluation guided largely by the needs of students, was part of a social mission inherited from Matthew Arnold (1822–88), who was by profession a school inspector. But Leavis' notion of authorship radically modified the Arnoldian tradition in a way that is often misunderstood.

Misunderstanding arises partly because he shared the modernists' resistance to offering a philosophical rationale for critical activity. All of those named above, as well as Henry James and W. B. Yeats, expressed similar convictions. In the latter half of the century, however, this came to be seen as theoretical naivety rather than intuitive adherence to a long-standing, and sophisticated, philosophical tradition. In the late twentieth century, Jacques Derrida became a principal theorist of the impossibility of reducing questions of vital quality or judgement to conceptual terms; a parallel with Leavis that has been noted by Stephen Heath (1989, p. 36). But whereas Derrida was overtly philosophical, Leavis was engaged in a practical programme of critical reassessment for which this was a premise rather than a primary interest in itself. In his later years, as his thought seemed to be not only losing influence but becoming incomprehensible, he sought to explain his conception discursively, as in *The Living Principle* (1975). Even here, however, he draws on his own readings of key authors so that a reader has to be tuned already to his critical points of reference. Most importantly, as with Derrida, his conception of literature is only comprehensible within his larger understanding of language as a problematic mode of personal presence.

The artist in language

Leavis provides an invaluable template by which to assess later twentieth-century conceptions of authorship, since he shared the common modernist reaction against a perceived Romantic over-emphasis on personality but, unlike some who took up the theme later, he did not throw out the baby with the bathwater. His core conception was a version of the creative impersonality variously promoted by the modern authors mentioned above. All emphasized the need to separate the significance of the work from the personality of the writer. For Leavis, however, there was more at stake than the internal dynamic of the art work: a Flaubertian disappearance of the author. The great work of literature was an embodied evidence of something more than itself, and in this regard only great works could be in question. The major artist is creative not just by personal expressiveness but also by becoming an impersonal medium through which new emotions, intuitions and forms of being 'for the race, as it were' come into existence (D. H. Lawrence's phrase, quoted in Leavis, 1969, p. 51). Seeing this quality, for example, in William Blake, made him, for Leavis, a great artist whatever the crankiness that pervades so much of his *oeuvre* (Leavis and Leavis, 1969, p. 77). Such a conception can only make sense, or compel conviction, in its concrete instantiations, and it is inevitably subject to many reductive or deceptive versions of itself. Even the word 'medium' here lends itself to such reduction, as in the chemical image by which T. S. Eliot sought to articulate his 'Impersonal' theory of poetry in 'Tradition and the Individual Talent' (Eliot, 1961, p. 18).

In *The Living Principle* (1975), Leavis was scathing about Eliot's scientific rhetoric, both as an account of poetic creation and as a symptom of Eliot's personal condition. Later in the century, Roland Barthes was to shred and rewarm modernist thought on impersonality in his essay 'The Death of the Author' (1968) (Barthes, 1977a, pp. 142–8). The solemn attention accorded to Barthes' essay is a startling index of late twentieth-century cultural amnesia with respect to the modernist generation. Most significantly, where Barthes opens up the text to postmodern relativity by detaching it from an author, the modernist conception of authorial impersonality, as formulated by Leavis, emphasizes the responsibility of the authorial function. Impersonality is not the opposite of personality, but rather personality exercised at full stretch for a purpose beyond itself. The transcendence of merely personal implication in the text enables the presence of the author in a more powerful and important mode. Leavis was the major critical proponent of this modernist conception, largely because he realized that it was not so much an idea as a qualitative perception.

Although Leavis learned from the modernist literary generation, he was isolated philosophically in the Britain of his lifetime – the era of analytical philosophy and logical positivism. Unwittingly, however, he pursued important strains of German thought in the traditions of phenomenology, historiography and *Bildung*. Placing him against these traditions brings out the complexity and coherence of his thought, while also indicating his peculiarity, both personal and national. It also lifts discussion out of the provincialism by which he has been obscured, perhaps partly through a misreading of his emphasis on the native language. Roger Poole (*The Cambridge Quarterly*, 1996, pp. 391–5) has argued the relevance of Edmund Husserl (1859–1938) to Leavis. But, in respect of creativity in language, the late essays of Husserl's successor, Martin Heidegger (1889–1976), on the interrelations of poetry, language and thought, provide the closest and thickest parallel (see Heidegger, 1971a and 1971b; for a comparison with Leavis, see Bell, 1988, pp. 27–56).

Heidegger saw in the very nature of language a creative potentiality that only the great artist brings to realization. We commonly think of using language to express ourselves, but, in Heidegger's view, rather than *we* speaking in language, language largely speaks *through* us. This may lead to an illusion of thought as if we are merely an unwitting function of the collective as embodied in language. Indeed, that rather reductive conception became a late twentieth-century commonplace. But the great literary artist, in the Heideggerean conception, turns this condition to positive account. Such an artist manages truly to listen to the language, and to bring the process of its speaking partially into consciousness. Not too fully into personal consciousness, of course, or the contact with the historical collective would be lost. For Heidegger, if poetry expresses a potentiality in language itself, it is because this, in turn, reflects a larger history of the loss, or forgetting, of what his translators capitalize as Being. For human beings, language is the condition of 'world' and Heidegger gave his own inflection to a tradition in German thought since the Enlightenment, whereby the ancient Greeks enjoyed an un-alienated relationship to themselves and the world. With the growth of Socratic ideals of knowledge, however – in other words, with the very principle of Enlightenment – the world became a congeries of external entities susceptible to scientific explanation and technical manipulation, while the normal condition of the self was an increasing lack of authenticity. Such a relationship to the self and to other beings was part of a forgetfulness of Being. On this account, the critique of modernity was not just a banal and temperamental conservatism, but rather signalled a larger predicament of the race. There is a strong parallel with Leavis, who adopted the insight encapsulated in T. S. Eliot's phrase 'dissociation of sensibility' to argue that behind our immediate modernity lies an historical process of alienation within the self, a coming apart of thought and feeling (Eliot, 1961, p. 288). This had its collective aspect in what he called the 'Technologico-Benthamite' culture for which Heidegger's central term was *Gestell*, or equipment.

Yet there are great differences in the thought-worlds and cultural contexts of Heidegger and Leavis. Heidegger argued philosophically a case that Leavis largely assumed, because he was more practically concerned with cultural intervention. For all his concern for 'world', Heidegger proved during the Nazi period to be fatally unworldly in a more obvious sense, and with a mixture of ordinary worldly self-interest to boot. Considered philosophically, apart from political overtones, the arbitrariness and vulnerability of his arguments suggest an encompassing myth; if the word designates, not a falsehood so much as a world-view. His philosophical vision is obviously so much greater than the sum of the specific cultural-historical evidence that readers have, if not to ignore this, then to accept its essentially illustrative status. His true concern is quite evidently a philosophical vision derived from reflection on language and Being. By contrast, Leavis' account grows from a detailed and polemical engagement with literary texts within their historical contexts, and any bracketing of his historical claims is, therefore, less appropriate. His larger narrative, lying between a grand philosophical myth and a detailed historical case, is similarly more vulnerable to objectors. Hence, while the phenomenological tradition provides an important lens through which to appreciate his preoccupation with major literary art within the creative potentiality of language, the truer burden of significance lies with his historical claims. In that respect, he parallels closely the historiographical thought of Heidegger's partial forebear, Wilhelm Dilthey (1833–1911).

The artist in history

For Dilthey, the history of philosophy was the struggle for universal validity of competing world-views (*Weltanschauungen*), which cannot be grounded purely in philosophical reason. By the same token, to understand another individual or culture you must understand their world-outlook in a way for which purely rational criteria are insufficient. His life-work was centred on the attempt to produce, in the light of this recognition, an adequate conception of historiographical practice. This was linked to a concern with hermeneutics, or the science of textual interpretation, which he studied in particular in the work of Friedrich Schleiermacher (1768–1834). In that respect, he was an inverse parallel to Leavis. Seeking to understand the past, including its own self-understanding, Dilthey privileged the concentrated, inward evidence of art, especially literature, as the art of language. Conversely, Leavis valued literary criticism as an inward reading of history. His judgements of relative literary importance are not by some independently aesthetic order of consideration but as concentrations of historical significance. Above all, he shared with Dilthey a belief in history's mode of self-creation in the collectivity of language, a process concentrated particularly in producing great works of literature.

Post-Enlightenment culture had developed a powerfully historical, as opposed to universalistic, understanding of almost all fundamental aspects of human life. Yet, for Dilthey, the understanding of history itself was still pre-critical, and required an equivalent of Kant's foundational critiques. Dilthey contested contemporary models of historical reason, in which he distinguished principally the metaphysical, the pragmatic and the scientific. The metaphysical conception was most strikingly exemplified by G. W. F. Hegel's view of history as a gradual realization of world-spirit. In so far as this was the survival of a theological model into a secular age, it was not perhaps the major opponent except that psychological formations live on in partly unconscious ways. Pragmatic history seeks to avoid such habits and assumptions but, to do so, it requires the more self-critical and principled alternative Dilthey was seeking to articulate. Meanwhile the powerfully seductive model in modernity was that of the natural sciences. Dilthey argued for the inadequacy, or inappropriateness, of a scientific model with respect to history. His *Introduction to the Human Sciences* (1883), the first volumes of a projected critique of historical reason, sought to place the humanities on a proper disciplinary footing distinct from the protocols of the natural sciences. Leavis similarly insisted on the discipline of English as having a strictness comparable to the scientific. Dilthey placed great weight on the word 'understanding', since part of the difference between history and the natural sciences is that we can understand human beings inwardly, even if they are of a different culture or period; although we cannot explain them. In contrast, science allows us to explain the non-human world significantly, but not to understand it in the sense that we understand our fellow beings. Where science gives certitude and predictability, history gives a depth of empathic understanding within protocols of interpretation. It is noteworthy that this German tradition distinguishes and limits the claims of science but does not demonize it. Leavis did not demonize science either, though he was frequently construed in that way in Britain, which has a long history of disciplinary polarization in its education.

Dilthey was one of several late nineteenth-century thinkers concerned with the inadequacy of historical self-reflection. Friedrich Nietzsche (1846–1900) provides, in 'On the Uses and Disadvantages of History for Life' (1874), a striking example with a prescient relevance to the modernist generation. Dilthey, seeking a positive model of historical understanding, gave full weight to the last word of Nietzsche's title: 'life'. For life is the ultimate category underwriting the significances of history, and of the textual forms through which it is often most crucially known. But as Leavis was aware, ' "Life" is a large word', whose importance is reflected in its near unusability (Leavis, 1969, p. 51). It is the four-letter, Anglo-Saxon 'f-word' that most truly designates the unspeakable. For life is not a self-evident category that can be inter-subjectively invoked in itself, and neither Dilthey nor Leavis subscribed to a generalized philosophical vitalism (Leavis, 1969, p. 52). Life represents a qualitative judgement to be made only in its concrete manifestations. Dilthey, therefore, accorded special importance to what he called *Erlebnis*, or 'lived experience'; a close parallel for Leavis' Jamesian phrase 'felt life'. The German words *Erfahrung* and *Erlebnis* both translate as 'experience', but whereas the former is connected etymologically to travelling, the latter is cognate with life. One can travel without deeply internalizing the experience it offers, while a stay-at-home can live an apparently limited experience more intensely. Part of the difficulty in taking stock of Leavis, who lived in Cambridge virtually all his life, is that he consciously limited his claims to cultural *Erfahrung* while exercising a formidable intensity of *Erlebnis*. His most forceful judgements were sometimes prefaced by cultural disclaimers that distinguished his concentration on the essential from educated distraction. What has been said so far also indicates why Leavis saw the critic as having a special access to, and responsibility towards, the native language. Personally, he was interested in Eugenio Montale, Paul Valéry and Friedrich Nietzsche, but he wrote with hesitation on topics outside his native tongue.

In contrast to Dilthey as theorist, but in consonance with his theory, Leavis gathered his meditation on history into the intuitive complex of his praxis, as a creative writer might do. Yet he was far from being a creative writer *manqué*, in the sense that T. S. Eliot diagnosed in the 'imperfect' critic who reads his own frustrated creativity into the work of others (Eliot, 1960, pp. 6–7). Rather, he brought to the act of reading an intense participation in reliving the author's creative process, as if the work were being freshly created each time in the reading. This is less easy than it sounds. Great works are precisely those that are now so much part of the world that it is hard to imagine them as not existing; and, especially so, if you are sensitive and self-conscious with respect to their historical impact. Dilthey recognized this difficulty. He invoked Schleiermacher's notion of interpretation as 'reconstructing a work as a living act of its author', and saw such reading as a form of 'divination' which 'apprehends an author through the same creative act – albeit conceived as receptivity – that generated the work in the first place'. Properly to appreciate a work of genius requires a measure of 'congeniality' (Dilthey, 1989–96, vol. 4, pp. 130, 158). Similarly, Leavis typically places himself within the imagined standpoint of the original creative act, and privileges moments in Shakespeare where the poetic thought seems still to be unformed, as if caught for ever in mid-process.[1]

This conception of reading as a re-living (*Nacherlebung*) of the original creation catches both the crucial significance for Dilthey and Leavis of the individual artist, along with the transcendence of personality that was crucial to their mutual sense of historical evolution. In Rudolf Makkreel's words: '*Nacherlebung* is the highest mode of historical understanding' (Makkreel, 1975, p. 361). Similarly, for Leavis, the literary, so often taken as a counter term to historical, is the fullest form of the historical. In the first volume of *Scrutiny* he expressed his resistance to Marxist explanation in economic and class terms (Leavis, 1933, pp. 205–14). Instead, like Dilthey, he saw collective purpose working itself out dispersedly in history, and therefore not as a knowable, and still less as a predictable, teleology. The creativity of great writers is a crucial means through which this process happens. As Leavis put it in *The Living Principle*:

All writers of major creative works are driven by the need to achieve a fuller and more penetrating consciousness of that to which we belong, or of the 'Something other than itself' on which the 'physical world ultimately depends'... The English language in the full sense is alive, or becomes for the creative writer alive, with hints, apprehensions and intuitions. They go back to earlier cultural phases. The writer is alive in his own time, and the character of his response, the selective individual nature of his creative receptivity, will be determined by his sense – intensely individual – of the modern human condition.... He needs all the resources of the language his growing command of his theme can make spontaneous – can recruit towards the achieving of an organic wholeness: his theme itself is (being inescapably a prompting) an effort to develop, in realizing and presenting it, living continuity... The 'living principle' itself is an apprehended totality of what, as registered in the language, has been won or established in immemorial human living. I say, 'an apprehended totality', for, in the nature of things, there can be no one total upshot; for every major writer it is different – there are many potentialities and no statistically determinable values. We call a writer major when we judge that his wisdom, more deeply and robustly rooted, represents a more securely poised resultant, one more fully comprehensive and humanly better centred – considerations bearing crucially on future growth – than any ordinarily brilliant person could offer us. (Leavis, 1975, pp. 68–9)

Dilthey had a similar conception of great art as impersonally serving the collective:

in the struggle of practical interests every expression can be deceptive and its interpretation changed with the change in our situation. But, in great works, because some content of the mind separates itself from its creator, the poet, artist, or writer, we enter a sphere in which deception ends. No truly great work of art can, according to the conditions which hold good and are to be developed later, wish to give the illusion of a mental content foreign to its author; indeed it does not want to say anything about its author. Truthful in itself it stands – fixed, visible, permanent: and, because of this, a skilled and certain understanding of it is possible. Thus there arises in the confines between science and action a circle in which life discloses itself at a depth inaccessible to observation, reflection and theory. (Dilthey, 1992, vol. 8, pp. 206–7; (Rickman's translation), 1961, pp. 18–19)

Dilthey's description of artistic impersonality here is closer to T. S. Eliot's emphasis on separation as of the author, whereas Leavis stressed the higher form of sincerity required in the author in discovering his own deepest intuitions. He saw this in the opening of Eliot's 'East Coker' (1940); and he always used the word sincerity in this impersonal sense. Leavis combined the impersonality of the process emphasized in Dilthey with D. H. Lawrence's sense of personal struggle in his formula 'Never trust the artist. Trust the tale' (Lawrence, 1924, p. 2). This conception places a heavy burden on the critic, who may be as rare as the major artist. Yet, as the etymology of the word arbitrary suggests, one person's considered act of grave public judgement is another's imposition of personal whim. This brings us back to the opening question of the imbrication of the personal in Leavis' criticism, and helps to explain a further aspect that is commonly misunderstood.

Impersonality and judgement

Leavis was accused of imposing an unacceptably narrow taste, as in the exclusions that take up the first part of *The Great Tradition* (1948). But, like Dilthey and Heidegger, he rather invokes a criterion of historical significance which few writers in any generation could satisfy. It is not a matter of mere taste but of an order of significance. His criterion is not just whether an author embodies an historically representative sensibility, or whether the work is even extraordinarily brilliant, but whether it is a genuinely desirable growing point in the culture. Underlying the historical judgement of representative significance is a life judgement on the fundamental tendency of the author. James Joyce, Ezra Pound and Wyndham Lewis, for example, are evident candidates for historical significance in the sense of encapsulating their epoch, but Leavis saw them as reflecting, and even exploiting, the predicament of modernity rather than making a truly creative response to it. For Leavis, a work achieves such historical significance through its impersonality, its transcendence of an author's personal preoccupation and self-image. In his view, however, the very techniques of impersonality associated with Joyce are rather the symptoms of his artistic will, a will-power that conflicts with the deeper process of creativity 'for the race'. This may be a serious under-estimation of Joyce, but it is not merely trivial or incomprehensive. If Joyce is truly significant it must be by such a criterion.

If great art, as Dilthey and Leavis believed, is crucial to historical self-creation, and therefore to self-understanding, then it is necessarily elusive to protocols of certitude. There is no alternative to judgement, and this judgement will always be more than an aesthetic one; hence their shared emphasis on the individual as the inescapable locus of both significant artistic achievement and responsible criticism. Summarizing the Enlightenment's development of historical consciousness, Dilthey puts much of the Leavisian view in a nutshell:

> And . . . the point was finally reached where the conception of society according to the natural system passed into a true historical consciousness. Herder found in the disposition of the individual person that which changes and constitutes historical progress. The medium through

which the nature of this progress was studied in Germany was art, especially poetry. (Dilthey, 1989–96, vol. 1, p. 215)

Similarly, their mutual emphasis on the individual as the creative focus of
the collective led them to reflect on the ambiguity of the word 'mean'. As
Leavis put it:

> The focal words for me at present are 'mean' and 'meaning'. The ease
> with which one shifts from one force of the word 'mean' to another is
> significant. The protest, 'Oh, but that isn't what I meant by the word',
> might very well have issued as, 'But that isn't what I meant to mean'. . . It
> seems to me that some presence of the force of 'intend' is necessary to
> the meaning of 'means'. . . . Thought about language should entail the full
> and firm recognition that words 'mean' because individual human beings
> have meant the meaning, and that there is no meaning unless individual
> human beings can meet in it, the completing of the element of 'intend'
> being represented by the responding someone's certitude that the last
> condition obtains. (Leavis, 1975, pp. 37–8)

As soon as words leave the dictionary, they take on purpose, and the
dictionary only records the semantic upshot of such purposes in the past.
Linguistic meaning is always underwritten by a purposiveness, which can
only be manifested through individuals; and yet is inseparable from the
general life and potential of meaning in the language at large. This truth,
Leavis suggests, is immediately self-evident and yet, for that very reason,
overlooked. Dilthey develops the same recognition: 'There is a relation,
strange as it is important, between purpose and meaning, which we have
already noticed in the life of the individual, and which asserts itself in
history' (Dilthey, 1961, p. 163).

The acknowledgement of intentionality as being specific to all linguistic
acts and diffused within the language at large bears crucially on the practice
of criticism and interpretation. All uses of language, including literary texts,
are freighted with intentionality. This rules out the postmodern notion that
a text is simply open to all readings; that the purposiveness of its creation can
be ignored. At the same time, it enforces the equally important recognition
that the meaning of the text may well differ from the conscious intention
of the author. Dilthey adopted Schleiermacher's formula that we may know
the author better than he knew himself; a recognition that has become a
primary emphasis in critical practice since the modernist generation, and is
pervasively exemplified in Leavis.

While Dilthey and Leavis both sought to understand the intentionality
of the text in an empathic spirit, Dilthey was more aware of interpretative
obstacles and Leavis of the seductions of the text. For Leavis, the difficulty
lies in adequacy of response rather than determining between competing

intentionalities. In resisting the emphasis on interpretation in relation to literary texts, Leavis was perhaps eliding a real problem; yet there is a point of practical wisdom at stake here. His working assumption that there is a tangible core of meaning to be found in the text acts as a sheet anchor against the open-ended relativity of much subsequent low-level academic practice which actively seeks originality of interpretation as a presumed good in itself. Above all, however, the judgements that Leavis sought to make were of quality rather than meaning in the sense suggested by interpretation. To appreciate this, it is useful to invoke another aspect of German tradition, the notion of *Bildung*, in contrast to a common reading of the Arnoldian model of culture.

Bildung and culture

Matthew Arnold believed in the civilizing power of humane culture. Knowledge of 'the best that is known and thought in the world' is ennobling, and imparts a detachment from merely material and sensuous considerations (Arnold, 1960–77, vol. 3, p. 282); although Arnold (as in the Preface to his 1853 Poems) acknowledged a virtually unbridgeable gap between his ideal of personal culture and the values of contemporary life (Arnold, 1960–77, vol. 1, pp. 1–15). His culture was based on universalistic values seen pre-eminently in the classical literatures, and while many modernists (such as T. S. Eliot, James Joyce and Ezra Pound) claimed to represent a classicizing turn against Romanticism, they were in many respects enacting an internal development of the Romantic tradition. In effect, this generation experienced the relative waning of classical dominance as the native tongue acquired a richer significance. This was also the period in which university English studies, notably at Cambridge, shifted from having a philological emphasis to a critical reading of the vernacular literature. Leavis' conception of a constant historical process of creativity within language is part of this shift and reflects the gulf between him and Arnold on what it means to be in possession of culture.

In assessing writers who might meet the criteria of major significance outlined above, Leavis made a judgement of their fundamental nature and tendency. This, once again, may be confused with a response to the author's personality in a temperamental or social sense. Consider, for example, his differing responses to T. S. Eliot and D. H. Lawrence. Both have manifest points of vulnerability, Lawrence the more strikingly so. To some observers, therefore, late Leavis seemed to adopt an increasingly uncritical identification with Lawrence and an irrepressible hostility to Eliot, as if his critical judgement were distorted by personal sympathy. But whatever the element of justice in this charge, there were reasons for his emphasis. Throughout Leavis' lifetime, Eliot enjoyed a high reputation in the academy, while Lawrence for the most part did not; and he was taken up in the 1960s in a way that was, for Leavis, even worse than the former condescension. Apart from tactical considerations, however, the true rationale for this difference arises from the logic of his criteria as already outlined. Leavis continued to see Eliot as the supremely important poet of his generation; one who achieved general new recognitions out of his personal struggle with language. But the weaknesses he found in him, as in parts of the *Four Quartets* (1935–42), were moments of archness, of self-protectiveness, and of flinching from life, especially sexuality, all of which interfered with the impersonality that enabled his true creativity. Eliot's failings mattered because they touched the essential. By contrast, the extremity, absurdity and turgidity to be found in Lawrence did not, in Leavis' judgement, damage what was essential in his creativity. In fact, they were often necessary to his heuristic openness, the practical condition of his capacity for self-righting. Above all, his heurism was not hampered or distorted by a concern for self-image.

As well as the distortion of creativity arising from concern for self-image, which Leavis saw in James Joyce and W. B. Yeats as well as T. S. Eliot, he also emphasized the damaging effects of class feeling, not as a matter of explicit ideological or political commitment, as of relevant depth of experience. This consideration bears particularly on the Leavises' response to the writers associated with Bloomsbury and its most notable literary instance, Virginia Woolf. The plural is necessary here as Q. D. Leavis, F. R.'s only life-long collaborator, was the most cutting in her treatment of Woolf for what the Leavises saw as her class-bound ignorance of common human experience, including that of women (see Leavis, 1938, pp. 203–14). Q. D. Leavis was a strong champion of women and had a wide knowledge of women's writing over several centuries although her conservative view of what was of value in women's lives and activities has excluded her from being generally recognized as a pioneer in this sphere. Her objection to Woolf, therefore, was not for her championing of women, but for her class-bound conception of the cause. Similarly, F. R. Leavis had promoted George Eliot as one of the supreme writers of the English tradition. Although Leavis did not argue it as a specifically gender-based case, Eliot's experience as a woman was clearly relevant to her achievement as he describes it. When he argued that her creation of Gwendolen Harleth was superior to Henry James' of Isobel Archer, this was because of her more acutely critical insight into the female ego of the character (Leavis, 1948, p. 111). The thrust of the Leavises' critique here has become obscured by the late twentieth-century supersession of class analysis by identity politics, and by the upward evaluation of Woolf by a later generation of feminists.

Leavis, then, was far from supposing that there was a generalized culture that could educate and ennoble where human experience and personal moral quality were lacking, and this explains his significant transformation of the Arnoldian tradition. Although Leavis' early study *Mass Civilization and Minority Culture* (1930) was squarely Arnoldian, his subsequent career indicates a further order of problem internal to culture itself, and here it is useful to compare the parallel fate of the German tradition of personal culture known as *Bildung*. Thinkers in France and Germany, with their different histories, had already recognized a radical problem in the notion of culture: where culture is spread it may, rather than ennoble, be merely vulgarized. Even J. W. Goethe, the classic representative of *Bildung*, was more sceptical of it than is commonly recognized outside specialist circles. In the latter part of the nineteenth century, Friedrich Nietzsche saw in the formal acquisition of culture a generalized philistinism or, for more profound spirits, nihilism. Hence, where Matthew Arnold contrasted culture and philistinism, Nietzsche spoke of the *Bildungsphilister*, the cultured philistine (Nietzsche, 1997, pp. 7–10, 35–40). Gustave Flaubert gave withering expression to the same perception in France. Leavis was to see an equivalent phenomenon in British academic and literary culture and, far from supposing that mere exposure to high culture was sufficient to produce the cultured individual, he concentrated on the quality of reception, the capacity to internalize appropriately in reading.

This explains further the special importance of D. H. Lawrence to Leavis, which he made explicit in the essay 'Wild, Untutored Phoenix' (Leavis, 1952, pp. 233–9).[2] Lawrence was highly cultured. He had a formidable knowledge of English and several other literatures, including French, German and Spanish in the original and Russian in translation. He reviewed acutely on a wide range of topics, had a keen appreciation of European art, and wrote a still significant early interpretation of American literature. But few people, including his strongest admirers, would think to describe him as cultured, because what was significant about him was more a mode of being than a body of knowledge or range of skills. Indeed, he retained a highly personal idiom, as if actively protecting himself from conventional cultural forms. Conventional readers have to attend carefully to register the range, weight and delicacy of perception, as Leavis sought to show by comparing T. S. Eliot's essay on *Hamlet* with Lawrence's description of a village production in Italy (Leavis, 1969, pp. 148–57). Lawrence as a critic is typically concerned with personal wholeness, both in the author's text and in his own response.

Lawrencean wholeness is the inverse of *Bildung* in a way highly pertinent to the internal deconstruction of that ideal effected in Goethe and Nietzsche. If the *Bildung* tradition disintegrated at the core, this was because of two interrelated aspects: it sought a roundedness of individual culture, and it grew from an Enlightenment belief in the individual as the microcosmic form, or growing tip, of an overall human development. The individual was a function of the whole. Hence, the tradition depended on its most vulnerable points: the quality of individual life that it promotes, and its reflection in the general quality of the social culture. Lawrence started at the other end. His commitment to truth of individual feeling, when taken in a spirit of full responsibility, had inevitably to encompass a whole world of essential culture, including the art, literature and thought of the past. But he judged this from his own standard of wholeness. In comparison, even those who meditated most critically on the tradition of *Bildung*, such as Nietzsche, were still inside its terms. Lawrence's relevance, arising from his being so comparatively *sui generis*, is by the same token harder to spot. The more fully one becomes cognisant of this quality in Lawrence, as happened only gradually for Leavis, the harder it is to think of real antecedents or equivalents.

Yet although Leavis' growing commitment to Lawrence is inseparable from his understanding of creativity and history, he could perhaps not fully learn from Lawrence's example. Lawrence, as a creative writer, showed a healthy instinct in keeping himself free of conventional cultural forms and settled social existence however much he also suffered, creatively as well as personally, from his lack of an audience. By contrast, Leavis had a settled existence centred in pedagogy within a university, although he too experienced this as an embattled isolation. Both suffered a crisis of authority which, in Leavis' case, returns us to the opening question of disentangling his essential vision and critical practice from its institutional circumstances and personal style.

Critical authority and the common pursuit

Before resigning his university chair, Nietzsche analysed the near contradiction of conducting humanistic education on an institutional scale. This echoes Leavis' embattled distinction between the ideal and the actual Cambridge. His felt need to exemplify the responsibility of critical practice, to be the ideal Cambridge, placed a revealing strain on his own wholeness and impersonality; the qualities he had learned to value in Lawrence. His best criticism undoubtedly has these qualities and remains exemplary. But contrary to the usual case, he seemed to achieve this at the expense of the personal dimension in himself and others. Even in radical disagreement, Lawrence acknowledged other centres of life such as Il Duro, in *Twilight in Italy and Other Essays* (1916), or the con-man, Maurice Magnus (Lawrence, 1994, pp. 173–8; 1968, pp. 303–61). In comparison, Leavis' sympathy was narrowly confined.

By his own terms, Leavis had to exercise a judgement at once highly personal and deeply representative, commensurate with the import of great literary art. For a critic, this cannot occur merely as an unconscious by-product of major creative work, nor is there a created object in which to embody the given order of values. It was to Leavis' credit that he constantly highlighted the risky ambition of his own writing. He always performed his demanding conception demonstratively and, in doing so, he threw its internal tension into relief. Since fundamental life values are *ex hypothesi* not open to other forms of grounding, it is difficult, and dangerous, to negotiate them. Any compromise risks the whole. Where such an intense and unnegotiable purity of judgmental attention is of the essence, however, it may narrow into embattled certitude and obsession very different from either Goethe's Olympian elusiveness or Lawrence's underlying insouciance. Despite the 'Yes, but . . .' principle of the 'common pursuit', the collaborative circle was narrowly drawn and it is hard to escape the impression that anyone who truly challenged was held to be disqualified (Leavis, 1969, p. 47). By the same token, it was hard for disciples, even highly independent spirits, not to appear antagonistic.

For whatever mixture of intrinsic and circumstantial reasons, Leavis increasingly broke relationships even with close and loyal collaborators.[3] In so far as his philosophical and moral posture had a paranoid potentiality at its core, it has a significant forebear in Jean-Jacques Rousseau (1712–78). As educator, Rousseau repressed the tension between his authority and the pupil's absorption of moral truth. His imaginary pupil, Emile, was to be taught as if by the immediate reality of nature, yet had to be subjected to elaborate manipulations (for discussion of this question, see Starobinski, 1988). Invoking a transparent value of life, while writing in an alienated social culture, Rousseau had to offer himself as being representative of full human beings. Leavis ends the era of Rousseau by rehearsing its central problematic with comparably intense internal strains. Within the pedagogical relationship, which was central to Leavis' practice, it can be hard to distinguish a pupil's failure to understand from authentic, if still immature, disagreement, but Leavis, like Rousseau, could allow virtually no scope for this distinction. Fundamental cultural quality was at stake and Leavis, like the modernist generation generally, felt himself to be fighting a rearguard action. By contrast, the latter part of the twentieth century largely abandoned the modernist belief in a single culture within which the discriminations of life quality and cultural value made by individuals of unusual wisdom and insight have, or should have, a representative force. In this respect, the mid-century 'two cultures' controversy arising from Leavis' 1962 Richmond Lecture on the novelist, scientist, and cultural commentator, Sir Charles Snow, is an emblematic watershed. Leavis' Diltheyan insistence on the commonality of culture underlying different disciplines within a linguistic community had become largely incomprehensible to many formally cultured people. If to later generations the whole argument seems merely quaint, this may, of course, signify precisely what Leavis foresaw as a 'major human disaster' (Leavis, 1975, p. 70): that the question of a common culture, and the authority of collective experience it makes available, is no longer even a matter of concern. It would be in the nature of such a disaster to be unrecognized.

In short, Leavis had a strong conception of authorship, and its responsibility, derived from a longer history of post-Romantic thought and honed by the new context of modernity. In developing the differing modernist models of authorship as impersonality, he rejected those associated with Joyce and Eliot and based on technique and detachment. These models involved a high degree of authorial self-image and imposition of will. Truly creative impersonality arises, for him, from a relationship to the general historical experience of the linguistic community in question. Where the same words have to serve, there is at once a hair's breadth and universe of difference between these different senses of the impersonal.

5
Mind that Crowd: Flann O'Brien's Authors

Joseph Brooker

'Where do you lave that crowd now?
I do not know.
A right crowd.
Yes.
And your other men. Where do you lave THEM?'

– (O'Brien, 1988a, p. 30)

Summer 1940, and a couple of letters have appeared in the *Irish Times*: the first bemoaning the lack of support for a production of Chekhov's *Three Sisters* (1901); the second blaming this state of affairs on the Irish people's love for American films, and on pro-Gaelic xenophobia among Dublin intellectuals. A response appears, signed 'F. O'Brien':

Sir,
I was interested in H. P.'s saucy letter of yesterday commenting on the poor attendances at the Gate Theatre's presentation of *The Three Sisters*. He is right when he suggests that overmuch Gaelic and Christianity, inextricably and inexplicably mixed up with an overweening fondness for exotic picture palaces, effectively prevents the majority of our people from penetrating farther north than the Parnell monument. Heigho for the golden days I spent as a youth in Manchester! In that civilised city we had Chekhov twice nightly in the music-halls; the welkin rang all day long from non-stop open-air Hamlets in the city parks, and the suicide rate reached an all-time high from the amount of Ibsen and Strindberg that was going on night and day in a thousand back-street repertory dives. One politely mentioned one's view on Dick Wagner when borrowing a light from a black stranger, and barmaids accepted a chuck under the chin only when it was accompanied by a soft phrase from Pirandello. Nowhere in the world outside Sheffield could the mind glut itself on so much buckshee literary tuck. (O'Brien, 1988b, p. 187)

It could go on: and it does go on. F. O'Brien begins to reminisce about a childhood in which Henrik Ibsen, Algernon Swinburne and Joseph Conrad would come round for tea and discuss George Moore with his grandfather. 'I need scarcely add', he adds, 'that "Conrad" was only a pseudonym (or pen name), for that seafaring man hailed from a far land which has since encountered still another of the slings of destiny' (O'Brien, 1988b, p. 188). 'Pseudonym (or pen-name)', indeed.

After this, a deluge: for weeks the letters pages of the *Irish Times* were occupied by irritable exchanges about the real Ibsen and Conrad, and a host of other literary figures from the recent past. Lir O'Connor corrects F. O'Brien on the subject of Conrad:

> Josephine Cuminsky or Joseph Conrad as she was afterwards called, was born and spent the earlier years of an exciting life dreaming the hours away on the gentle slopes of the Galway mountains. Cool, slim and unhurried, this lissom slip of a girl had the sea in her blood, and willingly, nay eagerly, she answered to its call. (O'Brien, 1988b, p. 193)

O'Brien replies:

> It is news to me that this great gentleman was a lady. Great as my surprise would be if this were proved, it would be nothing compared with the chagrin which Ibsen would endure if he were alive to hear the proof. That unprincipled foreigner spent many hours of his life closetted alone with Conrad, doing nothing more or less than discussing George Moore. (O'Brien, 1988b, p. 195)

There is a lot more where that came from: contributors to the controversy, as well as H. P., O'Connor and O'Brien, included Whit Cassidy, Paul Desmond, Luna O'Connor (sister of Lir) and Oscar Love. One month after that mysterious figure had penned a limerick to end the exchange, another debate started up. The occasion was a book review by Patrick Kavanagh: soon the list of correspondents included 'F. L. J.' from Glasnevin, N. S. Harvey, Judy Clifford, Jno., O'Ruddy, Hilda Upshott, The O'Madan, 'South American Joe', 'Lanna Avia', 'Na2 Co3', and F. McEwe Obarn, not to mention the same characters who had held the initial contretemps about Josephine Conrad.

To the best of our knowledge, almost all of these correspondents were fictitious. The exact sources of this crowd of opinionated characters are still not certain: but we know that the man who wrote as F. O'Brien was responsible for a good many of them, and that his associate, Niall Montgomery, wrote several of the rest. There is much to be said about the letters' content: they engage with national and international politics, conservative accusations against the filthiness of modern literature, and James Joyce's recently completed *Finnegans Wake* (1939), which is parodied more than once. But we should also consider the form of the controversy, the peculiar genre that confronts the reader here. In one sense it is inherently a thing of fragments, a chance collection of bits to be placed in chronological sequence. It has no predetermined order, no destination inscribed in it from the start: it is a text whose end its first author cannot foresee. At the same time, the controversy possesses a kind of continuity: the comic spirit that runs through the whole is a signal asking not only to be received and interpreted correctly, but to be appropriated and redirected. The debate tacitly asks those who get it to join in and extend it: to pick up the tone is to enlist in a restricted club. A kind of unitary work – though one without a central narrative – is fashioned: but this is done by a calculated accident. The chancy nature of the letters column, which might always attract another uninvited author, is taken into account, chosen as the very basis of the enterprise. The fake controversy is built on the vagaries of the public textual space offered by the newspaper: it acknowledges and invites the irruption of contingency and surprise.

Most importantly in the present context, its authors are multiple, though part of the point is that we cannot be sure how multiple. The controversy is double-sided, an uncertain pattern of difference and sameness. For even as it appears to announce a stream of outlandish new authors, one bizarre figure succeeding another, the suspicion simultaneously persists that some of the letters come from the same pen. In this respect, the presence of F. O'Brien amid the correspondents is significant: for it nods us in the direction of the better-known works of Flann O'Brien. In the absence of major modern novels by Lir O'Connor and Hilda Upshott, it is almost as though O'Brien annexes the controversy to his own *oeuvre*, leaves his mark on it and invites us to trace the paper trail across to *At Swim-Two-Birds* (1939) and *The Third Policeman* (1967). This is especially true for us six decades on; but even at the time of the letters' publication, the first novel bearing O'Brien's name had briefly topped the Dublin best-seller list the previous year.

We are thus invited to think of the epistolary controversies in the context of O'Brien's literary career. We could indeed go further than that, and view them as among that career's exemplary moments. The formal features noted above – comedy, fragmentation, the occupation of public space, the cultivation of esoteric references, the openness to contingency – are characteristic of this writer, but find as pure a realization here as anywhere. And more vividly and drastically than any other moment of Flann O'Brien's career, the *Irish Times* debates make play with authorship: with fantastical names, fabricated voices, uncertain origins and multiplicity. This chapter will focus on this dimension of O'Brien's writing, and with what it does to our ideas of authors.

This name or something similar

But one cannot go further down this path without noting the dubious ontological status of Flann O'Brien himself. In *At Swim-Two-Birds*, we read that the novelist William Tracy has invented the practice of 'aestho-autogamy', in which literary characters are born fully-grown and in their twenties, on the basis that

> Many social problems of contemporary interest...could be readily resolved if issue could be born already matured, teethed, reared, educated, and ready to essay those competitive plums which make the Civil Service and the Banks so attractive to the younger breadwinners of today. (O'Brien, 1967, p. 41)

It is therefore appropriate that Flann O'Brien should have been, as his commentator Robert Tracy (presumably no relation) says, 'born on 13 March 1939, on the title page of *At Swim-Two-Birds*', hence already in his late twenties (Tracy, 1994, p. 2). 'Flann O'Brien' was conjured by Brian O'Nolan (1911–66), a man from the North of Ireland who spent the middle of the century making himself into one of the era's quintessential Dubliners. 'Brian O'Nolan' is relatively stable ground, the hard rock to which discussion of this writer retreats from the shadowy waters of the pseudonym: when books on the man start talking about 'Brian', we know that we are as close to the real world as we are going to get. But even this name has its shadows. Like his father, Michael O'Nolan, before him, Brian multiplied versions of even this simplest of tags. According to his biographer, Anthony Cronin, in 1935 he sat the entrance examination for the Civil Service as 'Brian Ó Nualláin'; but the report for his first day at work stated that 'Mr Nolan reported for duty today' (Cronin, 1989, p. 79). When he made an official complaint about being addressed as 'Nolan', he remarked that 'My own name is one of the few subjects upon which I claim to be an authority' (quoted in Cronin, 1989, p. 78).

By then he was busy making it into the kind of subject upon which one could be an authority. In 1939, shortly after the publication of his first novel *At Swim-Two-Birds*, he wrote to the *Irish Press*, disclaiming authorship of the book:

> Your information apparently derives from a rumour spread by two gentlemen called Sheridan and O'Brien who charge me with the author-ship of a book of this name or something similar. The cream of this elaborate 'joke' is that the supposed book is anti-clerical, blasphemous and licentious and various lengthy extracts from it have been concocted to show the obscenity of the work. I have joined in the joke to some extent myself but I naturally take strong exception to the publicity given by your paragraph, which associates me by name with something which is objectionable, even if non-existent. I must therefore ask you to with-draw the statement. I would be satisfied if you merely mentioned that a graduate mentioned in your last Notes is not the author of any book

mentioned and has in fact no intention of publishing any book. (O'Brien, 1988b, p. 178)

Facts and fictions begin to swirl together. 'Sheridan' refers to Niall Sheridan, a close friend of O'Nolan's who was also a contributor to various joint projects – and thus a part of the ambiguous compound of authorship to which O'Nolan's writing lays claim.[1] Indeed, at O'Nolan's request, he had undertaken to edit *At Swim-Two-Birds*, excising a fifth of the text (Cronin, 1989, p. 85). His role might thus be compared with Pound's as *il miglior fabbro* on T. S. Eliot's *The Waste Land* (1922) – a comparison which re-emphasizes the complexity of authorship in O'Nolan's writing. If he had a hand in making the text, Sheridan is also represented in it as the narrator's literary confidant, Brinsley. In a memoir, he recalls that, as he and O'Nolan discussed the progress of the novel, O'Nolan wrote their discussions into the manuscript: 'I found myself (under the name Brinsley) living a sort of double life at the autobiographical core of a work which was in the process of creation' (Sheridan, 1985, p. 74). Discussion of the book went into the book, becoming part of the object under discussion. A peculiar circularity is involved here, a feedback loop which makes *At Swim-Two-Birds* radically open-ended and self-consuming; it also emphasizes the unusual fluidity of movement between the book's authors and characters, a fluidity which we shall see mirrored in the text itself.

While Sheridan is represented in the letter by his real name, O'Nolan is figured by a fiction: not the novel's narrator, whose anonymity matches his deliberately colourless voice, but its putative author, the fabricated Flann O'Brien. The name, O'Nolan wrote to his publishers in November 1938, 'contains an unusual name and one that is quite ordinary. "Flann" is an old Irish name now rarely heard' (Cronin, 1989, p. 88). In that sense it was a more flagrant fiction than his suggested alternative, the comparatively dull 'John Hackett' (Cronin, 1989, p. 89).[2] In any case, the imaginary O'Brien joins the real Sheridan as a rumour-monger making trouble for Brian O'Nolan. Beyond this, again, the letter weirdly combines two possible worlds: the novel is 'objectionable even if non-existent'. In an indirect anticipation of the following year's mock letters, the fiction of a fiction is substantial enough to cause complaint. As for the truth, by the time we reach the last sentence it is hard to keep in mind. But 'I would be satisfied if you merely mentioned that a graduate mentioned in your last Notes is not the author of any book mentioned and has in fact no intention of publishing any book' says that O'Nolan will be satisfied if the newspaper retracts the truth, and replaces it with a formulaically false set of negations. The request reflects the civil servant O'Nolan's professional need for anonymity in his literary work; but it also multiplies public falsehoods in a manner characteristic of his writing.

At Swim-Two-Birds meditates more or less directly on a series of literary issues, with authorship central among them. But O'Nolan was to become better known in Dublin through a different fabrication. On the basis of the letters-page controversies, the editor of the *Irish Times* offered him his own column from 1940.[3] O'Nolan picked the name Myles na gCopaleen from Dion Boucicault's play *The Colleen Bawn; or, The Brides of Garryowen* (1860), itself an adaptation of Gerald Griffin's novel *The Collegians* (1829). It was apt that O'Nolan's most persistent, prolific authorial identity should derive from two levels of intertextuality. With deliberate Gaelic pedantry, he spelt the surname with a small g and capital C. The sliver of yet another name emerged when the column, entitled *Cruiskeen Lawn* (1940), went over exclusively into English and Myles began to hope for international recognition: now he was Myles na Gopaleen, with a plain capital G.[4] To that extent there were at least three major identities in play: Brian O'Nolan, Flann O'Brien, Myles na Gopaleen, each of them involving variants. Yet in an autobiographical piece late in life O'Nolan suggested that a writer, outdoing T. S. Eliot's cats, might need even more than three names:

> [In] 25 years I have written ten books (that is, substantial opera) under four quite irreconcilable pen-names and on subjects absolutely unrelated. Five of those books could be described as works of imagination, one of world social comment, two on scientific subjects, one of literary exploration and conjecture, one in Irish and one a play (which was produced by the Abbey Theatre). (quoted in Cronin, 1989, p. 225)

It is characteristic of O'Nolan that, as he claims to be telling the bare truth about himself, he pulls from his sleeve four books that biographers have not been able to locate. In 1939, he was disavowing authorship of the one novel he had written: in 1964, he is fabricating authorship of books that he apparently hasn't. In both cases truth is merely an inconvenience, to be waved away by the authority of style.

In an intriguing passage in the same text he makes a more programmatic demand:

> [A writer] must have an equable yet versatile temperament, and the compartmentation of his personality for the purpose of literary utterance ensures that the fundamental individual will not be credited with a certain way of thinking, fixed attitudes, irreversible techniques of expression. No author should write under his own name nor under one permanent pen-name; a male writer should include in his impostures a female pen-name, and possibly vice-versa. (quoted in Cronin, 1989, p. 225)

Perhaps this was what Josephine Conrad was up to. It is notable that O'Nolan refers here to 'the fundamental individual'. The purpose of pen names, it seems, is to protect the real self beneath – to protect it, specifically, from falling into fixed modes of expression, from being typecast. In one sense we can, and should, say that Brian O'Nolan was the real man behind the writing, though it is not clear that he did manage to avoid a certain ossification of the personality. O'Nolan would sometimes refer to his personae as discrete individuals: when Anthony Cronin suggested, in the 1950s, that he publish a novel under the old name 'Flann O'Brien', O'Nolan replied 'I don't know that fellow any longer' (quoted in Cronin, 1989, p. 197). But writer and persona might not be so swiftly dissociated. John Wyse Jackson's formulation is elegant: 'For the first ten years, say, between 1930 and 1940, he was seeking a voice. During the next ten years or so, he had found it. After about 1950, he had become that voice' (O'Brien, 1988b, p. 8). The mask of Myles became harder and harder to remove, to distinguish from any underlying face.

No doubt it was Brian O'Nolan, not Flann O'Brien and still less Hilda Upshott, who drank himself slowly to death through the 1950s and 1960s, even if some of his friends thought it was a practical joke when they heard of his death on April Fool's Day 1966 (Costello and van de Kamp, 1987, p. 140). But to put it this way does not quite get at his evasive essence. The identity of this writer does not reside simply in his brute reality, the curmudgeon whose appearance demystifies all his aliases out of existence. We need instead to understand the aliases as part of the identity: to say that in a sense O'Nolan became more himself, and more than himself, in writing. He found his voice by putting on voices: he enjoyed himself by making up selves.

A suitable existing puppet

Such a dynamic view of writing finds vivid realization in *At Swim-Two-Birds*, a novel in which a man writes a novel in which another man writes a novel, and whose characters take over the writing of the novel and take revenge upon their author. The images of Chinese boxes or Russian dolls, each smaller than its predecessor, come readily to hand for this book of books. Like Policeman MacCruiskeen's boxes in *The Third Policeman*, stories nestle within other stories, and each narrative layer opens successively on to the next in a *mise en abyme* effect (O'Brien, 1988c, pp. 72–6). Nor does *At Swim-Two-Birds* maintain a straightforward, easily grasped relationship between narrative levels. It cuts back and forth frequently between the frame story and the fictional worlds that lie within it; it multiplies and leaves uncertain the number of fictional worlds that coexist on a given level; it invents new rules for the relations between (fictional) author, text and characters, then abruptly alters them, pulling the rug from under the reader. And from under one or more of its authors – for a corollary of the novel's multiple narrative lines is that different authorial voices jostle for textual control of the book. My assumption in the account that follows is that there are three different narrative layers, which for convenience will be dubbed A, B and C. The man who, before writing this novel, had invented a means for translating Gaelic into algebra might have understood (O'Brien, 1988b, pp. 56–61).

The primary narrative (A) is delivered in ten 'Biographical Reminiscences' by a student in his final year at University College Dublin, where O'Nolan had spent the first half of the 1930s. The first-person voice of this nameless figure is effectively the frame for everything else in the book. (Sue Asbee has pointed out that the anonymity of the narrator is itself a wilfully awkward aspect of the book: any account of the story must labour clumsily with the non-name 'the narrator' (Asbee, 1991, p. 23).) Here, he will be dubbed 'the student', in order to make it easier to discuss the novel's multiple voices. Significantly, the student is an author, engaged in 'spare-time literary activities' (O'Brien, 1967, p. 9): he is writing a novel, which he spends much of *At Swim-Two-Birds* expounding and discussing. It is worth noting the effect of this narrative level's prose style on the relationship between real and fictional authors. The student's authorial voice has the stiffness of a policeman reading from his notebook. Simple facts are described with as elaborate a precision as possible: 'The weather in the following March was cold, with snow and rain, and generally dangerous to persons of inferior vitality' (O'Brien, 1967, p. 59); 'Innumerable persons with whom I had conversed had represented to me that spirituous liquors and intoxicants generally had an adverse effect on the senses and the body and that those who became addicted to stimulants in youth were unhappy throughout their lives' (O'Brien, 1967, p. 21). It is a purposely cold prose, meticulously drained of abbreviation and colloquialism. As Anthony Cronin remarks, the narrator seems to be writing English as a dead language. A kind of depersonalization, Cronin adds, takes place (Cronin, 1989, pp. 106–7). In its way, this squares with O'Nolan's penchant for persona and mask: in writing as a first-person narrator who attends his own alma mater, he deliberately makes it difficult for us to identify with the student, or to see the figure as a warmly nostalgic version of himself. Depersonalized style is an escape from the facility of the familiar, the ease of the intimate personal voice. English as a dead language keeps us away from the author's life. The style thus refuses the seductions of the memoir, almost as Samuel Beckett's flip into French refused him what he considered the too easily won warmth of Hiberno-English.

But it is in its proliferation of narratives that *At Swim-Two-Birds* leaves behind decisively the consolations of the memoir. The student offers the frame-story, but we cannot necessarily say that his fate is at the centre of the novel. On the contrary, we might say that the frame is just where one would expect it to be: on the edge, a mere structure for holding something else in place. The student is writing a novel (B) about an author named Dermot Trellis, who is in turn writing a book of his own (C). Trellis' work is to have a moral purpose, albeit deviously executed, as the student explains:

> Trellis . . . is writing a book on sin and the wages attaching thereto. He is
> a philosopher and a moralist. He is appalled by the spate of sexual and

> other crimes recorded in recent times in the newspapers. . . .He realizes
> that purely a moralizing tract would not reach the public. Therefore he is
> putting plenty of smut into his book. (O'Brien, 1967, p. 35)

Trellis' book is to function as literary aversion therapy: the characters and
deeds it depicts will be so depraved as to repel its readers into righteousness.
   We are therefore dealing, in effect, with three different texts: the story of
the student (A), the novel being written by him (B), and the novel being
written by Trellis (C). The novel by Flann O'Brien – himself a kind of
fiction – already includes two different fictional authors. But as we near the
third level, things become still more complicated. Within the world of the
student's novel (B), fiction moves in mysterious ways. 'Characters' have a
physical existence: 'authors' cannot simply write them into existence, but
must employ them, picking them up from other books and paying for their
presence. A literary character is not a textual construct whose every word
and gesture is at the command of their author, but a hired hand, engaged
to participate in a story. The characters who are to populate Trellis' novel
are something like cinematic or dramatic actors: to some extent under the
instructions of the author, but always liable to protest at their treatment or to
improvise a narrative of their own. As the student puts it in an explanation
of his own literary theory,

> Each [character] should be allowed a private life, self-determination and a
> decent standard of living. This would make for self-respect, contentment
> and better service . . . Characters should be interchangeable as between
> one book and another. The entire corpus of existing literature should
> be regarded as a limbo from which discerning authors could draw their
> characters as required, creating only when they failed to find a suitable
> existing puppet. The modern novel should be largely a work of refer-
> ence. (O'Brien, 1967, p. 25)

The last line of the above quotation is applicable not only to *At Swim-
Two-Birds* but also to O'Nolan's writing as a whole. What it implies here
is that the author is an editor. Yet the authors on level B are something
slightly different. The most vivid instance of the book's alternative laws of
authorship is the point where *At Swim-Two-Birds* momentarily enters the
Western genre.[5] Paul Shanahan is among the characters enlisted by Trellis
for his book: in the past he has appeared in the fiction of William Tracy.
We hear of Tracy via Shanahan's reminiscence ('there was a rare life in
Dublin in the old days'), then via a *'Relevant excerpt from the Press'* recording
the death of 'the only writer to demonstrate that cow-punching could be
economically carried on in Ringsend' (O'Brien, 1967, p. 53). Tracy, a second
excerpt explains, has also developed extensive grazing land in Dublin, having
'had 8,912 dangerous houses demolished in the environs of Irishtown and

Sandymount to make the enterprise possible' (O'Brien, 1967, p. 56). He thus exemplifies something of the position of the author in *At Swim-Two-Birds*, as power-broker and businessman. When the cowboys, responding to a message, travel to see Tracy in Drumcondra 'to get our orders for the day', he tells them that it is a false alarm: 'Get back to hell to your prairies, says he, you pack of lousers that can be taken in by any fly-be-night with a fine story' (O'Brien, 1967, p. 54). There is some irony here: the cowboys' whole commission is the enactment of a story, fine or otherwise, and the false alarm has diverted narrative control away from Tracy. It has been seized by a rival practitioner: the rustler Red Kiersay, who has nabbed Tracy's cattle in the cowboys' absence, 'was working for another man by the name of Henderson that was writing another book about cattle-dealers and jobbing and shipping bullocks to Liverpool' (O'Brien, 1967, p. 54).

The comedy of a moment like this relates closely to its breaking of narrative order. Authors (Tracy, Henderson) ought to be safely beyond the stories that they produce, inventing and crafting fictions at will. But here the conventional fence between the author and the contents of his text has been removed: authors are also characters, embedded in the same world as their creatures, dealing and bargaining rather than writing and deleting. To write here is comically redefined as man-management; to be an author is to be an entrepreneur. This is a fantasy of authorial power, as well as one of weakness. In one sense, the literary artist gains the worldly sway that a life of second-hand typewriters and rejection letters denies him; yet the relationship of Tracy and Henderson to their characters lacks the omnipotence that an author should rightfully enjoy over his own creations. In this respect, the novel actualizes a recurrent, not always fully articulated feeling about the writing of fiction: that it is beyond full authorial control, liable to sweep the author's pen away like a galloping horse disobeying an incompetent cowboy. The student's friend Brinsley remarks later, apropos of his novel, that 'the plot has him well in hand' (O'Brien, 1967, p. 99). Brinsley echoes directly his concrete counterpart, Niall Sheridan, who in June 1935 had told the readers of *Comhthrom Féinne* that O'Nolan was 'engaged on a novel so ingeniously constructed that the plot has him well in hand' (quoted in Cronin, 1989, p. 82). The problematics of authorship were not wholly fictional: they reflected, and created, O'Nolan's own literary labour. The novel's breach of the bar between author and text – its problematization of authorial power – is echoed by, or echoes, a parallel process in the real world, in so far as that term can be used within range of O'Nolan's name.

We have already encountered the book's other, equally strange model of authorship and characterization: aestho-autogamy, in which characters can be created from thin air, 'from an operation involving neither fertilisation nor conception' (O'Brien, 1967, p. 40). Lacking a suitably bad man to play his villain, Trellis must conceive of John Furriskey himself, as a spoof newspaper extract reports: 'Stated to be doing "very nicely", the new arrival is about five feet eight inches in height, well built, dark, and clean-shaven. The eyes are blue and the teeth well formed and good, though stained somewhat by tobacco' (O'Brien, 1967, p. 40). Aestho-autogamy, as Anne Clissmann has noted, is a deliberate *reductio ad absurdum* of the idea of 'creating a character', and is of a piece with the way that O'Nolan's japes play upon the conventions of realist fiction – as influentially sketched, for example, by E. M. Forster in *Aspects of the Novel* (1927) (Clissman, 1975, pp. 40–1). It is as though Flann O'Brien has taken those conventions at their word, and written the novel that they logically imply but have never hitherto produced. To that extent, the flagrant fantasies of *At Swim-Two-Birds* have their roots in an immanent critique of the realist novel: by taking that form's terms literally, it turns it into a textual circus that is the very opposite of literary realism.

The relation between textual levels proves profoundly unstable. A central event in the student's manuscript is the birth of Trellis' illegitimate son, Orlick – who arrives, perhaps unsurprisingly in this book, as a 'stocky young man' in 'dark well-cut clothing', his first words a piece of oratorical eloquence (O'Brien, 1967, pp. 145–6). The other characters – notably the 'plain men' Furriskey, Shanahan and Lamont – are by now chafing under Trellis' regime, and seek to punish him for their poor treatment. Having drugged Trellis into sleep, they thus persuade Orlick – who has inherited Trellis' literary gifts – to take up the author's pen and seize command of his father's story. He readily accepts, as the student records in the course of another synopsis:

> Smouldering with resentment at the stigma of his own bastardy, the dishonour and death of his mother, and incited by the subversive teachings of the Pooka, he agrees. He comes one evening to his lodging where the rest of his friends are gathered and a start is made on the manuscript in the presence of the interested parties. Now read on. (O'Brien, 1967, p. 164)

What follows is Orlick's manuscript: a radical departure in which we see the author, Trellis, turned into a character in someone else's story. This development throws the structure of *At Swim-Two-Birds* into reverse. Until now the conceit has been that one character (A) writes about another (B), who writes about another (C): each narrator possesses at least some of the authority befitting an author. But Orlick's narrative exploits the conditions that pertain within the student's novel: the ontological plane that Trellis and his minions share. If characters are as real as their author, then why should they not be able to script his activities, rather than the other way around?

The process that results requires us to shift our conception of how writing works. What follows is the most dynamic depiction of writing that *At Swim-Two-Birds* has to offer. 'Tuesday had come down through Dundrum and Foster Avenue', Orlick begins, 'brine-fresh from sea-travel, a corn-yellow sun-drench that called forth the bees at an incustomary hour to their day of bumbling' (O'Brien, 1967, pp. 164–5). This ornate and circumlocutory prose persists for two pages describing Trellis' awakening, until the story is interrupted:

> I beg your pardon, Sir, said Shanahan, but this is a bit too high up for us. This delay, I mean to say. The fancy stuff, couldn't you leave it out or make it short, Sir? Couldn't you give him a dose of something, give him a varicose vein in the bloody heart and get him out of that bed? (O'Brien, 1967, pp. 166–7)

We are thus brought back from the third narrative level (C) to the second (B): and the next forty pages or so are spent cutting between these two. In one sense we have simply seen authorial power change hands – as if, back in contemporary Dublin (A), the narrator's uncle had taken over the writing of Trellis and company (B). But the situation is more disturbing than that: for it appears that what Orlick writes as fiction actually happens to Trellis. The characters' glee at seeing him mauled by the Pooka and hauled before a judge and jury is not an imaginary compensation for his treatment of them: it is an actual revenge, which is intended to lead to his physical destruction. Narrative has become a weapon, not just metaphorically – a means, say, of damaging another's reputation – but literally.[6] To return to the earlier theatrical metaphor: it is as though Orlick and friends have become directors who can order Trellis to perform dangerous stunts, and he is powerless to refuse. For he has now become 'just a character in a novel', in precisely the way that Furriskey, Shanahan and the others managed to avoid.

Towards the end of the novel, then, narrative levels seem to implode into one another: the demarcation between them becomes hard to locate. In a final irony, though, Trellis escapes his scripted fate through a loophole in the book's weird laws. The student has already brought his own narrative (A) to an end, when we encounter the '*Conclusion of the Book, penultimate*' (O'Brien, 1967, p. 215). Teresa, Trellis' maidservant, casually makes a fire with 'several sheets of writing which were littered here and there about the floor':

> By a curious coincidence as a matter of fact strange to say it happened that these same pages were those of the master's novel, the pages which made and sustained the existence of Furriskey and his true friends. Now they were blazing, curling and twisting and turning black, straining uneasily in the draught and then taking flight as if to heaven through the chimney. (O'Brien, 1967, pp. 215–16)

Immediately, a bedraggled Trellis appears outside the front door. The implication is clear: in destroying written descriptions of the characters, Teresa destroys them altogether. It has seemed until now that characters have a certain autonomy. Suddenly, they appear to be paper tigers, as fragile as the sheets they're written on: less than a pack of cards. The narrative of *At Swim-Two-Birds* has been stripped from three levels to two: both of which, as a sickly Trellis retires to bed again, are now ended. 'You could easily get your death, Sir', Teresa warns (O'Brien, 1967, p. 216). But the death of the author is not quite staged in the novel: what we get to see is his weary and sickly survival. Victory over these characters has proved to be somewhat pyrrhic.

Your name on the title page

Authorship is not such a self-evident concern in any of Flann O'Brien's subsequent novels as it is in his first. But on closer inspection, a preoccupation with the ownership and provenance of textuality repeatedly becomes apparent. *The Third Policeman* merrily digresses into footnotes recounting the thought of the savant de Selby: these expand into debates over the true authorship of not only his work but that of his commentators too. 'It is now commonly accepted', we are informed,

> that Hatchjaw was convinced that the name 'du Garbandier' was merely a pseudonym adopted for his own ends by the shadowy Kraus. It will be recalled that Bassett took the opposite view, holding that Kraus was a name used by the mordant Frenchman for spreading his slanders in Germany. (O'Brien, 1988c, p. 174)

The authorship of du Garbandier's output looks to be as uncertain as that of Oscar Love's letters. O'Nolan thus characteristically lets his own play with names find an echo in the novel via the marginal means of the footnote. The book that followed, *The Poor Mouth* (1941), uses a different paratextual device to analogous effect. It begins with a Preface from '*The Editor*', claiming that

> This document is exactly as I received it from the author's hand except that much of the original matter has been omitted due to pressure of space and to the fact that improper subjects were included in it. Still, material will be available ten-fold if there is demand from the public for the present volume. (O'Brien, 1993b, p. 7)[7]

That last line may be less comic than the rest: it bears something of O'Nolan's recurrent anxiety for commercial success (see Cronin, 1989, p. 95). But the note also manifests a characteristic sense of text as 'material' to be multiplied, cut, edited. The Preface concludes that 'It is a cause of jubilation that the author, Bonaparte O'Coonassa, is still alive today, safe in jail and free from the miseries of life.' The authorial claim to have received one's manuscript from another hand, the true history of an absent character, has its familiar place in the history of the novel. But it is again thoroughly characteristic of O'Nolan to fall back on that venerable device, placing a layer between himself and the novel's first-person narrator. The gesture at once displaces O'Nolan from the narrative and transplants O'Coonassa from the fictional plane to the real. Once again, authors are being multiplied, though not with the gay promiscuity of *At Swim-Two-Birds*. The name on *The Poor Mouth*'s jacket, as it happens, was Myles na gCopaleen. Its title page now reads as follows:

> Flann O'Brien
> *The Poor Mouth*
> *(An Béal Bocht)*
> *A bad story about the hard life*
> Edited by
> Myles na Gopaleen
> (Flann O'Brien)
> Translated by
> Patrick C. Power
> And illustrated by
> Ralph Steadman. (O'Brien, 1993b, p. 3)

In the present context, we may elect to disregard the last pair of names – though the page does plausibly grant them some share in the book's creation. But it is striking that even O'Nolan himself is cited three times, under two different guises (one of them spelt differently from its original appearance), two pages before anonymously disavowing authorship of the text. On the original Irish publication of the novel in December 1941, Myles na gCopaleen advised the readers of *Cruiskeen Lawn* to 'Refuse all substitutes. Every genuine copy bears the name, "Myles na gCopaleen"' (quoted in Cronin, 1989, p. 129). There is deadpan humour in this insistence on the authenticating quality of so blatantly inauthentic an identity.

Even the late novels of the 1960s replay in altered form O'Nolan's tendency to multiply and muddle authorship. Much of *The Hard Life* (1962) is taken up with letters from the narrator's brother, Manus, which take over the tale in a strange echo of *At Swim-Two-Birds*'s authorial battles (see O'Brien, 1983, pp. 82–6, 91–4, 96–7, 98–9, 103–5, 106–7, 107–12, 115–17). (This was perhaps becoming a recurrent tendency: even the manuscript of Flann O'Brien's final and unfinished novel, *Slattery's Sago Saga* (1973), ends with a lengthy letter, read by the protagonist and interpolated to fill in the story (see O'Brien, 1991, pp. 59–64).) The brother himself makes money through the copying and replication of other people's texts, which he sells to a credulous mail-order public as the work of the 'London University Academy' (O'Brien, 1983, p. 72). The first instance of this method is his guide to tightrope-walking, which Finbarr reads and reproduces for us: 'It were folly

to asseverate that periastral peripatesis on the *aes ductile*, or wire, is destitute of profound peril not only to sundry *membra*, or limbs, but to the back
and veriest life itself' (O'Brien, 1983, p. 40). Here is O'Nolan's characteristic
delight in stylistic performance, and in the pseudonym: the extract is attributed to 'Professor Latimer Dodds', which Finbarr considers a mere cover for
Manus (O'Brien, 1983, p. 41). As the operation expands, Manus republishes
material like the 'Odes and Epodes of Horace done into English Prose by
Dr Calvin Knottersley, D.Litt (Oxon)', drawn from 'his private mine, the
National Library' (O'Brien, 1983, p. 57). When he reaches London, he sends
Finbarr a long list of subjects in which he now offers correspondence courses:
Boxing, Oil Prospecting, Railway Engineering, and much more, including
the giveaway 'A Cure For Cancer' (O'Brien, 1983, p. 82). 'We really aim',
Manus writes, 'at the mass-production of knowledge' (O'Brien, 1983, p. 83).
Education, like the modern novel, should be a work of reference; and like
a faint echo of *At Swim-Two-Birds*, Manus' schemes proliferate personae and
deal in borrowed writing.

The question of authorship arises in a more direct sense in O'Brien's last
completed novel, *The Dalkey Archive* (1964). The novel's most innovative
jest is to stage the return of James Joyce, alive and old and living in Skerries,
a seaside resort North of Dublin. Tracked down by the protagonist Mick
Shaughnessy, he emerges as a pious Catholic who wants to join the Jesuits.
As for *Ulysses*:

> I have heard more than enough about that dirty book, that collection of
> smut, but do not be heard saying that I had anything to do with it. Faith
> now, you must be careful about that. As a matter of fact, I have put my
> name only to one little book in which I was concerned. (O'Brien, 1993a,
> p. 165)

That book is *Dubliners*, co-written with Oliver Gogarty. *Ulysses* itself was a
practical joke concocted in Paris by Sylvia Beach: 'Various low, dirty-minded
ruffians . . . had been paid to put this material together. Muck-rakers, obscene
poets, carnal pimps, sodomous sycophants, pedlars of the coloured lusts of
fallen humanity. Please don't ask me for names' (O'Brien, 1993a, p. 167).
Joyce is appalled to be informed that this farrago was eventually published
with his name on it.

It is easy enough to see the novel's treatment of Joyce as O'Nolan's final
revenge on the writer who had pre-empted so much of his own talent and
potential material.[8] What has been less often remarked is the persistence of
O'Nolan's distinctive attitudes to texts and authors into the fictional figure of
Joyce. As far back as the mid-1930s, O'Nolan had floated the idea of writing
a novel by committee. Niall Sheridan recalls his proclamation that 'the principles of the Industrial Revolution must be applied to literature. The time
had come when books should be made, not written – and a "made" book had

a better chance of becoming a best-seller'. Sheridan, O'Nolan, Denis Devlin and Donagh MacDonagh were the putative authors of 'the Great Irish Novel', to be entitled *Children of Destiny*. The four, O'Nolan proposed, would write the book in different sections, 'then stick the pieces together in committee'. As much as possible of the book would be borrowed and rehashed from elsewhere. As such, '*Children of Destiny* would be the precursor of a new literary movement, the first masterpiece of the Ready-Made or Reach-Me-Down School' (Sheridan, 1985, pp. 72–4). In reality, the book that emerged from that period of anarchic experiment was not *Children of Destiny* but *At Swim-Two-Birds*. But *The Dalkey Archive* imagines *Ulysses* being fabricated by similar means, collated from the work of many hands. There could hardly be a more obvious candidate for the title of Great Irish Novel.

One of the evident ironies here is that *Ulysses* really is a little like that – really is made of many parts, borrowed and travestied styles. It was James Joyce, not Flann O'Brien, who called himself a scissors-and-paste man. In this sense, O'Nolan's satire differs from the real less wildly than may appear. Perhaps he recognizes this in Joyce's account of the theological investigation that he is writing: 'Writing is not quite the word. Assembly, perhaps, is better – or accretion' (O'Brien, 1993a, p. 125). In another irony, the mischievous misattribution of works to Joyce oddly echoes O'Nolan's history as an author. The existence of *Ulysses* for Joyce is bad enough: the fact that, as Mick tells him, it has 'your name on the title page' (O'Brien, 1993a, p. 167) is disastrous.[9] But the whole scenario revives the sense of authorship's instability that had always been among O'Nolan's themes. Much of his writing had disavowed, or at least disguised, his role in its creation. Flann O'Brien, Myles na gCopaleen, Brother Barnabas, all were masks, distancing devices: and the same goes tenfold for the *Irish Times* correspondents of 1940. Joyce's discreet request, 'Please don't ask me for names' (O'Brien, 1993a, p. 167), reverses the career of Brian O'Nolan, who was never short of names and supplied them in abundance. But Joyce's refusal to be identified with the works bearing his name echoes, most strikingly, O'Nolan's 1939 letter to the *Irish Press*. We may look at it again:

> The cream of this elaborate 'joke' is that the supposed book is anti-clerical, blasphemous and licentious and various lengthy extracts from it have been concocted to show the obscenity of the work. I have joined in the joke to some extent myself but I naturally take strong exception to the publicity given by your paragraph, which associates me by name with something which is objectionable, even if non-existent. (O'Brien, 1988b, p. 178)

That disavowal might almost be spoken by O'Nolan's fictional Joyce twenty-five years later. Perhaps the cream of this elaborate joke is that O'Nolan had already treated *At Swim-Two-Birds* publicly as his imagined Joyce treats

Ulysses. Indeed, for the last decades of his life, O'Nolan dismissed *At Swim-Two-Birds* as a schoolboy prank, much as he had earlier done in that insincere letter (see Cronin, 1989, pp. 211–12, 247). The parallels between himself and his last conjuring of Joyce are in this sense more intricate than has usually been noted, and were probably invisible to O'Nolan himself. What they share is a desire to escape from authorship – from the burden of being answerable for texts which make them uncomfortable but stubbornly bear their names.

Gaelic masks

By the 1960s, radical revisions of authorship were on the agenda. *The Dalkey Archive* was published four years before 'The Death of the Author' (1968), which appeared two years after the novel's author had in fact died. Declan Kiberd writes that *At Swim-Two-Birds* found improved favour in 'the post-modern 1960s' (Kiberd, 2000, p. 519) – which places the full emergence of that discursive formation rather early, but still carries some cogency. Perhaps narrative experiment was to *At Swim-Two-Birds* as sexual transgression was to *Lady Chatterley's Lover* (1928), and both books had to wait almost until the Beatles' first LP to become more totemic than eccentric. It is not too difficult to find suggestive parallels with O'Nolan's work in Roland Barthes' famous essay. 'For him, for us too, it is language which speaks, not the author; to write is, through a prerequisite impersonality . . . to reach that point where only language acts, "performs", and not "me" ' (Barthes, 1977a, p. 143): Lir O'Connor on Conrad, Lanna Avia's letter to the *Irish Times* (O'Brien, 1988b, pp. 193, 221). 'The text is a tissue of quotations drawn from the innumerable centres of culture' (Barthes, 1977a, p. 146): 'The modern novel should be largely a work of reference' (O'Brien, 1967, p. 25). 'His only power is to mix writings, to counter the ones with the others, in such a way as never to rest on any one of them' (Barthes, 1977a, p. 146): as the Greek epigraph of *At Swim-Two-Birds* has it, 'All things yield each other place' (O'Brien, 1967, p. 7). '[A] veritable "distancing", the Author diminishing like a figurine at the far end of the literary stage' (Barthes, 1977a, p. 145): thus Myles na gCopaleen stays on the margins of his book, and passes responsibility for the tale to Bonaparte O'Coonassa, himself a rewrite of existing Gaelic memoirists.[10]

Kiberd's assertion that O'Nolan was 'way ahead of his time' is thus unarguable. Yet in other respects this description does not quite fit. O'Nolan was in some ways a conservative thinker, nervous of novelty, quick to scorn progressive schemes as being callow and pretentious.[11] What he would have made of Barthes and Michel Foucault themselves, had he lived long enough to hear a Kiberd or Richard Kearney promote their ideas at his *alma mater*, hardly bears thinking about. He was also reputedly a withdrawn, sometimes morose individual, in later years creatively unfulfilled and a quietly professional alcoholic. The blitz of fictional authors is compensatory as well as joyful, a defence mechanism as well as an adventure. His writing, as Barthes or Trellis might have understood, had a life somewhat beyond his ken: the anarchy of *At Swim-Two-Birds* loosens notions of authorship in a way from which he later recoiled, and Hugh Kenner has pondered O'Nolan's apparent nervousness at what he had unleashed in *The Third Policeman* (Kenner, 1997, pp. 69–71). There is, then, a troubling yet enabling gap between O'Nolan and *At Swim-Two-Birds*, the civil servant and the polyphonic spree: the textual play generates possibilities that the man might not have countenanced. And that fact is one of those possibilities.

The abstract character of Barthes' provocation has long been apparent.[12] One thing we have yet fully to understand is how O'Nolan's dallying with styles and selves might fit into a national literary tradition. For his dynamic sense of writing, and of the function of persona, is a notion with a particular Irish pedigree. F. R. Leavis, in a late essay on W. B. Yeats, found himself trying to describe the effect of the poet's posturing and role-playing, which seemed to Leavis in some way a peculiarly Hibernian tendency:

> It is characteristic of Yeats to have had no centre of unity, and to have been unable to find one. The lack is apparent in his solemn propoundings about the Mask and the Anti-self, and in the related schematic elaborations. It is there, an essential theme for the critic, in that habit of cultivating attitudes and postures which makes one – if an Englishman, at any rate – remark that Yeats is a fellow-countryman of Wilde, Shaw and Joyce (I am thinking of that photograph of Joyce with his walking-stick outside Shakespeare and Co.) (Leavis, 1969, p. 75)

The moment has come to seem comically apt, a summary of Anglo-Irish perceptions: the English puritan Leavis trying to articulate the level of performance and staginess which seemed to him innate in Irish writing and identity. For all that he occludes religious and political differences between the writers he names, he may be on to something – some way in which the Irish writer had historically felt the need to perform his Irishness, his literariness, or both.

The paradigmatic figure here is Oscar Wilde, at whom the name 'Oscar Love' surely nods, whoever coined it.[13] Sean O'Faolain, targeted by O'Nolan's satire in 1940, disparaged 'Flann O'Brien' as 'the man in the Gaelic mask' (Cronin, 1989, p. 107). We may find ourselves thinking five decades back in time. 'Man is least himself,' wrote Oscar Wilde in 1890, 'when he talks in his own person. Give him a mask, and he will tell you the truth' (Wilde, 1992, p. 144). More thoroughly and vividly than any of his contemporaries, Wilde developed and aired the idea that the self was a kind of fiction, a series of poses. The Wildean self is a matter of art rather than nature: like the work of art, it evades and triumphs over the dreary repetition of the social, as much as the natural, world.[14] As Leavis knew, a Wildean doctrine of the mask had also been adopted by Yeats. Richard Ellmann notes that the Yeatsian mask 'includes all the differences between one's own and other people's conception of one's personality. To be conscious of the discrepancy which makes a mask of this sort is to look at oneself as if one were somebody else.' The mask, Ellmann adds, has martial qualities: it is a defensive armour for the self, and a 'weapon of attack' which exalts the self's capacities (Ellmann, 1961, pp. 175–6). It is hard to think of a more different artist from Yeats than Brian O'Nolan: but the image of the mask has its own afterlife in O'Nolan's career. It is almost as though the self-dramatizing subjectivity of Yeats, with its collection of enigmatic and heroic poses, finds a comical echo in O'Nolan, with his bank of ridiculous personae.

If anything, O'Nolan's writing outstrips the sense of artifice already present in these precursors. Like them, he uses the mask – the persona – to assert the self and to disguise it simultaneously. It hides the self, works as armour: but it also facilitates extravagant attacks and polemical grandstanding. But the residual romanticism of his Protestant precursors is stripped from O'Nolan's practice. Give a man a mask and he will tell the truth, said Wilde; but give a man a mask, imply the pages of the *Irish Times*, and he will lie more entertainingly than usual. To put the difference another way: O'Nolan lacks the aestheticist doctrine of Wilde. His only guide is pragmatic, the number of pen names an author should have at his disposal, like fake passports in the event of a quick getaway. Yet O'Nolan, despite lacking the anti-metaphysical metaphysics that Wilde had fashioned, practises the dissolution of the self in his writing in a purer fashion. Rather than the honing of a persona of perfect wit and sensitivity, his writing offers a series of voices, caricatures, accents, discourses. In the passage from Revival to Free State that underpins so much of O'Nolan's character as a writer, we have also moved from the religion of art to its parodic denigration: yet the forging of writerly identity has become more, not less, central.[15]

No Irish writer endorsed the religion of art more emphatically than a fictional one: Stephen Dedalus. The artist, he decrees in one of modernism's embedded manifestos, 'like the God of the creation, remains within or behind or beyond or above his handiwork, invisible, refined out of existence, indifferent, paring his fingernails' (Joyce, 1992, p. 233). Dedalus, it is well known, reprises a formulation of Gustave Flaubert's, for whom

> the illusion (if there is one) stems from the *impersonality* of the work. That is one of my principles, you must not *write yourself*. The artist in his work must be like God in creation, invisible and all-powerful; you can sense him everywhere but you cannot see him. (Flaubert, 1997, p. 248)

Given its most programmatic statement in T. S. Eliot's 'Tradition and the Individual Talent' (1917), the disappearance of the author into the work would come to be seen as a definitive strand of modernist aesthetics (Eliot,

1975, pp. 37–44).[16] The contingency of the authorial life is absorbed into the necessity of the achieved work, which thus gains a certain enigmatic autonomy, freed from any simple accountability to a personality beyond it. It was primarily via Joyce that the formula of impersonality was transmitted to O'Nolan. Joyce, as we have seen, was O'Nolan's agonistic target as well as his inspiration: and Dedalus' formula, while suggestive, is not quite right for O'Nolan. The work of art for O'Nolan is rarely serenely self-possessed: writing, for him, is more often a trade plied in the public discourses of satire, journalism and polemic. If the eccentric voices of *Cruiskeen Lawn* take an estranging distance from the world, their roots in it are unmistakable.[17]

In relation to ideas of authorship, O'Nolan is similarly tellingly divergent from prevailing models of impersonality. For in *Cruiskeen Lawn*, the *Irish Times* letters or *At Swim-Two-Birds*, the author has not disappeared but proliferated: rather than the autonomous artefact abandoned by an indifferent god, we have a circus of fictional authors and styles, set up to collide and squabble with one another. O'Nolan practises less the withdrawal of the author than his dispersal. He cannot be fitted into a doctrine of modernist impersonality because he has too much personality: or rather too many personalities. These seem to have offered Brian O'Nolan not so much an escape from himself, more an escape into his selves: even if he might, by the ailing end, sometimes have felt that he had escaped into a stylistic prison as well as a Stillorgan bungalow.[18] As Eliot never quite said, only those who have multiple personalities and artificial emotions know what it means to want to escape from these things.

6
Authorship in the Writings and Films of William S. Burroughs

Polina Mackay

> 'To all the scribes and artists and practitioners of magic through whom these spirits have been manifested... NOTHING IS TRUE. EVERYTHING IS PERMITTED.'
>
> — (Burroughs, 1982, p. xviii)

The publication of *Naked Lunch* in 1959 turned William S. Burroughs from a Tangiers-based drug addict into a global brand, every bit as carefully designed and promoted as the Nike trainers advertised by Burroughs on US television in 1994. The book is framed by Burroughs' politically charged interpretation of its title as 'a frozen moment when everyone sees what is on the end of every fork' (Burroughs, 1993, p. 7). At the time, the book was a reaction to 1950s America, the decade that saw the meaning of the American dream redefined as a celebration of consumerism and urban lifestyle, comfort and conformity in the context of post-Second World War prosperity. In this context of simultaneous economic affluence and social oppression, a new generation of writers was emerging, the now infamous Beat Generation. Jack Kerouac's literary road movie *On the Road* (1957), Allen Ginsberg's anarchic poem *Howl* (1959), and Burroughs' textual experiment *Naked Lunch* went on to spark the counterculture of the 1960s in America, an era that, as Marianne DeKoven has shown in *Utopia Limited: The Sixties and the Emergence of the Postmodern* (2004), still informs the way Americans live now.

But Burroughs claims that he has no 'precise memory' of writing *Naked Lunch*, one of the most influential books of post-Second World War American fiction (Burroughs, 1993, p. 7). While this is primarily a reference to the fact that, at the time of writing, he was going through drug withdrawal sickness, which affected his memory, it is also an instance of denial of authorship of the book. This is not an isolated moment in Burroughs' work. As I shall show here, his writings and films are profoundly concerned with the author-function. His work gives us the opportunity to examine the relationship between postwar American literature and postmodernism, the literary and the cinematic, and the revisiting of the cultural history of authorship in contemporary fiction. My main aim here is to provide a better understanding of the curious fifty years that produced writers who disinherit their own books, and critics that are in the habit of announcing their own deaths.

First, it is important to note that connecting Burroughs' work to the study of authorship is not a surprising move. Indeed, *Naked Lunch* expresses an innovative theory of authorship, which pre-dates even Roland Barthes' and Michel Foucault's highly influential work on authorship. 'I am not an entertainer', the 'author' of *Naked Lunch* claims, but 'a recording instrument'. . . I do not presume to impose "story" "plot" "continuity"' (Burroughs, 1993, p. 174). In a simple reading, this statement could be labelled a 'reaction to conformity', which advocates anarchy as opposed to state-sponsored order. In this respect, *Naked Lunch* resembles the ideology expressed in other novels of the same period. An example is Hubert Selby's anarchic novel, *Last Exit to Brooklyn* (1957), which explores anti-conformity through the violent lives of immigrants, transsexuals, workers on strike, and people who live in 'the projects' (the 1940s American version of British council estates). However, what separates *Naked Lunch* from *Last Exit to Brooklyn* is the explicit theorization of how a countercultural text gives birth to such a peculiar form of authorship, an author who is not an entertainer and does not impose anything. As a recording instrument, the author's function is to orchestrate a literary narrative, itself merely a distorted recording. Despite a presumed (objective) truth that might be hidden in the idea of 'recording', this narrative does not conform to a Romantic ideal. It is not the expression of a unique personality, as in Wordsworth's theory of poetry (Wordsworth, 1895, pp. 935–41); nor is it 'an escape from personality', which would connect Burroughs' work to the modernist projects of, for example, T. S. Eliot (1932, pp. 17–22). Rather, Burroughs' narratives are a seemingly badly organized plethora of fragmented and blurred visions, desires, fantasies, anxieties and deliberately underdeveloped thoughts of a speaking subject, who is not a residing genius but merely an addict always looking for a quick fix.

True to this framework, *Naked Lunch* has no beginning and no end, no developing stories or characters. It ends with a section titled 'Atrophied Preface' in which Burroughs gives his definition of a 1950s novel: 'You can cut into *Naked Lunch* at any intersection point. . . I have written many prefaces. They atrophy and amputate spontaneous' (Burroughs, 1993, p. 176). The word 'you' at the beginning of this extract is indicative of Burroughs' understanding of the dialectic between the author, the text and the reader. The direct address to the reader is a plea that boils down to this: *I* have written the prefaces but *you* choose where to begin. The reason for this possibility is the author's function as a medium through which the text passes, a theoretical position that Burroughs summarized years later in *Painting and Guns* (1992): 'A writer or artist is simply someone who tunes into certain cosmic currents. He's a medium. The less of his "I", his "me", that gets in there, the better' (Burroughs, 1992, p. 44).

A way of lessening the 'I' of the author is to situate him/her as a character in the text. In his introduction to *Queer* (written between 1950 and 1952 but not published until 1985), Burroughs links the protagonist's addiction to drugs and withdrawal sickness to his own evolution as a writer and concludes with merging the author with literary character: 'While it was I who wrote *Junky*, I feel that I was being written in *Queer*' (Burroughs, 1986a, p. 12). As Oliver Harris argues, the use of this introduction to create a seemingly uninfringeable link between literary character and the figure of the author would replicate Burroughs' refusal to separate character from author, an act that has the potential to 'depoliticize the title and the text of *Queer*' (Harris, 2003, p. 88). Though Burroughs' introduction cannot be used as a sacred insight into the text, for that would sanctify both the author and his text, this merging cannot be ignored. For Burroughs' understanding of history and the political moment is based on the blurring of the boundary between fiction and reality, the real and the imaginary, the possible and the impossible, the ordinary and the absurd: 'What happens when there is no limit?' Lee asks in *Queer*. 'What is the fate of The Land Where Anything Goes? Men changing into huge centipedes . . . centipedes besieging the houses . . . a man tied to a couch and a centipede ten feet long rearing up over him. Is this literal? Did some hideous metamorphosis occur?' (Burroughs, 1986a, p. 92).

Indeed, the metamorphosis of the author into a recording instrument in *Naked Lunch* is as gruesome and shocking as it gets: in becoming an instrument in the writing process, the author is irrevocably an integral part of the text. *Naked Lunch*, which was once described as 'Glug glug . . . it tastes disgusting', is full of images of gruesome death, bodily dismemberment and cannibalism (Willett, 1991, p. 42). Thus the author is also an expression of these features. And here comes the part the reader must play: you can (or have to) cut into the text at any intersection point. On the one hand, this invitation determines the text as material, an object almost that is continuously cut and edited. On the other hand, it invites the reader to be part of the text; in other words, to be fictionalized. Since in Burroughs' fiction the text is always likened to the human body, this invitation is also to realize our presumed predatory nature, to succumb to the desire to dissect not only this material text that we now hold in front of us, but also its author, a seemingly passive voice who, though he claims not to impose anything on the narrative, is sitting in the middle of the page with a huge grin. But this is an emotional reaction to Burroughs' invitation to cut-into his text. In critical terms, Burroughs is asking the reader to be aware that the author no longer exercises absolute authority over the text, because two things have happened: first, like the text, the author is an exclusively discursive sign; and second, meaning is opened up, because the reader always acts as an editor, as he or she is now given the option of beginning to read at any point in the narrative. These complex schemas Burroughs is offering here are the parameters upon which his 1950s vision of a new kind of textuality and author is based.

More specifically, Burroughs' challenge to authorial mastery is based on an all-encompassing absence of authorial signature. There is no such thing as an authorial signature, Burroughs seems to argue. How else would one explain his extensive use of the 'cut-up method' – the application of the montage method to writing – whereby he copied material from all sorts of sources – for example newspapers, books, manuals and so on? His first cut-up was with Brion Gysin, Sinclair Beiles and Gregory Corso in *Minutes to Go* (1960). He was later to produce his own cut-up trilogy: *The Soft Machine* (1961), *The Ticket That Exploded* (1962) and *Nova Express* (1964). Who is the author of a cut-up text, one is tempted to ask? Cut-ups signify an authorial voice that is non-monolithic, conflicted and conflicting, and above all collaborative. Thus the technique is challenge to the authority, the integrity and the unity of the authorial voice. Burroughs made this point emphatically in a letter to Ginsberg, in which he asks his fellow Beat to cut-up his letter:

> Take the enclosed copy of this letter. Cut along the lines. Rearrange putting section one by section three and section two by section four. Now read aloud and you will hear My Voice. Whose voice? Listen. Cut and rearrange in any combination. Read aloud. I can not [*sic*] choose but hear. Dont [*sic*] think about it. Dont [*sic*] theorize. Try it. Do the same with your poems. With any poems any prose. Try it. You want 'Help.' Here it is. Pick up on it. And always remember. 'Nothing is True. Everything is permitted.' (Burroughs and Ginsberg, 1963, p. 60)

This extract expresses Burroughs' aesthetic position on authorship: by questioning his own voice and simultaneously asking his audience to 'listen', and by instructing the listener to 'read aloud' – that is, to legitimize – the words of that same voice Burroughs has already challenged and dethroned, he explains authorship in terms of a struggle for authority, where it is the author's authority that is being deconstructed. This endless struggle for authorial dominance is repeated in *Naked Lunch* in a moment reminiscent of M. C. Escher's lithograph 'Drawing Hands' (1948) of one hand writing the other (Escher, 1972, p. 69): 'Last night I woke up with someone squeezing my hand. It was my other hand...' (Burroughs, 1993, p. 66). Are we to take this as a moment in postmodernist fiction, where we finally see an author constructing his own writing as exclusively self-referential? There is evidence against interpreting Burroughs' work as solipsistic, autobiographical. It lies primarily in his attempt in *Naked Lunch* and the cut-ups to destroy all identities that presuppose a one-to-one correspondence between the individual and his or her environment, the author and his material. 'You were not there for *The Beginning*', the narrator of *Naked Lunch* tells us, 'You will not be there for *The End*... Your knowledge of what is going on can only be superficial and relative' (Burroughs, 1993, pp. 173–4). This absence and the contradictions embedded in one (writing) hand squeezing the other point to the incompleteness of writing, to the mapping of the novel as a territory where *all* contradictions are possible, even the writer consciously denying himself authorial mastery.

Let's say we accept this denial. What kind of an author are we left with? The answer to this question is found in the definition of the 'third mind', a concept Burroughs and Gysin coined in their collaborative work, also entitled *The Third Mind* (1979). Here, Burroughs and Gysin, another advocate of the cut-up technique, argue that an author always writes from the perspective of a third mind: an intersubjective and fragmented voice constructed by several conflicting discourses (Burroughs and Gysin, 1979, p. 19). The way they define this concept points to the lack of correspondence and immediate context that characterizes the third mind: ' "No two minds ever come together without, thereby, creating a third, invisible, intangible force which may be likened to a *third mind*". "Who is the third that walks beside you?"' (Burroughs and Gysin, 1979, p. 25). Parts of this extract are lifted from Napoleon Hill's *Think and Grow Rich* (1937), a book about self-taught capitalism. The question they insert at the end is from T. S. Eliot, who Burroughs and Gysin use here to determine the third mind as heterogeneous, an illustration of collaborative consciousness not always agreed by all contributors (see Eliot, 1974, p. 77). Thus the third mind is designed to abolish absolute binaries, such as that between canonical literature and popular non-fiction. Since the third mind is another name for the authorial voice that is constructed in the context of collaborative writing, this abolition of boundaries aims specifically to destabilize the relationship between the writer and the text. Power no longer lies with the author, because textuality is opened up as a working transcript of a set of ongoing collaborations.

The writer as a recording instrument – as a medium through which many texts sprint, the use of the cut-up method to interrogate the unity of the authorial voice, and the peculiar intersections and collaborations that these processes breed, are the three pointers we have inherited from Burroughs, which comprise what we may call Burroughsian authorship. On the whole, authorship no longer signifies authority, origin and unity. This position determines Burroughs' vision in the 1950s and 1960s as one of disconnectedness, a vision of detachment from the presumed objectivity of an authorial subject and the real world, a world that cannot and should not be represented in its entirety or totality. Instead, Burroughs and other American writers of the post-1945 period celebrate fragmentation (of the text, experience and the self). The reason for this difference is simple; as the narrator of Donald Barthelme's story 'See the Moon?' (1964) put it concisely: 'Fragments are the only forms I trust' (Barthelme, 1969, p. 157). Burroughs' dispersal of authorial signature, the ambiguity of signs in Thomas Pynchon's *The Crying of Lot 49* (1966), and Kathy Acker's partial and blurred retellings of Miguel de Cervantes' famous romance in her own *Don Quixote* (1986) all advocate fragments as opposed to any kind of unified whole. But the idea of fragments is not merely a formal device in postwar American fiction; it is also a metaphor for the diversity and perhaps the disintegration of the American dream; as Don DeLillo put it in *Americana* (1971): 'There were many visions in the land, all fragments of the exploded dream' (DeLillo, 1989, p. 129).

One can argue that the trust in fragments was a specifically postmodern project, or a project of and for postmodernity that postwar authors adopted and explored. It is hard to miss the similarities between Burroughs' portrayal of the author as an instrument of discontinuity, and the theories of authorship that were emerging from the middle of the twentieth century onwards. Indeed, the 'third mind' coincides with Roland Barthes' concept of 'third meaning', which 'open[s] the field of meaning totally, that is infinitely' (Barthes, 1977b, p. 55).[1] In Burroughs, the aim of the third mind is 'to leave the Word-God behind' (Burroughs, 1985, p. 103), or as Barthes puts it: 'We know now that a text is not a line of words releasing a single "theological" meaning (the "message" of the Author-God) but a multi-dimensional space in which a variety of writings, none of them original, blend and clash' (Barthes, 1977a, p. 146). Thus both writers treat the author as being neither godlike nor the absolute controller of the text, allowing him to enter 'into his own death [when] writing begins' (Barthes, 1977a, p. 142).

However, Burroughs was not aware of this theoretical framework when he was writing, for the simple reason that he was writing before its expression. Rather, his revolutionary ideas about the function of the author are a direct response to contemporaneous social and cultural changes in America, a point that is often missed by critics too keen to stress Burroughs' postmodernism. Consider the 'Talking Asshole' routine in *Naked Lunch*, the infamous tale of corrupt physician, Dr Benway. The 'Talking Asshole' is about a carnival man who teaches his anus to talk, developing this as a ventriloquist performing act. Things start to go wrong when the anus begins to talk on its own, grows teeth and starts to eat, eventually eating its way out of the man's pants and shouting out in the street for 'equal rights' and how it 'want[s] to be kissed like any other mouth'. In the end, the man's mouth is sealed off with a kind of jelly tissue, his brain died and 'eyes *went out*' (Burroughs, 1993, p. 110). On the one hand, the tale is a metaphor about authorial control ('"It's you who will shut up in the end. Not me. Because we don't need you around here any more. I can talk and eat *and* shit"', the anus tells the man (Burroughs, 1993, p. 110)), about who and what controls language: in other words, about who assumes the role of the author. Thus the story can be linked to the theory of the 'ventriloquial voice', which, according to Steven Connor, 'is the voice speaking from some other place, reorganizing the economy of the senses, and embodying illegitimate forms of power' (Connor, 2000, p. 43). On the other hand, and away from the highly theoretical, the carnival man's story refers to a material condition that would briefly readjust the boundaries of artistic expression in America; this is what follows immediately after the tale: ' "That's the sex that passes the censor, squeezes through between bureaus, because there's always a space *between*, in popular songs and Grade B movies, giving away the basic American rotten-ness"' (Burroughs, 1993, p. 111). More so, then, the tale refers to a form of censorship that would change the landscape of American cinema: the Production Code, or as it is better known, the Hays Code. The Hays Code, which determined what was morally acceptable in films, was adopted in 1930, started being implemented in 1934 and was abandoned by 1967.[2] Its period of implementation coincided with the writing and publication of *Naked Lunch*, a book that in the years between 1959 and 1966 was censored by the literary academy, the US Post Office, the US Customs Service, state government and local authorities (Goodman, 1981, pp. 247–9). When the proscription of *Naked Lunch* was lifted in 1966, it ended the censorship of works of literature on the grounds of obscenity in America. In the context of the Hays Code's implementation, the story of the 'Talking Asshole' signi-fies the complexity of censorship, its temporality and, to some extent, its presumed uselessness.

But there is a more crucial point to the story of the 'Talking Asshole'. It is an indication of the increasing interest in cinematic culture, whereby literary experiments such as cut-ups are aligned with experimentation in film. Responding to this, Burroughs would go on to make his own films and write his own film scripts. The filmic, I argue next, introduces new possibilities for the author-function, and, if we are to go by Burroughs' films, a new take on the Barthesian death of the author.

Authorship and film

Burroughs' experimental films, which he made with Anthony Balch in the 1960s, explore the concept of the mediated identity, the self configured as existing exclusively on the screen. Such an identity introduces a new framework for the study of authorship. Before I turn to Burroughs' filmic experiments, it is important to note that turning to cinematic authorship requires a change of gear, as film history and criticism differs from literary history. In the 1950s and 1960s, film critics were wrestling with questions of 'auteurism' (Truffaut, 1976, pp. 224–37; Sarris, 1962–63, pp. 1–8): according to *auteur* theory, the *auteur* (a French term for 'director') is the artist whose personality is meant to be 'written' in his or her films. *Auteur* criticism, then, looks to read an individual's artistic vision, which is perceived as being unique and subjective, as it is expressed in the work. The centrality of the concept of unique self-expression gives rise here to legitimate comparisons between the *auteur* and the Romantic artist. Wordsworthian Romanticism is what comes to mind here, and its belief that full authorial intention is found in poetic expression (Wordsworth, 1895, pp. 935–41). These questions would seem relevant to a discussion of Burroughs' films, especially since the author co-wrote, co-directed and starred in all of them.

However, in Burroughs we find a dispersion of the auteur's unique personality, a mode that Pam Cook sees as a characteristic of avant-garde films. Cook points out some of the difficulties of seeking the auteur in avant-garde film-making: while the idea of self-expression, she argues, suggests that these films become primarily personal, experimental films, like Hollis Frampton's *Nostalgia* (1971) and Michael Snow's *Wavelength* (1967), instead 'perform a . . . dispersal of the personal' (Cook, 1981, p. 277). This is due to a split in the psyche first brought to attention by Freudian psychoanalysis, which determines self-expression:

> not as the full expression of the artist's voice, but rather in the manifestation of a fragmented discourse, polysemic and polyphonic, suggesting a partial autonomy for the film-maker which allows space for her or his unconscious and conscious concerns, without suppressing the personal, but without privileging the discourse of the artist. (Cook, 1981, p. 279)

The personal expression and simultaneous dispersal of this expression is exactly what we find in Burroughs' films.

In the 1960s, Burroughs collaborated with Balch on four short experimental films: *Towers Open Fire* (1963); *Bill and Tony* (1963); *William Buys a Parrot* (1963); and *The Cut-Ups* (1966), which consisted of rolls of film that were literally cut-up and reassembled.[3] The films feature Burroughs, Balch and sometimes Brion Gysin, Ian Somerville and Alexander Trocchi, among others (for example, in *Towers Open Fire*) in various situations: Burroughs shooting family photographs with a ping-pong gun (*Towers*); Balch masturbating (*Towers*); Burroughs and Balch as interchangeable talking heads (*Bill and Tony*). There has been renewed interest in the films following their first DVD release in August 2004. Tim Cumming's article in the *Guardian* quotes Genesis P-Orridge's explanation of the films' artistic significance: '[Balch and Burroughs] edited everything mathematically . . . Regardless of any narrative or linear sense, in order to erase the concept of the author, and so that what they called 'The Third Mind' would kick in and become the driving force of whatever happened'. And in terms of the films' cultural legacy:

> People have a great trust in the [cut-up] method and the process, which has become so all-pervading in popular culture and the mass media that its vital future generations understand and are aware of the source material, and the original thinking behind what may now be mundane. (quoted in Cumming, 2004, p. 9)

Implicit in P-Orridge's assessment of the cut-up technique is the assumption that the cinematic is the same as the novelistic, and, by association, literary authorship corresponds to the film-maker. Is cutting-up film the same as cutting-up text? Burroughs justifies his cross-over from text to film by determining film as narrative, and, equally, novelistic prose as a series of disconnected images. He points up a fundamental link between word and image, or rather the equation of the two: 'the written word *is* an image' (*my emphasis*), he announces in his essay on the potentials of cinema (Burroughs, 1991, p. 55), a claim he made numerous times in his fictional work as well (see, for example, Burroughs and Gysin, 1979, p. 159).

So it is not a surprise, given the strong links that Burroughs saw between the cinematic and the novelistic, that his films are meant to be filmic images of his cut-up experiments with text, and more generally his writing style. In fact, *Towers Open Fire* is based on drafts for Burroughs' cut-up novel, *The Soft Machine*. Thus the films are non-linear, consisting of flashes of images that the audience is invited to connect. The link that Burroughs finds between writing and film transcription is the reason why we need to look first at his distinctly cinematic prose. The aim of this kind of writing, I argue, is to construct an exclusively mediated reality, which would render all identities, including authors, as technological artefacts.

Naked Lunch uses filmic terms such as 'cut', 'fadeout', 'flashback' and 'play it back on the screen' throughout. It cuts from one image to the next, and because of its fragmentary narrative style, it simply reads like an unedited film, signifying America of the 1950s, as Don DeLillo put it in *Americana*, as a 'long, unmanageable movie' (DeLillo, 1989, p. 205). A filmic scenario of *Naked Lunch* appears in *The Third Mind* supplemented by stills from Burroughs' and Balch's film *Cut-Ups* (Burroughs and Gysin, 1979, pp. 150–8). Challenging Burroughs' authorial right over *Naked Lunch*, the section is attributed to Gysin. While this may also be a reference to the fact that the film *Cut-Ups* is meant to be a cinematic representation of Gysin's *Dream Machines*, it is more likely that Burroughs and Gysin attribute the section to the third mind, the symbol of collaborative authorship. Another amalgamation of the filmic with the novelistic is found in Burroughs' novel *The Wild Boys* (1969), which begins by describing itself in terms of a film: 'The camera is the eye of a cruising vulture flying over an area of scrub', and continues this motif throughout with statements such as 'the camera zooms past', 'the camera dips and whirls and glides tracing vultures higher and higher spiraling up' (Burroughs, 1969, pp. 3, 18), and so on. An even stronger example are Burroughs' two film scripts, *The Last Words of Dutch Schultz: A Fiction in the Form of a Filmscript* (1969) and *Blade Runner: A Movie* (1979), which build on the technique noted in *Naked Lunch* and *Wild Boys*, supplementing the text with sample shots and images. It is clear, then, that Burroughs' narratives aim to be primarily visual. Given the absence of plot and character development that characterizes Burroughs' work, the aim is simply to impose a certain degree of disorientation on the reader/viewer, a technique that aims to constitute the text as a deliberately distorted image of contemporaneous culture.

Visual narratives are located at the intersection point between literary narrative and contemporary (postmodern) culture.[4] David Lodge's influential work *Working with Structuralism* (1981) begins its 'Contemporary Culture' section with an analysis of the relationship between visual culture and fiction. Talking of Ted Hughes' visual narrative in his collection of poems *Crow: From the Life and Song of the Crow* (1970) and pointing out the similarities between the poet's work and the contemporary comic strip or animated cartoon, Lodge discusses this technique in terms of how 'the adapted cartoon-style conventionalizes the experience, frames it ironically, puts it at a distance and thus makes it manageable' (Lodge, 1981, p. 173). The same can be said of Burroughs' use of cinematic elements (filmic terms, perspectives presented through photographic snapshots) in his prose: reality is seen through a lens and thus represented indirectly. In this context, there is no author-ity one can call upon, for a simultaneous freedom and limitation characterizes this disorientating filmic prose.

The merging of the novelistic with the cinematic is a concern that other twentieth-century American writers share with Burroughs: examples include Don DeLillo, Thomas Pynchon and E. L. Doctorow. The filmic imagery of Pynchon's *Vineland* (1990), which is used to revisit the troubled 1960s, or the series of disconnected images in DeLillo's *Libra* (1988) that recount the most cinematic event of all – Lee Harvey Oswald's murder live on American television in 1963 following the assassination of J. F. Kennedy – are stark examples of this technique. Reality here is presented as informed by the amalgamation of the 'real' with the 'imaginary' in order to signify a distorted version of reality or, as Burroughs puts it in *The Soft Machine*, to 'Wise up all the marks everywhere Show them the rigged wheel – Storm the Reality Studio and retake the universe' (Burroughs, 1986b, p. 151). Brian McHale has rightly pointed out that, in this context, reality is presented as a filmshot. The critic labels this 'cinematic discourse', which he sees as a characteristic of postmodernist fiction:

> Cinematic discourse [is] a series of metaphors for textual strategies; but it can also be read as the sign of narrative level interposed between the text and the 'real'. By this reading, texts such as *Gravity's Rainbow, Projet pour une revolution* or *The Wild Boys* do not directly represent a reality, but rather represent a *movie* which in turn represents a reality . . . Burroughs makes explicit what can only be inferred from other postmodernist cinematic writing, namely the *thematic* function of the interposed ontological level of the film. Reality in Burroughs is a film shot and directed by others; we are actors in the movie, our lives scripted and fixed on celluloid. (McHale, 1987, p. 129)

In the context of postmodernist thought, McHale's interpretation of Burroughs' use of cinematic discourse is absolutely correct. At the same time, the representation of reality as a filmshot in Burroughs, Pynchon and DeLillo aims to constitute reality as a product of commodified, consumerist and capitalist culture. And this kind of reality is uniquely American: 'Into the Interior', Burroughs urges us, an interior that is made up of 'a vast subdivision, antennae of television to the meaningless sky', an interior where 'there is no drag like U.S. drag'. 'You can't see it', he continues, 'you don't know where it comes from'. 'Take one of those cocktail lounges at the end of a subdivision street – every block of houses has its own bar and drugstore and market and liquorstore. You walk in and it hits you' (Burroughs, 1993, pp. 12–13). Characteristic of what James Annesley has termed 'blank fiction', Burroughs' prose points to an almost apolitical vision, where everything appears as it is: violent, ruined, blank (Annesley, 1998, p. 3). That naked moment again, when everyone sees what is at the end of every fork. The danger is, and this is why Burroughs urges us to 'wise up the marks', that if we accept these conditions we shall all fall into the comfort of consumerist conformity.

Any resistance to this kind of conformity, consumerism and capitalism, is to be found in media, more precisely in mixing media in order to instigate an 'electronic revolution'. *Electronic Revolution* (1971), Burroughs' report of his experiments with cut-up tapes and images, is more generally an attempt to alter the basis of identity through mixing media. But this mixing does not signify unity; rather, it points to conflict. Another mixing of sorts takes place in Burroughs' *The Book of Breething* (1974) and *Cobble Stone Garden* (1976), where illustrations by other artists accompany Burroughs' text. But these illustrations are the opposite of what is usually meant by 'illustration', as they hardly correspond with Burroughs' text. Here, we see a struggle for authorial dominance similar to the one we observed earlier in *Naked Lunch*. Simultaneously, the incompatibility of discourses is a strategy that constitutes 'the text' as a few sample shots, deliberately randomized, with no authors and, again, no authority to fall back on.

This snapshot-like narrative is similar to the prose of *Naked Lunch*, which the narrator describes as a 'book that spill[s] off the page in all directions, kaleidoscope of vistas' (Burroughs, 1993, p. 180). Crucially, this definition is framed by the author-function, as only a few pages before Burroughs defined the novel, he defined its author:

> There is only one thing a writer can write about: *what is in front of his senses at the moment of writing* . . . I am a recording instrument . . . Insofar as I succeed in *Direct* recording of certain areas of psychic processes I may have limited function . . . I am not an entertainer. (Burroughs, 1993, p. 174)

While this statement expresses a postmodernist position, an argument I pursued in the first part of this essay, it also frames the author in filmic terms. For this author is not only an instrument of fragmentation and discontinuity of the postmodernist kind, but also a tape recorder, a camera: 'You are a programmed tape recorder set to record and play back', the narrator announces in *The Ticket That Exploded* (Burroughs, 1962, p. 213). His text is also a tape, a shot, a film. In novels like *Naked Lunch* and the cut-ups, the author is still somewhat present, for this textually explosive environment is orchestrated by him: '*I* have written many prefaces' [*my emphasis*], he tells us in *Naked Lunch*. The authorial 'I' here gives up some of its power to make room for the text to 'spill off in all directions', to be read, that is, from any intersection point; simultaneously, the 'I' remains in relative control of this spilling-off. It is this vestige of control that Burroughs would erase in his films.

Burroughs' film work signifies a profound concern with authorial identity, how this identity is constructed, and how it is heard and listened to. In his prose, identity is determined by a struggle for authorial mastery, whereby many and conflicting authorial voices are allowed to be heard. In his films, identity is more clearly split. The best example of this is found in *Bill and Tony*, the short film that Burroughs made with Balch in 1963. Here, Burroughs and Balch, the 'authors' of the film, appear on screen reading from a variety of sources (for example, from a Scientology Auditing Manual and from Tod Browning's 1932 classic film *Freaks*). *Freaks* is one of few films that manages to 'cross over' from horror into the avant-garde and the countercultural canon, a cross-over that Burroughs and Balch are invoking here. They experiment with image and speech by playing the voice of one to the face of the other. As Burroughs' voice is projected on to Balch's face and vice versa, a crucial reversal is taking place: as Baldwin has noted, 'here voice and image are reversed so that the nature of filmic identity is interrogated by the medium itself' (Baldwin, 2002, p. 166). Since Burroughs and Balch are also the 'authors' of *Bill and Tony*, their appearance in the film as transposable talking heads identifies authorship with mediated identity – an identity that is visually and literally fragmented.

Here it is not only the authority of the speaking subject that is being challenged. Burroughs and Balch are aiming to call into question 'History'. This aim is evident in Burroughs' description of the film:

Anthony Balch and I used another device to bring up the whole matter of identity in a film called *Bill and Tony*. We showed Anthony's face projected onto mine and mine onto his. When his face was projected onto my face, the image looked like him. Then we switched the voices around, so that sometimes Anthony's face and my voice and sometimes his face and my voice, and so on. It was all done with projections. Now, this technique, which can only be done with color, not black and white, could be used for all kinds of Jekyll-and-Hyde effects, as well as for horror stories. A lot of what passes for historical fact may be, in fact, distorted. History – a lot of it – is simply rumor and hearsay. (Burroughs, 1991, p. 81)

The aim of the film, then, is to constitute history, and by extension, reality, as a distorted version not of a real reality but as one in a series of many distorted versions. Thus history and reality are placed in the realm of the double, the space where the self is also found. Burroughs expresses this idea more clearly in *Electronic Revolution*: 'Whatever you may be, you are not the verbal labels in your passport any more than you are the word "self". So you must be prepared to prove at all times that you are what you are not' (Burroughs, 1979, pp. 154–5). This comment illuminates what Burroughs and Balch attempt to do in *Bill and Tony*: the *auteur* simultaneously appears and disappears on the screen in disconnected flashes and images, always in the face of another. Thus his personality is never fully expressed, because he has no *one* personality to be expressed in the first place. As in Jean-Luc Godard's film *JLG/JLG: Self-Portrait in December* (1995), which Kaja Silverman discussed beautifully in 'The Author as Receiver' (2001), the mediated subject, who also happens to be the author of the film, gestures towards 'authorial suicide'. The film or text is made to accommodate an author who 'erases himself as a bodily presence', an author who communicates an 'auto-portrait' and 'biographical erasure' (Silverman, 2001, pp. 21, 23, 19, 24). Authorship, then, is determined as self-inflicted death, a process that does not necessarily give birth to readers. The connection Burroughs makes between his filmic experiment and the concept of history, moreover, expresses this authorial suicide in political terms. In this context, avant-garde film-making is realized as political critique: more precisely, a critique of the authority of (hegemonic) culture, identity and textual/cinematic canons.

This representation of the author aims specifically to instigate a new kind of doom for authorship, a new kind of death:

> Remember, i [*sic*] was the movies, the door flash-bulb or orgasm ... Fadeout overtakes a rotting pier – Young faces turn faster through dead nitrous streets – Open shirt in the bath cubicle – The street blew rain – You is coming in the death trauma? . . . sound identity fading out. (Burroughs, 1962, pp. 73, 68)

Deliberately downgrading the 'I' to an 'i' is a strategy that articulates the 'death of the author' in linguistic terms. More pointedly, Burroughs seems to suggest, in an increasingly mediated and technological world, which he embraced with his film-making, it is only as technological artefact – 'sound identity' – that identity can begin to fade out.

What is the point of this cinematic fadeout? To kill the Author-God, to leave him behind, yes. And then? Ultimately, it is about achieving a freedom, an escape from the constraints of identity and authorial control. Burroughs' and Balch's filmic experiment, *Bill and Tony*, is the visual manifestation of this freedom and the possibilities and limitations that it instigates, like a new breed of selves endlessly simulated on the screen, situated in the realm of the double, the uncanny and the monstrous, a 'Jekyll-and-Hyde' situation, as Burroughs rightly describes it. 'The death of the author' is in this context, as Silverman writes, 'better understood as an ongoing process than as a realizable event' (Silverman, 2001, p. 34). As an ongoing process, the author's death involves a simultaneous engagement with the past, the present and the future. Enhancing this point is Burroughs' last full-length novel, *The Western Lands* (1987), which revisits a cultural history of authorship. The meaning of this in terms of the study of authorship is my main concern next.

Looking back

Burroughs' 1980s novels, *Cities of the Red Night* (1982), *Place of Dead Roads* (1983) and *The Western Lands* (1987), now generally known as the Red Night trilogy, are concerned explicitly with the figure of the author. All main characters in the trilogy are 'forger-writers', a kind of guerrilla writer who simultaneously transcribes and falsifies other people's writings. In the first two books of the Red Night trilogy, their aim is to forge historically effective and valuable scripts in order to rewrite history. In *The Western Lands*, it is revealed that William Seward Hall is the ultimate forger-writer, who controls all the other characters. This figure, who shares two names with Burroughs and is deliberately constructed as his alter-ego, has an impossible task from the outset: to 'write his way out of death', literally to locate the land of immortality, 'the western lands' (Burroughs, 1987, p. 3). This quest is quickly put out of focus as it becomes clear that its true purpose is to recount a history of authorship, from the ancient Egyptian scribe to the postmodern director of a film. Here I examine Burroughs' references to these forms of authorship in order to explore why an author like Burroughs, who, as I have shown previously, defines the author as a recording instrument and is concerned with how authorial identity is mediated on the cinematic screen, revisits a cultural history of authorship. To put it another way: why does Burroughs go back? What does he hope to find?

There is much confusion in *The Western Lands* as to what is the primary purpose of the narrative. For a start, there are three overlapping layers of narrative that are never developed fully or resolved. On a meta-level, there is Burroughs' novel. Second, there is the book that Hall is writing, which is a novel about a posthumous pilgrimage to the Western Lands – the land of immortality. Finally, recalling Burroughs' technique of mixing media, there is a film on which Hall is collaborating. But more than anything else, *The Western Lands* is about the old writer's situation, his writer's block and what he does to overcome his desperation. 'The old writer lived in a boxcar by the river', *The Western Lands* begins, a writer who forty years ago 'had published a novel which had made a stir, and a few short stories and some poems . . . After the first novel he started on a second, but he never finished it'. And it gets worse: 'Gradually, as he wrote, a disgust for his words accumulated until it choked him and he could no longer bear to look at his words on a piece of paper' (Burroughs, 1987, p. 1). This is a covert comparison between *Naked Lunch* and the late work, where *Naked Lunch* is glorified and Hall is realized as a bad imitation of the writer of *Naked Lunch*. The 'author' of *Naked Lunch*, here completely merged with the literary character, is no longer the orchestrator of a 'spill off' text, which subscribes to an energetic tone of the postmodernist kind (with its hectoring of the reader, grotesque imagery and the fragmented, discontinuous narrative style). All this is replaced by the passivity of the old writer.

This passivity results in the loss of direction and purpose; in other words, in the loss of identity. Hall is looking to create a new mythology for himself, a new way of overriding mortality, which he finds in the myth of the 'scribe', the writer. While in the first two books of the Red Night trilogy the characters are forger-writers, here they are described as scribes. Kim Carsons, the protagonist in the first two books, becomes Neferti, 'a Scribe, an elite class that is feared and hated' (Burroughs, 1987, p. 99); Abata is 'Assayer of Scribes, and since the number of Scribes was far in excess of the work available, he still exercised considerable influence, his position being more or less similar to that of a modern art critic' (Burroughs, 1987, p. 100). The connection between scribe and modern writing is made even more obvious in the passage that follows: 'The Scribes were divided into a number of schools: the Traditional, the Naturalistic, the Functional, the Situational, the Punctual, the Random, the Picture Puzzle' (Burroughs, 1987, p. 100). Here, then, Burroughs merges the writer with the critic, meeting both in the figure of the scribe. The purpose of this merge is fundamental to the story of the old writer in *The Western Lands*; as I will show, the signifier 'scribe' invokes three distinct forms of authorship: ancient/pre-classical; pre-modern/medieval; and (post)modern.

The primary use of the signifier 'scribe' in *The Western Lands* is in its ancient Egyptian sense – that is, the name for a public official concerned with writing as well as a chronicler of ancient Egyptian life, beliefs and tales.[5] Evidence for this lies in Burroughs' inspiration for the novel, which was Norman Mailer's book about ancient Egypt, *Ancient Evenings* (1983), in the numerous references to ancient Egypt and their ontology of the seven souls, and in the explicit quest of Hall's narrative, which is to find the Western Lands, the place the ancient Egyptians located as the home of the dead (Burroughs, 2001, p. 811). The scribe assumes a central position in this framework, because, in the book, the scribes are supposed to know where the western lands are and, by association, how to find immortality. Through the ancient Egyptian scribe Burroughs is invoking a mythology of the author as a figure that is valued and respected as the holder of divine knowledge. In ancient Egypt, the scribe was supposed to be the actual manifestation of the God Thoth, the God of writing. His primary task, which was to record history, is repeated by Burroughs in the description of Hall as the ultimate forger-writer. Simultaneously, a link is inserted here between the chronicler and the author as 'a recording instrument' in *Naked Lunch*. While the difference between the two is obvious – the author as recording instrument is a technological artefact, whereas the author as a scribe-chronicler works with pen and paper instead – the similarity is more fruitful: it suggests that the author as technological artefact (a primarily postmodernist assertion) is based on an ancient understanding of the author, one completely stripped of agency. At the same time, the ancient Egyptian belief in the scribe as the manifestation of the God of writing that Burroughs recalls here places the author in the context of myth and legend. This definition of the author is consistent with Burroughs' contemporaneous ideas about the writer in his non-fiction work. An example is *Painting and Guns*, in which Burroughs describes the author as a practitioner of magic:

> The purpose of writing is to make something happen. What we call *art* – painting, sculpture, writing, dance, music – is magical in origin. That is, it was originally employed for ceremonial purposes to produce very definite effects. In the world of magic nothing happens unless someone wants it to happen, *wills* it to happen, and there are certain magical formulae to channel and direct the will. The artist is trying to make something happen in the mind of the viewer or reader. (Burroughs, 1992, p. 32)

'A writer or artist,' Burroughs continues, 'is simply someone who tunes into certain cosmic events. He is a medium' (Burroughs, 1992, p. 44).

This description of the writer is in fact more consistent with the medieval view of authorship, which determines the author (*auctor*) as the scribe through whom the 'Divine script' was mediated.[6] As Seán Burke has pointed out, 'within the Medieval view, the human author of Scripture has no power to originate, and his text derives from the creativity and authority (*auctoritas*) of God' (Burke, 1995, p. xvii). Of course, in Burroughs' philosophy, the author would seem to have more agency, as his aim is to make things happen. However, what Burroughs calls 'creative observation', whereby the artist 'is making something exist by observing it', also depends on the same medieval assumption: that there is something 'out there', outside normal (and human) perception, that the author is called on to record (Burroughs, 1992, p. 39). There are other links between *The Western Lands* and medievalism, mainly the obsession with apocalyptic themes and the conception of death as being all-pervasive or as being 'tame', to use Philippe Ariès's term (Ariès, 1981, pp. 5–28). Similar connections can be found in the works of Kathy Acker, which are dominated by diseased bodies, dead mothers and fathers, and suicidal characters; or the death-obsessed Dennis Cooper novel, *Closer* (1989). These texts merge material cultures (consumerism, finances or media) with a distinct sense of millenarianism. As Elizabeth Young has rightly argued, literary examples such as these show that the 1980s in

America was a literary era that assumed the features of medieval plague and death (Young and Caveney, 1992, p. 1).

And this connection between medievalism and (post)modernity is distinctly visible in *The Western Lands*. One piece of evidence is the apocalypse described in the book, which at points is likened to a nuclear disaster; another lies in the (post)modernity of Burroughs' scribe, evident in the third meaning for 'scribe' found in the novel. The label 'scribe' is also used as a name for the Director of the film that is being written and made within the framework of *The Western Lands*. In the character of the Director, Burroughs amalgamates the ancient Egyptian with the medieval and the (post) modern:

> The ancient Egyptians postulated seven souls. Top soul, and the first to leave at the moment of death, is Ren, the Secret Name. This corresponds to my Director. He directs the film of your life from conception to death. The Secret Name is the title of *your* film. When you die, that's where Ren came in. (Burroughs, 1987, p. 4)

Here there is no visible concern with the *auteur* – a unique personality that can be expressed in a film. Instead, Burroughs is concerned with the ways in which authors of all kinds become institutionalized, resembling government institutions that have one aim: to control others. The subject, especially the addict, is subjected to bureaucratic control, whereby he becomes the host for bureaucracy, which is signified as a parasitic virus:

> Democracy is cancerous, and bureaus are its cancer. A bureau takes root anywhere in the state, turns malignant like the Narcotic Bureau, and grows and grows, always reproducing more of its own kind, until it chokes the host if not controlled or excised. Bureaus cannot live without a host, being true parasitic organisms . . . Bureaucracy is wrong as a cancer, a turning away from the human evolutionary direction of infinite potentials and differentiation and independent spontaneous action, to the complete parasitism of a virus. (Burroughs, 1993, p. 111)

Through these associations, the Director in *The Western Lands* is a sign of bureaucratic and institutional control, which determines the scribe in specifically postmodern terms. In this context, artistic creation, whether it is a novel or a film, is informed by capitalist control, movement of capital, and the resulting hierarchy of different financial or other institutions.

In the case of bureaucratic control, Burroughs offers this as the only way out: ' "Bureaus die when the structure of the state collapses. They are as helpless and unfit for independent existences as a displaced tapeworm, or a virus that has killed the host"' (Burroughs, 1993, p. 112). But in *The Western Lands* guerrilla-style 'resistance' is proving difficult, until the old writer gives up; these are his final words: 'The old writer couldn't write anymore because he had reached the end of words, the end of what can be done with words... "Hurry up, please. It's time"' (Burroughs, 1987, p. 258). The old writer may have hoped to find immortality – the only way out of death – but he found the end of words instead, the end of writing. It is significant that Burroughs chooses to end his last full-length novel in true Burroughsian fashion – that is, with the words of another, namely T. S. Eliot.[7] This final line recalls Eliot's connection between writing and death in 'Tradition and the Individual Talent' (1917). Here Eliot asserts that the poet finds the self, writing and life in the conception of death: 'What is dead,' he writes, is 'what is already living'; and by the same principle, the living are already dying, for they experience 'continual extinction' in the act of writing (Eliot, 1932, p. 22). In other words, artistic expression 'is a continual self-sacrifice, a continual extinction of personality' (Eliot, 1932, p. 17).

Burroughs' fiction and films point to this feature of twentieth-century authorship: as in modernist projects, the continuous extinction of the author in Burroughs is deliberate, visible in his challenge of authorial signature in *Naked Lunch* and the cut-up trilogy, in the erasure of the author in his film work and the death of the author-character, William Seward Hall, at the end of *The Western Lands*. Whereas in Eliot the extinction of personality is in order to give rise to the (modernist) literary work over authorial intention, in Burroughs it is in order to bring into question the work itself. Since the author in postmodernist fiction, the literature that Burroughs helped to bring about, is an exclusively textual sign, it is authorship that is being brought into question here; not just the authors of Burroughs' time, but the author in all his/her different historical formations. But like those modernists many years before him, who looked back to the literary myths of the past and – for example, like James Joyce – turned Odysseus into the modern Ulysses, Burroughs abolishes the myth of the author with a backward glance. But any purging presupposes a new beginning: perhaps the history of authorship that Burroughs recounts here through his revisiting of the scribe in *The Western Lands* is also a way of looking ahead and anticipating the new kinds of authors that the new millennium would bring.

But describing Burroughs as a prophet is a dangerous move. 'I may have limited function', he writes in *Naked Lunch*, which points to the limitations of authorship and its non-transcendental, temporal and at times oppressively contextual function. Perhaps it would be more appropriate to finish with Burroughs reminding us of that fact: 'As if I was usually there but subject to goof now and again... *Wrong! I am never here*... Never that is *fully* in possession, but somehow in a position to forestall ill-advised moves...' (Burroughs, 1993, p. 174).

Part III
Postmodern Culture

7
Postmodernism, Criticism and the Graphic Novel

David Punter

Talking about the graphic novel poses several difficulties. One, of course, would be about how worthy they may be of academic consideration in the first place; many of the others are, in one way or another, about time. For example, one might ask about the graphic novel as a genre and its relation to the future. There was a time, as it were – and it was not so long ago – when the graphic novel was being mentioned, along with that long-dead phantom of the future, internet fiction, as a necessary stage in the emancipation of the word, in the evolution of a wider history of the image; as a development that would take up the threads of narrative and weave them in a new way, a way singularly appropriate to a future present in which the word itself was insufficient to whet jaded appetites. But many mainstream bookshops have recently stopped stocking graphic novels, and they seem to have moved back into the *samizdat* world of the 'alternative' specialists.

The graphic novel then perhaps in some sense belongs to the past. Certainly if we consider the issue of naming we might take this to be so; because, of course, the name 'graphic novel' is not without its own difficulties; it signals a contested site. In the first place, one might wonder what a non-graphic novel might be – one, it might be supposed, that has eluded signification entirely. But, of course, the name graphic novel does not mean this: it does not refer directly to writing, neither does it refer to any particular strength or force of depiction, as in, for example, the phrase 'graphic violence' or, alternatively, in the phrase 'graphic depiction of whores', which might be one meaning of the word pornography. Rather it refers to a medium that mixes dialogue and occasional narrative with a certain pictorial stylization, the very medium which, of course, has long been known as 'the comic'.

Some practitioners of the graphic novel still prefer the name comic, which refers us not so much forward to the supersession of the naked word as back to a time of childhood, a time when word and picture were intertwined in all our reading matter. It may be that there has never been a narrative structure as complex as the *Rupert Bear* annuals, where, if the reader dares to admit to having read them, it will be recalled that each page contains a narrative in no less than five forms. There are, on each page, four pictures that tell the story. Beneath each picture is a two-line verse that tells the story again. At the foot of the page there is a prose narrative which goes into events in greater detail, and probably from a quite different readerly position, that of the older child. At the head of each page is a caption that summarizes the story in a few words. In each top corner is an icon that again summarizes the crucial interaction through posture and expression. Five levels, a quintuple narrative, which puts even the most complexly interwoven of graphic novels to shame.

Alongside these issues about time – because, of course, the multiplicity of *Rupert Bear* could also be referred to in terms of multiple times and strategies of reading – run similar difficulties about authorial identity, which perhaps are resolvable only in terms of time. Each graphic novel is usually credited to a team involving a writer, artists, inkers, letterers, colourists; the story, however generally, has temporal predominance in the process. With the visual images one is looking at a technique that is, strictly speaking, one of illustration, placing the graphic novel decisively apart from the work of one of its most frequently – and wrongly – mentioned forebears, William Blake. None the less, the multiplicity of authorial attribution does create its own set of assumptions and ambiguities; it is common, for example, to find different artists at work on the same text, with the result that the visual representation of a character is allowed to run through a series of changes, held together not by imagistic coherence but by a free-flowing set of pictorial changes secured only by a style and material representation of dialogue.

What, however, probably most importantly, lies behind these issues to do with time and complexity is nevertheless the question of the time for reading. What does one do with a graphic novel? From the very outset, the track of reading bifurcates. One track would take the reader speedily through the labyrinth. Treating the pictures as mere aids to keeping one's place, as it were, in the story, this track would be essentially recapitulatory, recon-structive; it would involve the reader, more or less consciously, in forming a simpler story out of the presented fragments, reducing the narrative to precisely the verbal form it would have had before the elaboration of a more complex system of significations. The second track, however, is more difficult to pursue; because, despite the pop-culture pretensions of the graphic novel, by a singular irony the reading habit it appears to require has long since been superseded. It invites browsing, the taking of time to form multiple connections, time to re-read and see new depths in the connections between pictures, time to allow visual representations to sink in, all those complex and in some cases apparently lost habits of temporality that we might asso-ciate either with the endlessly ambiguous moment of standing in front of a painting in a gallery, or with the eighteenth-century gentleman cruising his library for moments of beauty and delight (on the time of reading, see Derrida, 1978).

There is not enough space to elaborate fully on it here, but behind this unfolding series of issues to do with time there would also be something to be said about memory, about what and how the reader remembers in the graphic novel, what it is that he or she re-members, in the sense of reassembles, from the shards and fragments. One would also want to explore something about the child's memory and the memory of childhood; something further about the phrase 'leaving it to the imagination' and what that means, both generally and also more specifically in an age dominated by visual media. But perhaps more to the point, what one might say is that here at this juncture of narrative complexity, time and memory, one is already in some sense on the terrain of the postmodern.

One of the major writers of graphic fiction is Neil Gaiman, and among his works is a ten-volume novel – reassembled after the fact, as it were, from separate individual comic issues – called *The Sandman* (1996). The ninth volume, *The Kindly Ones*, contains an introduction by Frank McConnell, in which he talks a little about Gaiman's narrative techniques – and in which, it is also fair to say, he takes care to establish a discourse which refuses academic purchase on the text. The 'kindly ones' of the title are the Fates, and McConnell draws our attention to the way in which their conversation is *ab initio* constructed to 'refer to the act of telling'. To quote McConnell, partly quoting Gaiman:

> 'What are you *making* him then', asks Clotho of Lachesis in the third frame of the first chapter. 'I can't say that I'm terribly *certain*, my popsy,' she replies, 'but it's a fine yarn, and I don't doubt that it'll suit, go with *anything*, this will'. The story begins as a story about storytelling... In fact, eight of the thirteen chapters begin, in the first frame, with a thread of some sort running across the panel, and with a comment that applies equally to the telling of the tale and to the tale itself. (Gaiman *et al.*, 1996, p. iv)

McConnell's interpretation of this process is very much in the tradition of what we might call the 'postmodernism through the ages' school of thought: 'the great storytellers', he says, 'have always wanted to tell us as much about the business of storytelling as about the stories themselves' (Gaiman *et al.*, 1996, p. iv). Whatever the rights or wrongs of this view, it does at least place us in a certain position in relation to Gaiman's practice, which is in one sense essentially recapitulatory, and deals in precisely the manipulations of time and temporality we have already mentioned in a different context. To begin to look at this more closely, however, I want first to turn to a different work, *Witchcraft* (1996), by a team headed by writer James Robinson. *Witchcraft* is essentially a feminist revenge story running across different time-frames. In Roman Britain, a group of benevolent witches is set upon by a gang of (male) barbarians. One of those who is raped and killed cries out in the moment before her death to the goddesses. Here the figure of the three-in-one recurs, not exactly the Fates this time, but the triplicity that is held to have preceded the Christian usurpation of the trinity – and they are forced to provide opportunities for revenge, even though this is not immediately possible at the time. The story then unfolds in a variety of different scenarios as the character Ursula and her killer are reborn in various different guises, but on each occasion until the last one the achievement of vengeance is thwarted. However, finally that vengeance is achieved and the previous aggressor is sent back into the past, to endlessly relive the very pain he has inflicted on others, to endure as a perpetually repeated victim of sexual violence.

The strength of the text, however, would lie, as perhaps it always does in the graphic novel, in the repertoire of delay. I am not thinking here merely of the delaying devices conventionally employed to prevent an early denouement, plentiful though these are; but rather of the way in which some kind of parallel is achieved between narrative delay and the delay necessary in the reading process in order to keep our attention moving between word and picture.[1] An example would be a double page from towards the end of the text (Robinson, 1996, pp. 108–9). In this section, the aggressor has been reborn as a modern warlock, Martyn; Ursula is reborn as an elderly woman, Irene, and here I will need to go into a little further detail about this section of the story. While Irene was looking after her granddaughter, Fiona, the little girl disappeared, and was subsequently found dead; the shock of this has driven her into a traumatized silence (silence, I am going to imply later, is crucial to the graphic novel as a genre), and she now lives in a nursing home. The time, however, for the old story to be played out again has arrived, and this is signalled by the arrival of the triple goddess disguised in various ways in the nursing home. By this point in the story, we are also aware that it is in fact Martyn who has killed Fiona, his stepdaughter, but, as the first frame on page 108 makes clear, what is crucial is for Irene herself to identify, in some sense 're-member', the identity of the killer.

The crone, one part of the goddess, is trying to reawaken her memory; simultaneously, the nursing home television, in distinctive yellow dialogue boxes, is telling a further story, a story apparently about the habits of lions but, of course, designed further to alert Irene to what she knows but does not realize. The second frame, however, has meanwhile taken up quite a different thread of the story, and what we see is a priest who at some previous time has got in Martyn's way. The third frame takes us back to the television itself, with the voice-over of the nature programme and the voice of the crone starting to interlock. In the fifth frame a different incarnation of the goddess takes up the story, and in the seventh frame the youngest incarnation joins in. The identity of the silhouetted face that dominates the eighth frame is intriguingly unclear: the colour of the hair and the semi-prone position of the figure, as well as the positioning of the frame on the page, all suggest the priest, in which case the question 'Who?' (the only word in this frame) would be signalling from a quite different context from the goddess' previous utterance of the same word; but the fact that the face is not wearing glasses, and the femininity of line around the lips, seem to take one back to the youngest of the goddesses in the previous frame. There is also a similarity to Gaynor, the murdered girl's mother and Irene's daughter, who may also, in her uneasy sleep, be asking herself the same question, and I suspect that the image here is designed to draw together all these narrative and characterological threads, thus investing the question 'Who?' with a multiple symbolism, which is then burst apart in the identity revelation of the single frame which forms the second page, which shows Martyn, exultant and covered in blood, fresh from the murder of the priest.

What, however, one might want to dwell on for a moment on this second page is the relationship between the major picture and a small inset at the bottom, which shows Irene's moment of realization that Martyn is the killer; for that relationship is unclear, and unclear in a way that is probably only available to a mixed verbal and pictorial mode. The reader does not know whether, for example, Irene is seeing, in perhaps some kind of hypnagogic state, Martyn, as he then is, gorily shouting in the priest's bedroom, and thus inferring that he has also been the murderer of Fiona; or whether the temporal relation between the two pictures is simply one of coincidence. What is certain is that the pages depict what we might call a narrative of voices. By that I do not simply mean a narrative told through dialogue, but rather a dialogue where the subject matter is voices themselves, where voices interweave and float free, such that the readerly task becomes precisely the attribution of those voices – when that is possible, which is not always the case.

The story is also told, of course, through colour and tone: in this case, the night colours of the whispering in the nursing home, the more vivid tones of the priest's room, the black and white of the TV screen. It is told again in the pictorialization of the characters, the skull-like face of Irene forming a kind of counterpoint to Martyn's devil disguise. The story of the lions is obviously also Martyn's story, and reveals to us that the death of Fiona, his stepdaughter, has been necessary in order that a new, different birth might take place, a birth for which it is necessary that child and priest alike must die.

What is postmodern about this type of story-telling? A certain level of self-consciousness, clearly, albeit of a kind that one could extend to the comic in general, where an atmosphere of disbelief is assumed by the conventions of stylization. More importantly, perhaps, the assumption of a certain type of attention, whereby rapid interchange between threads of the narrative replaces internal exploration or character development; the story, we might say, becomes one of interplay between surfaces. Most obviously, this is a type of story-telling – as is by far the bulk of the graphic novel – where the boundaries between natural and supernatural have been wiped away: not 'magic realism', perhaps, but 'magic unrealism', although what is also interesting in *Witchcraft* is the way in which parts of the narrative are in fact woven around 'real people', biography is constantly implicated in invention.

The principal example of this is a long passage which deals with the life of the adventurer Richard Burton, who is figured in that section as the current reincarnation of Ursula. The violent barbarian figures as a man called Ithal, who is having an affair with Burton's mother. When Burton confronts him, he is hideously humiliated by Ithal, and this is seen as the motivation behind Burton's later career; coming across Ithal again in later life, and thereby encountering a further chance of revenge, he again flunks it in favour of fame and fortune, and the vengeance goes unachieved. Here, then, the narrative weaves its own explanations around historical events; but because, of course, it does not take historical time seriously, these events become merely items or instances in a longer history – in this case, of gender oppression; all falls under the sign of repetition and difference.

Witchcraft, then, we can certainly see as decisively not postmodern in one sense, in that it deliberately sets out to provide an interpretative master – or mistress – narrative by means of which particular events can be explained. Thus the shards and fragments of dialogue, while operating in a dispersive fashion at a local level, all tend towards a unification of narrative. The same cannot be said of the many graphic novels that exist in what we might call the aftermath of the superheroes. An example is the series of texts written by Grant Morrison under the name of *The Invisibles* (1999). The Invisibles are, as it were, superheroes for our age, postmodern superheroes prone to moments of extreme doubt about what they are doing and why they are doing it. To put it another way, these superheroes are robbed of narrative agency: as they go about their everyday work of killing and salvation, they are never sure whether in fact they are enacting someone else's narrative: whether, indeed, their script has already been written – and drawn – for them.

The obvious irony of this position – because, of course, their perception is in a sense correct – is underlined, in a volume of *The Invisibles* called *Counting to None*, by a character called King Mob, who is looking for a time machine – for reasons too complicated to explain – except that superheroes are always looking for time machines. – 'Sometimes I wonder if the time machine *causes* the end of everything', he says, and we can hardly fail here to pick up the resonance of the time machine as the process of narrative itself, as the process whereby freedom is destroyed in the very act of recounting:

Maybe it was something that never should have been made, like the *bomb* . . . I'm shooting people and it never seems to *end* . . . It was all those *Moorcock* books; I wanted to be *Jerry Cornelius*, the English assassin. I wanted the guns and the cars and the girls and the chaos . . . Shit. I've ended up a *murderer*. My karma's a bloody *minefield* (Morrison *et al.*, 1999, p. 54)

'Why does this have to be *us*?' complains Ragged Robin, his companion. 'Don't you sometimes wish you just didn't *know*?' (Morrison *et al.*, 1999, p. 54).

But lack of knowledge is not an option, just as an un-reading of these shades of Michael Moorcock is an impossibility. Such textual traces abound in *The Invisibles*, giving the characters a curious unfreedom, trammelling their footsteps even when they are engaging in Batmanesque feats of derring-do. Their self-awareness is simultaneously an awareness of the empowering and disempowering possibilities of language itself.

On pages 212–13 of the novel, five of the Invisibles are attacking the command centre of another power-hungry group, and in the background hang several phantoms; not only the comparatively harmless, if irritating, one of Michael Moorcock, with all the corresponding implications of post-modern new worlds, but also of Burroughs, Ballard and the implantation of paranoia. But the paranoia itself moves back into the past, into a specifically textual past which has at all points to do with the materiality of the word. The weapons that will be used against the Invisibles are precisely the verbal weapons of the 1960s situationists, which, *inter alia*, makes one wonder about the age and presumed education of the implied audience.

The Invisibles here are clearly part of somebody else's text. Invisible as they may themselves be – in some way that the text never takes the trouble to specify – here the problem is the invisibility of the authorship of the very words that comprise the text to which they are exposed. 'What if something *terrible*'s been going on here right under my nose', moans Mason, financier extraordinary to superheroic exploits; the 'scary part of the movie' which is starting to unfold is taking its shape within the background noise, like a 'hiss' on a 'speaker channel', and then we are into the full panoply of motifs from the conjunction of situationism and Parisian structuralism that marks a specific regress into the past (Morrison *et al.*, 1999, p. 212).

'Reality is all about language' says their pseudo-structuralist persecutor, and the 'demonstration' that ensues is all about a phenomenon that has been occurring unexplained throughout the story to date, a kind of Radio Alice writ large, here referred to as 'detournment or hijacking', whereby the media are interrupted by revolutionary messages (Morrison *et al.*, 1999, pp. 212–13). Here, however, this 'hijacking' has been internalized: 'we've just occupied the language processing areas of your cerebral cortex', barks the anonymous author-in-the-text, and the imagery moves into black and white, the mark of a certain academic simplicity at the same time as the mark of the point at which the superhero is at the mercy of a consciousness of his or her own constructed identity: 'The most pernicious image of all is the anarchist hero-figure. A creation of commodity culture, he allows us to buy into an inauthentic simulation of revolutionary praxis' (Morrison *et al.*, 1999, p. 213).

The archaic revolutionary provenance of the words is echoed in a graphic replication of the product of a faulty typewriter, the source of home-made theoretical praxis after the model of Gramsci: 'The hero encourages passive spectating and revolt becomes another product to be consumed' (Morrison *et al.*, 1999, p. 213).

Maddened, we might alternatively say, by the phantom of Jean Baudrillard, or at least by the spectre of Baudrillard's own past political credentials, the superheroes are at the mercy of a recapitulation of their own curious genesis, their own story hijacked by voices from past constructions. King Mob and his acolytes, as we learn from the ongoing *dramatis personae* at the beginning of the volume, do have a certain kind of knowledge, or perhaps a knowing kind of uncertainty; they know that 'all the conspiracies are true'; but in accordance with a postmodern recapitulation of conspiracy theory, such an awareness rebounds on the one who knows, and places the possibility of action in the context of a violent materiality of the word that is precisely part of the substance of the graphic novel itself.

As with *Witchcraft*, *The Invisibles* takes the task of the graphic novel to be the interweaving of temporal images. It brings visually and verbally alive a world composed of fragments from different time-scales, and finds objective correlatives for the disordering of time that is taken to be the mark of the postmodern. In this world, it is possible for the object of desire to transmute through times, histories and incarnations at the stroke of a pencil, at the merest change of a colour range: the fact that these may be crude indicators of temporal complexity takes its place in a world where crudity is the object of the lesson, where character has been burned away to be replaced by an interplay of self-conscious fantasies, ironized by an occasional awareness of the impossibility of finding any authorial position outside the texts that have already been written.

This ambiguous set of dealings with the author also forms the background to Martin Rowson's graphic version of *The Waste Land* (1990), an extremely funny recapitulation of T. S. Eliot in the guise of *film noir*. 'The book I most appreciated this year', wrote Peter Ackroyd in 1999, 'was *The Waste Land* by Martin Rowson, a comic strip version of the poem which is far funnier and perhaps more genuinely learned than the original' (Rowson, 1990).[2] More genuinely learned; perhaps not. But the structure of the book follows the structure of Eliot: 'The Burial of the Dead', 'A Game of Chess', 'The Fire Sermon', 'Death by Water', 'What the Thunder Said'. The sad detective who is trying to make sense of the hints and clues provided is one Chris Marlowe; Burbank and Bleistein, foreign bodies perhaps in the poem itself, figure as vice squad officers, Madame Sesostris and Sweeney, her butler – not to mention the character pleasingly known only as 'Wrinkled Doug' – make their appearances on cue. But these are characters who figure – or so the cast list tells us – as 'themselves'. More complexly, the so-called 'Mr Eumenides, the Smyrna Merchant', appears in the guise of Sydney Greenstreet, and the Water Babes are played by Dorothy Comingore, Lauren Bacall and Marlene Dietrich. Ackroyd himself is in there as a taxi driver, Ezra Pound, Craig Raine and Ernest Hemingway have bit parts, and there are set-piece scenes that include W. B. Yeats, Joseph Conrad, Gertrude Stein, Alice B. Toklas, Richard Wagner, William Shakespeare, Edmund Spenser, William Carlos Williams and, as we might expect, Eliot himself, as a barfly in a London pub.

This cross-referencing, however, is background, more hiss in the speakers. What is interesting about the central detective figure is the way in which he features also as the reader, as the incarnation of a process of moving through Eliot's *Waste Land* (1922) without guidance and without information. He speaks also as a voice from a quite different place, as a detective from Los Angeles who has found himself on a quest in a London of which he knows little and understands less. Towards the end of 'The Fire Sermon', he realizes that the track he has been on is leading him nowhere:

> Nothing was connecting...except maybe...I remembered the scrap of paper I'd found at the Porter dame's place. And there it all was. A crippled wino with bad eyesight and the short-term memory of a dressed crab sandwich could've worked it out, but not me. They were all in it together. Sesostris, Sweeney, the Minoan...I'd been doped, dumped, almost drowned, but worst of all I'd been treated like a sucker...LA, LA, that's where I should've been all along, not swapping sob stories with the soak sisters in some zero burg called Margate.

The scrap of paper, addressed from 'Carthage Novelties Inc.', constitutes the unravelling of the plot as the only text that can bring together the discrete fragments of the story; fragments, indeed, shored against the ruins, but here the very pasts of the poem are 'presented' – made, as it were, into a visual present – in the background of a London pub, in boats dimly glimpsed across the Thames, in half-seen pictures that appear out of a drab, black-and-white murk. Marlowe's visit to Mrs Porter, as we have seen suggested, is not a great success:

> It looked like I'd walked in on a moonshine and soda party where they'd gone crazy with the cocktail sticks. That or they'd been playing strip poker and someone had noticed the cards were marked. I wasn't planning to hang around in case Sweeney and the dames came back to life and fingered me to the cops. So I took the pearls, the chalice from the palace, one of the syphons and the list. It could have been a hit list; could've been a sucker list...maybe even a reading list.

What this list actually is, as we can see in the relevant frame, is a list of quotations, an assembly of sources – Jessie Weston, Sir J. Frazer, Petronius, Thomas Malory and so on; but what are also here are the broken, squalid bodies and the spray of tarot cards (foregrounding here, of course, the Last

Judgement); also the window, the sill, on which something or someone might squat, looking out – where else? – on to Rats' Alley.

What Marlowe needs, above all, is to crack the code; and for this he requires a library, a source of references to further explain the list, but all the library does when he visits it is to add further puzzles to the existing ones. Eliot is there himself, as, again, we might by now expect, asking for 'Volume Seventeen of the Encyclopaedia of Anthropology, from Ritual to Romance'; the librarian replies that he thinks 'you'll find that's from Rickshaws to Romanies', thus installing a misquotation, a suspect memory, at the heart of the problem. This misremembered – or perhaps one should say dismembered – book is flanked in the frame by two others: 'Editing and Dictation Made Easy', reminding us, among other things, of the fate of Eliot's *Waste Land*, its gestation and eventual publication as the result of a complex process of multiple authorship; and a volume called *Weird Detective Stories*, linking the pulp ambience of *Weird Tales* with the genres of *film noir* and detective fiction, but also with the names on its front cover, principally Verlaine, figuring here as a 'symbolist sleuth'.

There is much more that could be said about these particular frames and about Rowson's *Waste Land* in general. The principal point, however, would be to do with the visual imagery. What is attempted here is a gallery of grotesques that simultaneously bind themselves inexorably to a literary history; the anxiety of influence is always just over Marlowe's shoulder, as it is over the shoulders of the Invisibles, indeed it is the source of the self-conscious paranoia that infests the genre. The language of Eliot's poem and the language of Raymond Chandler and Humphrey Bogart are fused in a sequence of images that present a city seeping decay, a London darkly seen where half-remembered filmic images provide an overlay and a set of distortions between the reader and any attempt to make concrete sense of the narrative. This is indeed an 'unreal city', but its unreality consists precisely in the freight of symbolism it is obliged to carry, and in the uncertainty of the sources of that symbolism – and here even the notion of symbolism itself enters into the flux of images. There are Notes – as, of course, there have to be – at the end of the text, mostly in other languages, but the single Note to 'Death by Water' reads thus:

> During the filming of *The Big Sleep*, Bogart asked the director of the picture the significance of the dead chauffeur in the Packard dredged out of the ocean. Not knowing the answer, the director asked the scriptwriters. Equally in the dark, they phoned Chandler, who'd forgotten.

'Of equally great anthropological interest' claims the author of the Notes – whoever in the complex contexts of the text that may be – is an account of a passage from William Empson's inaugural lecture as Professor of English at Sheffield:

I was rather pleased one year in China when I had a course on modern poetry, *The Waste Land* and all that, and at the end a student wrote in a most friendly way to explain why he wasn't taking the exam. It wasn't that he couldn't understand *The Waste Land*, he said, in fact after my lectures the poem was perfectly clear: but it had turned out to be disgusting nonsense, and he had decided to join the engineering department. Now there a teacher is bound to feel solid satisfaction; he is getting definite results.[3]

This might be as good a point as any other to return to a contemplation of the question of whether reading and writing about graphic novels is a wise use of time. At the simplest level, I think that to 'refuse' the graphic novel would involve all the difficulties that have followed, in my view, from the comparable long-term refusal similarly to consider the significance of children's fiction, a refusal that is only now, and only to a certain extent, being rectified; but I think the cases of Rowson's revisionary version of *The Waste Land* and Gaiman's long sequence of texts might provide two very different, though equally emblematic, answers.[4] In the case of Rowson, it seems to me that what is presented visually provides a counterpoint, a counter-voice, to the 'original' poem; but it seems to me also that it provides evidence that one could argue that the graphic novel has a specific relationship to the postmodern which can bear comparison to the relationship between the postmodern and high modernism; or perhaps one could say that it represents a further stage in a general trajectory of fragmentation. In particular, I would want to describe this as a process of ruin. Eliot's own poem naturally deals in ruins, and seeks and develops its own aftermathic status, setting itself in a line that includes not only the 'reading-list' of quotations but also the very possibility of epic, C. F. Volney's *The Ruins, or, a Survey of the Revolutions of Empires* (1791), as well as the ruin of classical allusion. The postmodern comes – or perhaps we should now say 'came' – to break apart further the assumption of narrative completeness, to re-present those shards under the sign of a presumably perpetual deconstruction; but it comes, or came, also to remind us of the presumptions behind the eventual triumph of language, a triumph that the graphic novel places under question. Another way to explore these arguments would be by starting from the Lacanian assertion that 'the unconscious is structured like a language'.

That Lacanian approach, I would say, has now been altered decisively by the recent work of psychoanalysts such as, in particular, Jean Laplanche, who, in his *Essays on Otherness* (1992) asserts, firstly, that whatever the unconscious might be structured like, it can never be language, for the obvious reason that the evidence we have about the unconscious is not reducible to linguistic form; and second, that if, as Laplanche claims, it is better to think of the unconscious in the very different terms of a series of messages, then the form and medium of those messages will vary historically according to the technologically dominant form of the message (see

Laplanche, 1999; Punter and Bronfen, 2001, pp. 7–21). Laplanche claims, in essence, that the unconscious is itself formed of ruins. He says that it reverberates with the messages we received in childhood; but crucially, it contains – and continually seeks to rework – all those messages that were unintelligible, untranslateable, because they were essentially messages from the unconscious of the other, and their misunderstanding at source forms part of a chain of misunderstanding that can find relief – or a least re-living – only in the unconscious, only in dream.

According to this line of thinking, the disembodiment implicit in the reduction to linguistic form is therefore itself a recuperative activity; it necessarily seeks to disclaim the fullness, the terrible implacability and specificity, the vividness of the image, to subdue it to the dominance, not merely of the word, but of the word as an item in an intelligible and rule-bound system. In this light, we might reconsider the readerly position assumed in Rowson's text. We might, for example, say that a more capacious take on our reception of the message will necessarily move us beyond the confines of the word, will already have moved us beyond it, for reasons that are both historical and also related to the general status of the unconscious as ruin, as residue. This sense of the aftermath will only be impeded by the pretence of purity implied in the reduction to the verbal; it is here that the Notes to his text, cast in fact in purely verbal form, come to be seen merely as an ironic adjunct to the complexity of messages implicated in the text itself.

If Rowson's text can be referred to in this sense as 'aftermathic', then it seems to me that Gaiman's work – and, to a lesser extent, the assumptions behind such less erudite texts as *The Invisibles* – can be referred to suitably as 'after-mythic'. *The Sandman* (Gaiman *et al.*, 1996) recounts a tale instantly familiar from a host of myths and epics, one we could easily recognize as being centred on the displacement of the gods. His own pantheon, eclectically engaging Greek, Roman and Norse elements, and including figures such as Desire, Death and Delirium – herself an aftermath of a dead god called Delight – is thrown into turmoil by the mortal capture of one of their number, Dream; and the entire saga concerns the effects of this capture; or of, to put it another way, the difficult negotiations between Dream as an immortal (or, we might say, universal) and Dream as the outcome and representation of specific human and social conflicts.

In a typical moment of *The Kindly Ones* (Gaiman *et al.*, 1996, part 8, pp. 1–2), Dream moves through his disrupted kingdom, taking account of its condition, and in the first frames we can recognize the contours of the shards of history employed to resonate with folk tale, legend, myth:

> On Moonday, the king of dreams gave an audience to five small children, who had travelled a long way, seeking their lost mother. He met them in a hall filled with scarecrows, who whispered among themselves in the voices of the stars of the silent screen. (Gaiman *et al.*, 1996, part 8, p. 1)

But above and preceding this image, with the scarecrows themselves in eighteenth-century costume redolent of the ambience of the early fairy tale, are the scissors of the Fates, a silent reminder of the shadow that hovers over wish-fulfilment; just as the foregrounded misshapen fingers of the scarecrows silently 'frame' (or frame with silence) the apparent (almost) normality of the interview with the children. Here in this world of dreams, there are only more dreams and more stories; no solution, no resolution, only a constant dealing with desire that merely allows us to carry on – into a realm where death is omnipresent, where the end of the story always hovers, but where also there is always room for further elaboration, further narrative delay: 'At the end, he drew a door in the air with his finger, and the children walked through it, into the rest of their story'. There is then no complete story offered on these pages, only momentary effects from a multitude of stories, points of mythic intersection. The allusions are unclear, messages always liable to be misunderstood: 'He awarded the Magic Lantern Show to the Knight of Clouds, although he permitted the Body Politic to retain custody of the Screaming Stones and the Snows of Yesterday' (Gaiman *et al.*, 1996, part 8, p. 2).

Although the skills of the artists may be limited, there is none the less something of the untranslateable – one of Laplanche's favourite terms, and one beginning properly to resonate within postcolonial and 'alter-global' studies – about the relations among the frames. Dream can relativize the tribulations of the everyday, as with the final dream of the tortoise ('And then, to conclude the day's work, he gave an elderly tortoise, alone on her island these past two centuries, a dream of her love, roasted by passing sailors long since for his rich green flesh' (Gaiman *et al.*, 1996, part 8, p. 2)); but only in his own realm, and in a place – like dream – where words have no firm or systematic jurisdiction. In the last frame but one, for example, Dream appears to be a standing figure, his back to a tree, while the 'tribal gods' of a fantasized South Africa are silently shown to us as being ambiguously located between past and present, between an archaic dream of South Africa and its contemporary political reality. Similarly, in the sixth frame, Dream is content to let well alone; the expressions on the faces of the eastern gods depicted in the frame may be reassuring or menacing, but at any event they are designed to conjure difference, to suggest that there is no eternal content of dreaming, no master-interpretation, but instead a collection of processes each distinct from one another, each containable in its own frame, each framed in turn by a process of silence.

Perhaps it is on these questions of framing and silence that we should end. For it seems to me that the graphic novel can offer us a specific take on experience as being framed into discrete units, as passing between the doors of silence; that it can, alternatively, provide us with a perspective on ruin. It seems to me that one could refer to this as postmodern, but only if one is willing to grant the postmodern the terms of its own supersession, allow it to proceed to some of the conclusions of its own scepticism about textuality. However, there is always at this point the difficulty of a disjunction between the text and the interpretation, between discourses predicated on incompatibility; so perhaps it would be better to conclude, as Gaiman concludes *The Kindly Ones*, with a scrap of stained, greenish paper, carrying the legend, with no obvious relation to anything that has gone before: 'Was it a bear, or a Russian, or what?'

8
Authorial Identity in the Era of Electronic Technologies

Tatiani G. Rapatzikou

The expansion of electronic media has affected the status of the book as a material trademark of culture at the beginning of the twenty-first century. This chapter aims to examine the impact of the interaction of electronic and print media on postmodern literary production through its examination of William Gibson's work in relation to software design and digital art. Discussing Gibson's fiction in relation to other electronic and artistic media, it intends to draw attention to the centrality of interactive and hypertextual communities (MUDs) to his writings. What this particularized study is after is to form the basis of a wider examination of authorial identity in the era of electronic technologies.

Ever since the popularization of virtual technologies in the 1980s, computer networks and their functions have attracted the attention of the public. Computer technology is no longer regarded as obscure and abstract but as a medium of human interaction, communication and artistic creation. Computer networks are not simply connecting machines to machines but also people to people with the use of email, chat rooms, discussion lists, conferencing, games, e-book access lists, and digital art galleries. The impact that computer technologies have had on the notions of space and community has gradually led to the creation of conceptual spaces that extend far beyond fixed geographical boundaries. As a result, this has enabled the unrestrictive interaction between online users on a worldwide scale nowadays. In her study *Cyberpunk and Cyberculture* (2000), Dani Cavallaro argues that the electronically facilitated communities are 'less and less a nuclear structure and more and more a multilayered apparatus' (Cavallaro, 2000, p. 31). They function as a gateway to a much more diversified terrain of communication, creativity and sensory input, since ideas, impressions and viewpoints can be shared instantly by other people all over the world.

However, the experience of immersing in alternate realities should not be credited only to the newly emergent digital technologies. Artists and authors have often resorted to an array of spatial, temporal and typographical or illustrative techniques to enable their public to identify with the image shown or with the story narrated. For example, in Jean-Jacques Rousseau's *Julie, la nouvelle heloise* (1761) the immediacy of the characters' reactions and the constant interpretation of their actions add a communicative value to the novel, making it appear as all evolving. This is further enhanced by the supplementary publication of a separate set of illustrations. Also, Laurence Sterne's *Tristram Shandy* (1760–67) is characterized as a typographically innovative book with its blank pages, wiggly lines, loose chapters, detours and fragmented storyline published in instalments.

On a contemporary note, Mark Z. Denielewski's *House of Leaves* (2000) constitutes a hybrid novel in which an array of typographical innovations, illustrations, textual fragments and lengthy footnotes are combined in order to produce a spatially and temporally challenging novelistic and artistic experience. N. Katherine Hayles notes that this novel 'extends the claims of the print book by showing what print can be in a digital age' (Hayles, 2002, p. 781). Alongside *Julie* and *Tristram Shandy, House of Leaves* does not just exemplify how art and fiction fuse together through the use of a variety of media. The alternative pictorial and narrative patterns that these narrative examples employ rely on interactivity with the reader and immersion within the narrative without negating the corporeal nature of the artwork itself. Luca Toschi has observed that 'the history of writing serves to remind us that language continually strives to find diverse material representations . . . and tries to give new forms to space in order to extend its expressive potentialities' (Toschi, 1996, p. 191). Treating space both as textual and electronic, this chapter aims to reconsider the challenges that printed matter has been called to face nowadays as well as the potentials opening up for it.

One of the authors to revolutionize the novelistic form is the cyberpunk fiction writer William Gibson. His first novel *Neuromancer* (1984) pioneered in associating textual description with computer-generated realities.[1] The opportunity Gibson offers his readers to inhabit (alongside his characters) simultaneously an array of real and virtual spaces has made reading a much more challenging and interactive experience. This is because cyberpunk fiction encourages the reader to take an imaginative leap beyond the boundaries of the printed page, to explore new terrains of spatial and sensory diversity. Almost anticipating the interactive hypertextual communities (MUDs) that appeared in the late 1980s, this novel sets up a book model in which literary narration and technological mediation can co-exist.

Gibson's new novel, *Pattern Recognition*, published almost twenty years later in 2003, further exploits the possibility of communication as part of a global and internet facilitated market-place. Moving away from the understanding of the author as a sole creator, it attributes to the authorial figure the role of an experienced navigator who, similarly to an online user, experiences 'reality' as an assortment of images. In this sense, Gibson's books offer a new model of authorship that makes the printed text a window on to an electronically expansive world and a global network of intercultural and interracial communications. This enables the reader to take a step further from simply concentrating on the narrative structure of the text *per se*, to engage with a public and much more sociable activity. Jay David Bolter writes:

> The viewer or reader is supposed to fall through the frame or the page into another world, one that is either continuous with our world or has its own convincing logic. The work of art or literature is supposed to describe an *environment* that the viewer or reader can inhabit for the time in which she is enjoying the work. (Bolter, 1996, p. 267)

Bolter's reading of Gibson's novels has been influenced by Paul Cobley's *Narrative* (2001), which discusses the hypertextual feel of contemporary fiction. This is because of the variety of data that novels now contain, and the ease with which knowledge can be transferred instantaneously among the various locations and individuals that feature in their pages. What Cobley indicates though as 'one crucial factor in the development of narrative [is] the power of the reader' (Cobley, 2001, p. 205). In addition, Joseph Tabbi's views, as expressed in *Cognitive Fictions* (2002), should be taken into consideration, especially his claim that 'print narrative might then recognize itself, at the moment when it is forced to consider its own technological obsolescence, as a figuration of mind within the new media ecology' (Tabbi, 2002, p. xi).

Tabbi believes that the printed matter can capture the data that electronic media merely transfers. His understanding of print media as an effective counterpoint to the technologies of today is important to the present study of Gibson's fiction. Such view will help highlight how the kind of a novel Gibson has invented is informed by his reader's efforts to come to terms with the plethora of messages and types of discourse that flow in the virtual highway. What is the role that both the author and reader are invited to play in the case of these electronic and interactive communities? The extent to which their relationship to the text has been reformulated with the advent of electronic technologies will be discussed in the section that follows.

Hypertextual interactive communities

Bolter writes: 'Like printing in the fifteenth century, the computer today is a technology that challenges the traditional definition of the book' (Bolter, 1996, p. 254). However, electronic technologies still lack the ability to act autonomously, since they rely heavily on printed matter for the accumulation of their databases and construction of their web pages. What they offer in return, though, is flexibility and navigational freedom through a vast amount of information, as well as numerous creative opportunities that result from the manipulation of their various data resources. What matters in this case is the fact that the book as a cultural artefact is not rendered obsolete. It is constantly reinvented because of its interaction with today's evolving electronic technologies which, instead of diminishing, have in fact altered the way we now view print media.

Of particular relevance here is Michel Foucault's statement in *The Archaeology of Knowledge* (1972) that 'the frontiers of the book are never clearcut' since 'it is caught up in a system of references to other books, other texts, other sentences: it is a node within a network . . . [a] network of references' (Foucault, 1976, p. 23). This comment serves as a reminder of the fact that books have been considered to be the loci of a number of intersecting narrative paths. Due to the fascination of literary imagination with computing technologies, the notion of the text has broadened to give way to other textual formations known as hypertext. This term coined by the American Ted Nelson around 1965, is a kind of text which 'is experienced as non linear, or, more properly, as multilinear or multisequential' (Landow, 2001, p. 100). It is defined by its ability to organize textual fragments in a network of communication between related parts or different texts that are part of the same retrieval system (Aarseth, 1997, pp. 12–13).

The interactive communities known as MUDs (Multiple-User-Domains or Dungeons) constitute an example of such a hypertextual experience. They are worth examining here to appreciate the intersection of computing and textual strategies in Gibson's fiction. The name of these communities was invented by two English software programmers at the University of Essex, Roy Trubshaw and Richard Bartle, who designed an adventure computer game called *Dungeons and Dragons*, which many players could access simultaneously from many parts of the world. The first MUDs were destined for game-playing. From 1989 onwards, MUDs have enabled users to communicate more freely within their own personally designed virtual landscapes by employing collaborative textual strategies. It is important to note that MUDs are self-governing systems that are interested in communication between real people in real time. Anonymity is one of their main features, since users often resort to the adoption of multiple nicknames or favour gender-swapping without being hindered by conventional codes set by social class, sexuality and race.

What the users of MUDs are after is the creation of a virtual but liberating environment. Apart from the rules that the managers of MUDs need to apply to every new and potential user for security reasons, each MUD field allows room for play and pleasure facilitated through internet-activated text. This clarifies the fact that MUDs are textually mediated events, which 'makes them valuable to those interested in the development of new literary aesthetics and to those who want to study the conditions of written communication in the age of computers and telematics' (Aarseth, 1997, p. 146). As a result, the MUD users are after the creation of a virtual but unregimented environment which is not bound by any cultural, social or psychological restrictions.

MUDs are interactive and hypertextual communities, which offer possibilities for the enactment of various identities. Identity performance leads to the construction of diverse types of users whose multiple points of view result in the development of certain power relations between them. This chapter aims, in part, to envisage the degree of openness and interactivity that characterizes such environments. Of particular relevance to its scope is Mikhail Bakhtin's claim that the polyphonic narrative is that which is 'constructed not as the whole of a single consciousness, absorbing other consciousness as objects into itself, but as a whole formed by the interaction of several consciousness, none of which entirely becomes an object for the other' (Bakhtin, 1984, p. 18).

Bakhtin's description sheds light on how the MUD environments work. This is because their reliance on the incorporation of multiple points of view equally facilitates the formation of various spatial dimensions. Sherry Turkle describes MUDs as 'a mediaeval fantasy landscape in which there are dragons to slay...or it can be a relatively open space in which you can play at whatever captures your imagination' (Turkle, 1996, p. 355). It is clear from her description that MUD users can easily move in and out of certain spatial and temporal restrictions by inhabiting multiple environments and adopting variable identity characteristics. Their mobility and flexibility consequently increase the interactive value of the MUD medium. Structurally, a MUD is not limited to a single point of view, but open to a combination of experiences and textual prompts that continually open up new paths for interaction and spatial immersion.

In this respect, the success of the hypertextual interactive communities described here relies on the activity of their users as well as on the improvisatory and multivocal nature of their structures. It is the users who are responsible for the regulation and dissemination of the information offered by the designer of the MUD system. Importantly, their role is not just supplementary but in fact exceeds the boundaries of the 'user-only' label. Their input complements the one already provided by the initial designer, since the communication variables they are feeding into the MUD system enable its growth and development. In this sense, both the designer and the user share the same load as far as the running of the MUDs are concerned. They are interchangeably creators and consumers of the MUD hypertextual experience. However how does their relationship translate in the case of the novel for the author-reader? The next section will examine Gibson's *Neuromancer* in relation to hypertextual environments in order to assess the strengths and the weaknesses of both print and electronic media.

Cyberspace and the virtual reality medium

The creation of electronically-sustainable, interactive and reader-participatory environments is one of the concerns of digital art. Tina LaPorta's online projects entitled *Re:mote_corp@REALities* (2001), which shares similarities with Gibson's cyberpunk fiction, will facilitate the examination of the trajectory created between electronic and novelistic authorship. LaPorta concentrates mainly on the construction of internet-activated identities through the chatroom medium and multiple virtual environments with the use of web cameras. The combination of fragmented pieces of text, produced by the online discussions that the users have in their chatrooms, with live webcam images, creates an instantaneous textual as well as visual sensation. What LaPorta attempts to highlight is that the effectiveness of an electronically-mediated activity does not just rely on the sustainability of the system and the way it has been designed. It also depends on the collaborative spirit of its participants, who usually come from variable social and cultural backgrounds. However, the sense of freedom these users are experiencing while online is misleading, since all their paths of communication have already been conceptualized by the designer of the present programme. Tabbi comments on such a process by stating that '[t]he hypertext reader is not an author . . . but rather a rearranger of materials the author has selected and arranged' (Tabbi, 2002, p. 124).

In a similar manner, the electronic but literary worlds that Gibson describes in *Neuromancer* almost correspond to this newly-emergent tendency in digital art by which the viewing information or witnessing action takes place in intersecting or parallel environments in a non-linear fashion. The reader of such a novel should not ignore the fact that there has been somebody in charge of amassing all this information and facts. The study and appreciation of Gibson's computer-diffused environments and the role-play activities in which his characters are engaging could be read as futuristic parables and forerunners of a technologically-orientated cultural trend wishing to view authorship in the era of electronic technologies as a diversifying and collaborative experience.

The initial idea upon which Gibson's popular novel resides emulates hypertext practices regarding the 'degree of choice involved in the ways in which readers construct narratives' (Cobley, 2001, p. 205). When Gibson started working on *Neuromancer*, he was searching for a model that would allow action to take place simultaneously in parallel narrative plains. The idea was that his characters would be able to access these plains without being obstructed by space and time constraints. In an interview, he claimed:

> having really a lot of trouble in how I got the characters in and out of a room. Literally I was having trouble with getting them up and down the stairs. I could put them in the room and I could talk but I couldn't

move them around. So . . . I came up with a kind of formative cyberspace gadget that allowed me to jump-cut all of those things. (Rapatzikou, 2004, p. 228)

His idea of employing cyberspace as a formative gadget not only resolved the restrictions that a conventional linear narrative imposes. It also helped his characters to jump in and out of his electronically activated worlds, while his readers could visualize action through a textual plot line. By experimenting with character formation as well as with the construction of alternative spatialities, Gibson freed literary writing from the constrictions of the one-dimensional printed page. He made reading a three-dimensional experience, as envisaged in his own definition of cyberspace in *Neuromancer*: 'Cyberspace. A consensual hallucination experienced daily by billions of legitimate operators, in every nation, by children being taught mathematical concepts . . . A graphic representation of data' (Gibson, 1995, p. 67).

Gibson's characterization of cyberspace as 'a consensual hallucination' focuses on the electronic re-conceptualization of experience that this technological system offers by creating a spatially and temporally illusory effect. The 'reality' that cyberspace projects is nothing more than a simulated reproduction of real-life experiences reduced to mere images floating on it. In this way, attention is paid to *how* the images or data are represented, not *what* they represent. Lacking subjective substance, these images are regenerated for public consumption only, since the experience that they represent is nothing more than an accumulation of unrelated but life-like images. These images offer users the advantage of a visual point of view, or 'a graphic representation of data' as Gibson writes, which, as in a film sequence, makes users believe that what they see is real even though the sensory experience that virtual reality transfers is electronically constructed.

The way Gibson chooses to depict cyberspace adds another dimension to the way digital technologies are envisioned. It locates a difference in the relationship of old and new media with their reading public. Since the advent of print media, what brought readers together, independent of their social or geographical isolation from one another, was the circulation of printed matter. However, in the late twentieth century, and at the beginning of the twenty-first, the development of electronic technologies, such as cyberspace or virtual reality have changed the nature of media communication. By fusing the human with the technological, digitalization has created communities, worth exploring, equally imaginable and habitable. In this sense, the cyberspatial literary model Gibson proposes does not annihilate authorial identity. Rather, it creates a new type of novelistic authorship that is informed by technological change. Gibson's cyberspace, then, fulfils a social role that capitalizes on the interaction between diverse sources of information with creativity.

The narrative experience that *Neuromancer* embodies brings together its electronically active characters with the readers through a textual model the author has devised. In particular, the readers, coming from diverse geographical locations, are facilitated through language to follow the way the characters act and move within a cyberspatial environment that had been considered, according to popular belief, technically inaccessible. As a result, printed literature is not simply part of a media-run world but exists through it. Writers experiment with emerging social, technological and aesthetic modes of literary production by emulating language's graphic intensity and animating energy. The fact that the cyberspatial medium is textually, not visually, described, produces a different effect which questions the idea of language as a mode of representation. Gibson's novel allows readers to make their own connections between the events narrated and set their own reading pace while moving between chapters and narrative-mediated descriptions.

In *Neuromancer*, virtual reality serves as a database that characters can access when wired to a computer console. Gibson describes the procedure:

> [Case] settled the black terry sweatband across his forehead, careful not to disturb the flat Sendai dermatrodes . . . He closed his eyes . . . And in the bloodlit dark behind his eyes, silver phosphenes boiling in from the edge of space, hypnagogic images jerking past like film compiled from random frames. (Gibson, 1995, p. 68)

The experience depicted here should not be taken literally. The virtual and cybersptatial realms Gibson presents us with are only used metaphorically in order to induce an experience that is still communicated to us through the book medium itself. The 'random frames' and the 'hypnagogic images' the main character is envisioning appear to be far too arbitrary compared to the steps one has to take in order to set up an electronic connection. Technically speaking, in the case of a hypertextual or a MUD, players or users would connect to their multi-user environments by gaining access through their own computer. As soon as they logged on, they would connect to their own character formation or lexical commands, which would enable their participation in a number of pre-designed activities. As Tabbi notes, such practices can only be useful when employed for 'producing and retrieving information, and finding pathways through lexia that have already been mapped out by the author during composition or the reader during previous readings' (Tabbi, 2002, p. 121). In this case, the possibilities for action the MUD environment offers are not infinite. Certain existing parameters remind users of their limitations, since there are always lexical or informational indicators that regulate admission to a MUD domain and access to commands. This reveals that MUDs are not entirely devoid of power structures. The multiple scenarios with which they supply users are only reinforcing the fake sensation that it is the users who are in charge of the whole operation and no one else.

In the MUD's literary equivalent that Gibson's *Neuromancer* embodies, the reader is acquainted with a much more sophisticated and advanced model of communication practices. The confrontation of the human subject with the electronic technologies is not just digital but corporeal. In the case of hypertext or MUD, users are looking for other users with whom they are acquainted, or with whom they are engaging in conversation – total strangers who are, of course, registered members with one or another system. In Gibson's cyberspatial world, the interaction sought is far more intense and unpredictable:

> [Case] keyed the new switch. The abrupt jolt into other flesh. Matrix gone, a wave of sound and color... [Molly] was moving through a crowded street... fragments of music from countless speakers. Smells of urine, free monomers, perfume, patties of frying krill. For a few frightened seconds he fought helplessly to control her body. Then he willed himself into passivity, became the passenger behind her eyes. (Gibson, 1995, pp. 71–2)

From the description provided in the above quotation, both characters seem to be rather experienced and familiar with the processes involved in accessing the electronically-generated space. Their actions rely on their own initiative and they are not restricted by each other's interests and inclinations. Within their field of action, which seems to be developing in real time, there seem to be no commands that the characters need to adhere to. There are no predetermined descriptions about the characters they may run into and the type of landscape they might be envisioning. In other words, nobody is trying to impose his or her will on the other: action or movement in Gibson's cyberspace is unpredictable because of the constant synaesthetic effects fed into the system, which succeed in sustaining the readers' attention. The understanding of the text as a cyberspatial terrain makes character formation much more flexible. It increases the indeterminacy levels of the system with which these characters are interacting. As a consequence, narrative suspense rises because of the impulsive and almost unpredictable way the plot develops.

According to Aarserth's analysis of the interactive communities or MUD aesthetics, '[a] very important aspect is the ability to attach descriptions to the actions performed on an object' (Aarseth, 1997, p. 153). In Gibson's narrative, however, the opposite happens. Action always precedes language, which distinguishes the cybespatial activity of the characters from the textual information the readers receive. This may not be complying with the prescriptive language that MUDs and hypertext links usually employ, but it certainly reveals the kind of language to which Gibson resorts. This is endowed with cinematic qualities intending to create a three-dimensional real-time visual effect. The juxtaposition of these two variant but parallel forms of communication creates the illusion that both the characters and the readers co-exist within a simulated environment. Simulation allows them to view or communicate with one another through a far more descriptive and graphically inept rhetoric maintained by the novelistic form itself, as shown in the following cyberspatial description from *Neuromancer*: 'Disk beginning to rotate, faster, becoming a sphere of paler gray. Expanding – And flowed, flowered for him, fluid neon origami trick . . . transparent 3D chessboard extending to infinity' (Gibson, 1995, p. 68). Having blurred the boundaries between text and image, Gibson has succeeded in widening the scope of the novel. What he has constructed is a narrative that is able to capture the expansive and fluid sensation that electronic technologies create in textual terms.

Consequently, novel reading becomes far more creative and interactive, because it succeeds in helping readers to appreciate the effect that these technologies have on the the human mind. In this respect, attention should be paid to the title of the novel itself. David Porush, in his article 'Cybernauts in Cyberspace: William Gibson's *Neuromancer*' (1987), writes that the title 'puns on the idea of the literary text as a cybernetic manipulation of the human cortex' (Porush, 1987, p. 171). In particular, the novel functions as a textual and language-prompted mechanism that navigates the human mind through the electronic pathways it describes by sensitizing the emotive and intuitive centres of the reader/spectator. Readers are not asked to respond actively to what they see happening in *Neuromancer*'s cyberspatial terrains. Rather they are expected to observe intuitively how the characters act and react in a technologically-designed reality made familiar by the language and diction used in the novel. The narrative Gibson employs bridges the textual with the electronic by making the latter appear more alluring through the vividness of its portrayal.

Gibson's narrative is not simply aiming at celebrating electronic technologies but rather at highlighting their deceptive and disorientating character. Cavallaro locates this polarizing attitude towards computer technologies in the etymology of the word 'virtual':

> linked to the Latin root *virtus*, the virtual would seem to stand on the side of moral excellence . . . What this assessment leaves out, however, is a supplementary – yet no less momentous – encoding of *virtus*, which gained fame and indeed notoriety in the Renassaince . . . synonymous with expediency, opportunism, dissimulation and secretive-ness. (Cavallaro, 2000, p. 31)

In *Neuromancer*, Gibson compares the cyberspatial experience metaphorically to a drug addiction that possesses one completely, as shown in the following excerpt:

> [Case] felt a stab of elation, the octagons and adrenaline mingling with something else . . . Because, in some weird and very approximate way, it

was like a run in the matrix. Get just wasted enough, find yourself in some desperately but strangely arbitrary kind of trouble. (Gibson, 1995, p. 26)

The confusion that the human mind is experiencing, because of its engrossment by the artificially designed planes that cyberspace generates, is caused by the disorientation experienced. The justification is that it is not the human subject who has the initiative, but the machine which executes on the basis of a pre-designed set of commands that have already been fed into its system. In Gibson's fiction, it is Artificial Intelligence (AI) that controls all action in cyberspace, by preventing characters from achieving total informational control: 'Wintermute had built Armitage up from scratch, with Corto's memories of Screaming Fist as the Foundation' (Gibson, 1995, p. 241). What this quotation underlines is that the artificial intelligence systems described are innovatively designed computer programmes. They are powerful enough to construct AI-governed monopolies and hierarchical systems of technological control, whose supremacy exceeds the technical expertise of their users. This highlights that users, in this case, are not dealing with human-designed and human-regulated systems, but with technologies that can reproduce themselves independently and without human intervention. What Gibson confronts readers with here is a far-fetched example of technological supremacy that attempts to offer a contrasting reading of electronic technologies, which in his novel feature as media not only of freedom but also of control.

Of course, one should not forget that *Neuromancer* is nothing more than a novel made available to readers in a book form and signed with a particular author's name. It promotes in this way a collaborative writing model within which, as already noted, the textual and the technological can co-exist by covering each other's shortcomings and inadequacies. Similarly, the success of the interactive and hypertextual MUD systems we have already examined relies on their ability to bridge electronic technologies with already existing narrative traditions. They offer their participants space for experimentation and improvisation, though the textual practices they adopt are far from mastered. MUDs should be judged in terms of their literariness and their communal and participatory value, since in their realms a number of consciousnesses interact. Cavallaro writes that 'virtuality [is] inviting us to feel directly involved in the making of ourselves and of our environments by means of interactive technologies, and simultaneously retaining hierarchies and forms of discrimination', since the power with which electronic technologies are endowed is only superficial and deceptive (Cavallaro, 2000, p. 40).

Nevertheless, what do all these tell us about the linguistic potential of both media? What kinds of potentials do interactive communities, hypertext and print media offer to their users? As far as the online sustainable communities are concerned, Turkle writes: 'There are parallel narratives in the different rooms of the MUD; one can move forward or backward in time . . . Authorship is not only displaced from a solitary voice, it is exploded' (Turkle, 1996, pp. 355–6). The multiplicity of narrative lines that hypertext and MUDs generate rely on the multiple narrative input provided by its users, which may lead to the invention of further story lines or to the evolution of multiple other versions of selfhood. What is important, though, is that none of these systems can exist in total autonomy, since an electronic system that can sustain such a variable and complex input of information has not yet been constructed.

Gibson's computer-saturated worlds attempt to dramatize, in literary terms, the construction of a narrative that can easily divide into different spatial and temporal dimensions. This is because of the manipulation of variable points of view as well as because of the fusion of the borders between textual and image-generated narrative within the context of a book-bound experience. Tabbi claims that these kinds of narrative 'become not an escape from the world, but a way into it, and not a denial of realism in literature and philosophy, but its re-conceptualization' (Tabbi, 2002, p. xxvi). With *Neuromancer* having been published at the very beginning of the digital revolution, it is important that the relationship of the novelistic author to a global WWW community is assessed next. The following section will focus on the cross-pollination of digital and textual practices and their impact on book authorship.

The author and the global WWW community

With the publication of *Pattern Recognition* (2003), Gibson is confronting us with a novelistic authorship model that is very much part of a twenty-first-century global mentality. This is shaped by the multiple sources of information and images that flow from one email inbox to the next, and one database to another through a worldwide system of communication. This has the ability to preserve and transfer documents electronically, as well as visual or sound files with great ease and efficiency anywhere that internet access is provided. Within a World-Wide Web-mediated world, the author of printed literature faces a great challenge. According to Tabbi, his 'function is not to discover the real within a culture of simulations, but to model communicative pathways in a medial ecology' (Tabbi, 2002, p. 80). This becomes evident from the very first pages of Gibson's new novel, when the main female character, Cayce Pollard, finds herself surrounded by 'mirror-world' objects and 'simulacra of simulacra of simulacra', as well as of text which takes the form of slogans, emails, attachments, advertising logos and footage. This is a world whose technological infatuation is no longer imagined but part of life itself (Gibson, 2003, p. 17).

These interactive and cyberspatial domains offer their users the opportunity to explore different spatialities and manifestations of being. Yet, they portray a world that is totally fantastical and arbitrary. However, this is not always the case with contemporary novel writing which is defined by its engagement with external reality and the changes it undergoes. Gibson's *Neuromancer* could be nowadays regarded as probably an exaggerated paradigm of the cyberspace continuum. However when it was first published, his novel aimed to communicate to its reader its skepticism about the emergent, at the time, electronic technologies.

In *Pattern Recognition*, Gibson acquaints us with a different set of events triggered just after 9/11. The collapse of the Twin Towers in New York, a focal point of trading and commerce in the city, lies in the background of the story being narrated. This event metaphorically marks the end of cultural and economic fixity and stability in a world whose geographical boundaries and capital relations are constantly being challenged. As a result, the novel's plot, setting and characters reflect the dynamics of an emerging global community whose members are brought together through the various mass and media culture practices that affect the way they react and respond to a variety of situations. 'It's as though the creative process is no longer contained within an individual skull', Gibson writes in *Pattern Recognition* (Gibson, 2003, p. 68). In this sense, one can talk about the development of a twenty-first-century consciousness mapped by an abundance of trademarks – Weetabix, Fruit of the Loom, 501, Silk Cut, Neal's Yard – which only exist as mirror labels of the real objects, and a number of web-accessed search engines and email databases – Hotmail, Google, eBay. The writer's aim is not to portray a consumerist postmodern society in the fashion of 1980s fiction, but rather a global community that is ready to tell us more about itself. The email messages become the repositories of variable points of view, financial agreements, cultural experiences and emotions, all shared among the users on the World Wide Web.[2]

Cayce, throughout *Pattern Recognition*, is often viewed sitting in front of her laptop in order to check, read and reply to her emails: 'She needs to check her e-mail . . . plugs her iBook into the room's dataport. One e-mail. As it pops up in her in-box she sees that it's from Parkaboy' (Gibson, 2003, p. 168). Each email provides clues to the mystery of the footage, which Cayce is called to solve. It includes information of sentimental value, especially when the sender is her mother, which she either chooses to read on the spot or keep in her inbox. In this way, Gibson is making us all participate in this process of email sharing or of 'transferring information', as Cayce notes (Gibson, 2003, p. 63). All the emails the readers find dispersed through the narrative may not be of primary importance when they are read initially, since they do not appear in a sequential order, but they do succeed in getting the readers more and more involved in the story narrated. Working as a marketing consultant and trademark assessor, Cayce describes her job as follows: 'The client and I engage in a dialogue. A path emerges. It isn't about the imposition of creative will . . . It's about contingency. I help the client go where things are already going' (Gibson, 2003, p. 62). Could that probably be Gibson himself voicing his authorial intentions?

The novel-writing process, as presented in *Pattern Recognition*, is not looking to construct an alternative narrative model. Gibson is simply coming to terms with the reality that the new means of communication have created, a reality that is the outcome of a global consciousness. The narrative pattern the present book adopts is not the work of a sole creator as denoted by the material existence of the novel itself. Each character, and subsequently each reader, is the recipient of fragments of information, images and attachments that are constantly exchanged. This is dramatized by the footage trope that the novel employs. Being a computer art project, the footage consists of 'one hundred and thirty-four previously discovered fragments, having been endlessly collated, broken down, reassembled, by whole armies of the most fanatical investigators, have yielded no period and no particular narrative direction' (Gibson, 2003, p. 24).

The creator of the footage is not revealed to the readers until the final chapters of the book. Even then her work is not complete. The footage is nothing more than an electronically-sustained project in progress which she is inviting us to watch as it unfolds wordlessly on the screen. In this way, we all become part of it in the same way that we become part of Cayce's email messages. The type of authorial identity this novel promotes is not fixed, but is something fluid and dynamic that resists labelling. Gibson's writing style echoes Bakhtin's polyphonic and dialogic novel that has already been discussed in relation to the hypertext and MUDs. In *Pattern Recognition*, Gibson makes an argument for the impact of technological change on the changing character of literary, and more specifically, novelistic authorship. At a time when the future of the book is still to be considered and the World Wide Web has become an intimate space of communicating, storing and distributing information, Gibson's novel serves as a locus for evaluating the value of the printed vs. electronic matter. In this case, Gibson's novel and his fictional character Nora's online footage provide a terrain within which both the textual and the electronic can be juxtaposed and assessed.

Tabbi announces a 'shift from interpretation to observation, from a concern with an author's subjectivity to what is public and intersubjective' (Tabbi, 2002, p. xv). In other words, both the reader and the author are participants in the same process: observers as well as transcribers of the information posted on the web. Similarly to Laporta's digital art, the images that Nora, the footage creator, designs create both a visual and a textual sensation. In *Pattern Recognition*, Gibson does not simply write about Nora's art but he actually transcribes in narrative terms the visual information that her images contain. As Cayce states, 'arguing over whether or not the footage is intended to convey any particular sense of period, or whether the apparently careful lack of period markers might suggest some attitude, on the maker's part, to time and history' is not that important (Gibson, 2003, p. 57).

What matters here is the neutral and non-sequential make up of the footage that seems to be echoing the sudden and inexplicable (for the characters in the novel) collapse of the Twin Towers. This coincidence may not be accidental since it raises questions about temporality and spatiality:

> 'For us, of course, things can change so abruptly, so violently, so profoundly, that futures like our grandparents' have insufficient "now" to stand on. We have no future because our presence is too volatile.' . . . 'We have only risk management. The spinning of the given moment's scenarios. Pattern recognition.' (Gibson, 2003, p. 57)

The footage speaks of the emergence of a new value system in which nothing lasts and nothing holds. Its abstraction turns our attention from the process of its making to the uproar that its internet distribution creates:

> Parkaboy is de facto spokesperson for the Progressives, those who assume that the footage consists of fragments of a work in progress, something unfinished and still being generated by its maker. The Completists, on the other hand, a relative but articulate minority, are convinced that the footage is comprised of snippets from a finished work, one whose maker chooses to expose it piecemeal and in nonsequential order. (Gibson, 2003, pp. 46–7)

As a result, the creator of the footage, who probably functions as a mirror image of Gibson himself, plays a less authoritative role in the novel. The images that she creates are personalized from the moment somebody accesses them on the web and attempts to interpret them. As described in the excerpt above, the words 'Progressives' and 'Completists' could function as identity labels. They distinguish the members of these groups from the rest of the online footage fans as more convincing interpreters of the footage. Both Gibson and his fictional character, the digital artist Nora, denounce the power that authorship – whether novelistic or electronic – involves. The dispersal of power questions the idea of authorial identity as a concentrated source of power from which meaning originates. The potential that electronic authorship offers for the literary writer is dramatized in the novel through the depiction of a network of communication operating in the most geographically distant localities among diverse groups of people. For example, Cayce is often presented communicating electronically with characters that are in Japan and Russia. Through the World Wide Web all territories are equalized and each character chooses his/her own path of action independently of the place s/he comes from. In such a global terrain of action, the artist, Nora, and subsequently the writer, Gibson, are only detecting the likes and dislikes of the public by bringing together images and printed matter that could appeal to them all independently of gender, cultural, social and racial strictures.

Nora is often mentioned as the maker of the footage, which in the novel becomes an extension of her own existence, giving away no clues about her identity and gender. Gibson is almost invisible, since his role has been reduced to that of the note-taker or recorder of the events taking place or the information exchanged in the course of the narrative. What they are both trying to do is to direct our gaze at those facts that escape our immediate attention by concentrating on the process of their making and circulating across the World Wide Web. In this way, the digital art that Nora creates and the novel Gibson writes take on global dimensions without being restricted to the confines that Nora's studio or the novel's printed pages dictate. They are both made in order to be consumed by art lovers and avid readers of fiction worldwide. Their production is not seeking an instant capital gain but rather the expansion of their trade, which has been manufactured in order to be shared visually with other users online.

In this instance, a different type of consumerism is introduced. 'Any creation that attracts the attention of the world, on an ongoing basis, becomes valuable, if only in terms of potential', Nora's sister, Stella, claims (Gibson, 2003, p. 307). In the case of Nora's art, there is pleasure evoked when attempting to decode the message that each image carries. Similarly, when the readers of the novel are reading Cayce's messages, they are equally intrigued by the way the messages develop and the amount of information hidden in their attachments. This reveals their fascination with the technicalities of the writing process rather than with the actual message that it attempts to convey. It is exactly this kind of attitude that Nora's fans have towards her artwork, since their obsession with it is much more process than message related. Therefore, the notion of authorship is re-conceptualized here as a silent mode of creation or recording of inform-ation, since emphasis shifts from the subjectivity of the creator to the objective projection of the creation itself. What seems to matter now is the circulation of images that emerge from the artist's unconsciousness, or the depiction of the mind processes or speech patterns a character employs, as shown in the emails contained in the book. Everyone inside and outside the book becomes the recipient of various fragments of textual and visual data. Yet all come together again in their attempts to detect the pattern that regulates, governs or generates all the pieces of information that flow unobtrusively through the World Wide Web. This is exactly what the novel's title, *Pattern Recognition*, insinuates: the operation and design of systems that recognize patterns in data.

Consequently, the new trend that Gibson is attempting to record here is related to the enigmatic nature of the footage that succeeds in bringing in instantaneous contact users from culturally and socially distinct areas around the globe, such as Russia, London and Japan. The footage becomes for all of them their common code of communication that supersedes language and geographical barriers. It becomes a global object equally accessible and appealing to all interested parties, and which stays open to any kind of interpretation. Subsequently, Gibson is promoting a type of novel whose authorial identity has exploded and dispersed to a variety of centres scattered around a vast communication system. The present novel, then, is not simply narrating a story. In fact, it keeps note of all the information and messages that have been exchanged among the characters online, thus creating a mosaic that the readers are invited to consume.

Conclusion

The various narrative patterns with which the reader of this chapter has been confronted reveal how flexible and adaptable the book is, even at a time when electronic media dominate. The roles that the reader and author are called to play nowadays seem to be interchangeable. Both participate in the processes of reading and writing, although there is always someone who provides the information and someone else who is asked to decode it. Consequently, the cyberspatial practices operating today have become part of both the authorial and reading consciousness who mutually regulate and transfer knowledge to a number of users, all communicating with one another via the World Wide Web.

The text, whether appearing in a hypertextual environment (MUD), email or fiction, is always written down, printed or typed, which enhances its value as a material artefact. This proves that the author, artist or software designer do not act out of their own accord. What they produce does not simply correspond to their own personal taste, but to the demands of their time. The use of both the electronic and print media leads to the construction of much more rewarding narrative patterns combining the corporeality of the printed text with the vitality of the electronic one. In this way, conventional narrative is prompted to 'move beyond itself' and to learn from other media. This does not mean that the beauty of the bounded volume has to be anni-hilated. The chance that the book offers readers to 'dwell for some time on passages of narrative, re-reading . . . or simply musing on them' can now be reinvested with numerous possibilities (Cobley, 2001, p. 227). This process brings to the attention of the readers pieces of information that may have gone unnoticed, making them aware of the process of collating and piecing them together.

In the case of *Neuromancer* and *Pattern Recognition*, Gibson attempts to access and describe the electronic media from within by exposing its inner workings and making his readers conscious of the writing practices and narrative mechanisms the World Wide Web employs. In this kind of narrative style, the reader, through observation, becomes aware of the manu-script's own production, featuring as an ongoing process because of the different viewpoints, references and fragmented pieces of text the book itself contains. As a consequence, the author and the reader are not alienated from one another; rather they are participants in a process of textual recovery and preservation in their attempt to construct a repertoire of information that is not reserved for them alone. This justifies the fact that the narrative experience they are now invited to share redefines their roles as readers and authors. In the era of digital technologies, authenticity is an illusion since both can savour the pleasure and experience the animating energy that derives from the writing and interpretative process.

This justifies the fact that narrative patterns and authorial identity need to comply with the needs of an expansive world that is no longer characterized by singularity of vision but by plurality and dialogism. Due to the changing nature of the book within an era dominated by electronic technologies, narratives can now move between different levels of consciousness allowing both the author and the reader to participate in the decision-making process. Cobley believes that the book still has a lot to offer, always functioning in tandem with 'the specificities of the technologies in which it is embedded' each time. Although it is considered by some to be of a 'limiting action, it [still] harbours astounding complexity and . . . unlimited potential' (Cobley, 2001, p. 228).

9
Towards a Politics of the Small Things: Arundhati Roy and the Decentralization of Authorship

Maria-Sabina Alexandru

The God of Small Things, for which Arhundati Roy won the Booker Prize, was published in 1997, the year India celebrated fifty years of independence from Britain. Her novel was highly praised in the 23 & 30 June 1997 issue of *The New Yorker*, which recognized Indian fiction in English – both in the west and by its main representatives – as a field of study in its own right. Because of the promotional rhetoric of this issue, Roy found herself, rather unwillingly, occupying a central position in this recently established canon of Indian literature written in English as the first and only Booker prize-winning Indian woman author. Taking into consideration the need that Roy sees for decentralization in her writing, this chapter aims to explore her subversive role within such male-oriented tradition. It considers the possibilities that her perception of herself as a decentralized author offers for the study of postcolonial, and more specifically female, authorship.

The *New Yorker* issue helps contextualize the debate around Roy's female authorship in relation to the Booker prize. It sets the framework within which I will move on to examine her redefinition of the author-function for postcolonial writing. Importantly, this issue included an article by Salman Rushdie entitled 'Damme, This is the Oriental Scene for You' (1997), later reprinted in his 2002 volume of essays *Step Across This Line* (Rushdie, 2002, pp. 50–61). In this article, which provides an overview of contemporary writing, Rushdie places Arundhati Roy within the history of Indian fiction in English. Taking her to be a very strong, talented author with an original voice of her own rather than being his mere follower, Rushdie greets Roy's arrival into the world of letters with the assertion that *The God of Small Things* is 'full of ambition and sparkle...written in a highly wrought and utterly personal style' (Rushdie, 1997, p. 61).

In conjunction with John Updike's essay 'Mother Tongues' (Updike, 1997, pp. 156–61) from the same *New Yorker* issue, Rushdie's article presents *The God of Small Things* as one of the most important achievements which deserves a central position in the canon of Indian fiction written in English. His appraisal plays an important role in the treatment of Roy as a canonical author because of his authoritative status, which the *New Yorker* was keen to emphasize. Ever since, *The God of Small Things* has tended to be read as a fictional enactment of Roy's political beliefs regarding caste and gender. It has also been perceived as being representative of the stage that postcolonial authorship has reached.[1] This tendency was reinforced when later that same year the novel was awarded the Booker prize. A brief overview of Roy's critical stereotyping as a political author will help understand the role that the anniversary issue of the *New Yorker* and the Booker's own status as a politicized event, played in the canonization of her authorship and her attempt to redefine her author-function.

Graham Huggan describes the central position that Roy occupies within the history of the Booker as 'an instance of a neo-colonial "othering" process' (Huggan, 2001, p. 115). While Rushdie does not take into consideration Roy's gender, Huggan notes that her 'marketably exotic looks' and 'good interview value' are examples of a kind of postcolonial authorship that relies for its success on a double message: its political marginality in need of voicing, and its huge 'exotic appeal' (Huggan, 2001, p. 77). As suggested by the pictures on the covers of all the editions of her novel, Roy's personal charm easily meets a rather stereotypical view of Indian female beauty. According to Huggan, Roy's public fame is due to her postcolonial 'exotic' otherness more than to a fair acknowledgement of her value as a Booker-prize winner. This chapter aims to examine how Roy's claim for decentralization is keyed into her attempt to resist inclusion within ideologically determined categories. As the first Indian woman to have won the Booker, Arundhati Roy's work invites a reading of her understanding of caste and gender as forms of marginality in *The God of Small Things* within a wider feminist context.[2]

Despite her own refusal of feminism as a political agenda, Roy is widely considered to be the exponent of an effective feminist message. Madeleine Bunting, for example, labels Roy a 'grassroots gamine', who marks a point in the development of the feminist movement:

> What makes Roy so thrilling a political icon is that she represents the coming of age of feminism. It was the radical feminists of the 1960s who coined the phrase the personal is political, and now Roy, a celebrity in the global media, is bringing that insight to bear on the politics of globalization. (Bunting, 2002)

Bunting's perception places Roy in a doubly powerful position within the postcolonial arena, and particularly within Indian fiction in English, dominated as it is by strong patriarchal figures such as Rushdie. However, in most of her interviews, in essays and in public readings, Roy refuses association with fashionable Indian writers such as Rushdie or Vikram Seth, who are considered to be the authors of the 'great Indian novel'.[3] This chapter argues that Roy's authorship needs to be read in relation to her refusal to be positioned within any large political agenda, whether postcolonial or gender-related. To this end her writing aims to transcend givens, moving towards a more fluid, local difference-sensitive construction of meaning.

Roy does not agree to the association of her writing with controlling discourses that reassess India's role in today's postcolonial world in terms of an all too often discussed centre/margin set dichotomies. Even though her writing engages with wider social, political and religious issues, Roy makes it very clear that her subject matter is not 'big mother India' but the 'small things' in people's lives (as the title of her novel points out). Focusing on *The God of Small Things*, this chapter argues that Roy's shift from big to small topics allows her to develop a critical stance against set ideologies, any extreme 'isms'. Her pledge for attention to detail, which is often missed in the highly-politicized postcolonial space, is precisely what gives strength to her voice as a postcolonial woman author.

Importantly, Roy's implicit claim that the personal is political is connected to her distinct use of English, which is arguably the dominant language in contemporary Indian fiction. The use of language and national ideology are two aspects of Roy's authorship which can hardly be discussed separately. The use of English by Indian authors is in itself a strong political issue, especially in an age of electronic technologies where English has become the language of internet communication. Discussing Roy's position within the tradition of Indian writing in English, I intend to draw attention next to the extent to which her use of language is part of her attempt to break away from the centre/margin dichotomy in terms of which her authorship has been defined.

Writing in English

Roy is famous in the field of contemporary fiction in English as a one-novel writer. Her non-fictional writings touch on pressing contemporary issues concerning India. I find it important to read the fiction with the non-fiction in terms of their shared thematic concerns. Roy's *The Cost of Living* (1999) includes the essays 'The Greater Common Good' and 'The End of Imagination'. The former debates the controversial issue of dams in India, which displace many people in the name of questionable progress. The latter builds up an argument against India becoming a nuclear state, an opportunity Roy uses to attack 'Indian identity' as an umbrella term working to the detriment of individual rights. This small volume provides new insights into *The God of Small Things*. 'The Cost of Living' is also the title of the last chapter in *The God of Small Things*.

As I shall argue, this last chapter proposes a different plot from the main one of the novel. It does so through shifting the emphasis from the conventional chronological ending of the events to the apotheotic triumph of love over social prejudice. This double structural arrangement expresses Roy's message as a social critic. In the actual development of events, Ammu and Velutha are punished severely for having trespassed the rigidly established Love Laws of the community. However, the logic of Roy's argument ends the book non-chronologically with the love scene itself. This scene is celebrated as it is projected into the future. Thus the cause-and-effect pattern of punishment is turned into a triumphant act of defiance of the social order, which, in its application of this very punishment, is denounced as being severely wrong.

Roy's attempt to transcend the reductive categories in which this social order operates is inscribed primarily in her use of language. Born in Kerala, she writes in English rather than Malayalam. She explains her adherence to the long line of Indian writers writing in English (still a pressing issue in postcolonial writing as a whole) as a matter-of-fact situation rather than as a political decision:

> There are more people in India that speak English than there are in England. And the only common language that we have throughout India is English. And it's odd that English is a language that, for somebody like me, is a choice that is made for me before I'm old enough to choose. It is the only language that you can speak if you want to get a good job or you want to go to a university. All the big newspapers are in English. And then every one of us will speak at least two or three – I speak three – languages. And when we communicate – let's say I'm with a group of friends – our conversation is completely anarchic because it's in any language that you choose. (Simmons, 2002b)

Even though she rebukes the anxiety of influences, Roy implicitly continues Rushdie's project of 'conquering English' by writing in an English language sprinkled with words from Malayalam or with the development of her own language (portmanteau words, babytalk, poetic language) (Rushdie, 1991, p. 17). Focusing on the individual rather than the collective, Roy exploits the ambiguity inherent in language. In doing this, she joins a whole generation of contemporary Indian authors who reassert the status of English as the major Indian literary language rather than the language of the colonizer. This is part of a project of creating what was to become a whole new literature in English, whose growing openness to a worldwide audience is described by Meenakshi Mukherjee in the seventies in the following terms: 'Indian writing in English is the only form of modern Indian literature that is accessible to critical examination all over the country and even abroad' (Mukherjee, 1971, p. 7).

Mukherjee explains the ambiguity of the title 'twice-born', the phrase used to refer to the superior three Hindu castes, the *brahmin*, the *kshatriya* and the *vaishya*. This is not an attempt to promote contemporary Indian fiction to a superior caste (thus acknowledging an initial state of inferiority). Rather it is a way of signalling that her fiction belongs to two different parent traditions: Indian and British. The use of English as a language meant for creative purposes may have dated back a century at the time Mukherjee was writing. Rushdie locates its beginning in 1864, along with Bankim Chandra Chatterjee's novel *Rajmohan's Wife* – 'a poor melodramatic thing', as he calls it (Rushdie, 1997, p. 57). As Mukherjee notes, 'not until the third or fourth decade of this century was there a serious attempt to place such writing in its proper historical and cultural context and to evaluate its literature' (Mukherjee, 1971, p. 9). The common consensus is that Indian fiction in English was brought into the limelight by the extraordinary outburst of value represented by 'The Big Three' pioneer figures who emerged in the 1930s: Mulk Raj Anand, R. K. Narayan and Raja Rao (Thieme, 2003, p. 29). Rushdie singles them out within world literature at the time. He places Anand under the influence of 'both Joyce and Marx', and sees Rao as the starting point of that urge of making 'an Indian English for himself' (Rushdie, 1997, p. 57).

This issue has confronted every Indian author writing in English, including Rushdie himself. Rushdie bows to Narayan as 'a figure of world stature'. At the same time, he acknowledges the particular influence that G. V. Desani's puzzling *Tristram-Shandy*-esque novel had on him – the tricks he learnt in terms of forging a new English language recording the phrasing and rhythm 'of the bazaars' (Rushdie, 1997, p. 58). Rushdie then mentions a number of mid twentieth-century names (including Ved Mehta, Ruth Prawer Jhabvala, Anita Desai and V. S. Naipaul). He points out a rich plethora of styles, with the intention of celebrating the diversity of Indian writing in English and thus welcoming his younger contemporaries. He sees them as continuing his own endeavour to strengthen the tradition of Indian fiction in English. Therefore, he places them – and, implicitly, the very idea of contemporary Indian authorship – in the area of 'India's encounter with the English language', which, 'far from proving abortive, continues to give birth to new children, endowed with lavish gifts' (Rushdie, 1997, p. 61).

The 1997 issue of *The New Yorker*, discussed above, in its intention to celebrate contemporary Indian fiction in English, features a picture of the tradition's most important, world-famous writers: Vikram Chandra; Rohinton Mistry; Arundhati Roy; Anita Desai; Amit Chaudhuri; Kiran Desai; Ardashir Vakil; Vikram Seth; Amitav Ghosh; and the Sri Lankan author Romesh Gunesekera. They are all grouped around Rushdie (thus proclaimed, once again, the father-figure of the group). In his introductory article to the issue, entitled 'Declarations of Independence' and bearing the significant subtitle 'Why are there suddenly so many Indian novelists?', Bill Buford makes a point of noticing that most of these authors were meeting on the occasion of this group picture for the first time. The reason – they all came for the shot from very different parts of the world (other than India) – is suggestive of the status of contemporary writing in English (Buford, 1997, pp. 6–8). Though originating from India, this rich wave of fiction was proclaimed as being produced and read all around the world. Its stylistic and thematic richness had long attracted the attention of English-reading audiences (and many others, thanks to translations into other languages). From the group, Arundhati Roy, whose *The God of Small Things* had made a great impact on the literary world, is particularly singled out.[4] There is also a full-page portrait of Roy, which could not fail to remind one of the exposure of female authorship to judgement on looks rather than the book itself.

In his article for *The New Yorker* (Rushdie, 1997, pp. 50–61), Rushdie recognizes the central position he occupies within the canon of contemporary Indian writers. He frames his brief analysis of the current status of Indian letters in the light of an inevitable bond with the English language – what he calls an 'unexpected and profoundly ironic conclusion':

> This is it: The prose writing – both fiction and non-fiction – created in this period by Indian writers working in English is proving to be a stronger and more important body of work than most of what has been produced in the eighteen 'recognised' languages of India, the so-called 'vernacular languages', during the same time; and, indeed, this new, and still burgeoning 'Indo-Anglian' literature represents perhaps the most valuable contribution India has yet made to the world of books. The true Indian literature of the first postcolonial half-century has been made in the language the British left behind. (Rushdie, 1997, p. 50)

In this ironic conclusion, Rushdie seems to see a necessary precondition of the existence and visibility of all contemporary Indian authorship, including (or as inaugurated by) his own writing. Having established that, he acknowledges the 'musical' presence of all the other Indian languages in the consciousness of Indian authors writing in English (Rushdie, 1997, p. 57). But he can only deplore the limited extent to which vernacular language writers are known; he believes this can only be solved through English translations of their works. Rushdie was, in fact, making a very similar argument about the importance of writing in English (the former language of the British empire, now probably the main literary language in India) as early as *Imaginary Homelands: Essays and Criticism 1981–1991* (1991). Here, he coined the concept of 'the Empire writing back to the centre' which has, ever since, become emblematic of postcolonial writing in English as a whole (Rushdie, 1991, pp. 9–21).

In his editorial to the same issue of *The New Yorker*, Bill Buford signals two of the notable features of contemporary Indian fiction in English. One of them is its English expression (in which he sees a connection to the beginnings of American literature). The other is its internationalism, its amazing geographical and thematic spread around the world. Buford points out the important role played by Rushdie in all this. The year 1981 is considered to be the turning point of Indian letters, when *Midnight's Children* (1981) 'made everything possible', as it 'showed Indian writers that great novels could be fashioned from Indian stories, with an Indian sensibility and a distinctly Indian use of the English language' (Buford, 1997, p. 8). In stating this, Buford recognizes Rushdie's crucial position in the emerging examples of Indian writing in English. He expresses his belief in the legitimacy of such writing and compares it with the rise of American literature back in its own immediate post-independence times (Buford, 1997, p. 8). Thus Buford supports Rushdie's position, seeing writing in English as a welcome catalyst of success for highly qualitative fiction. Buford represents the friendly American critical view, wishing to associate, or at least, to compare, all successful enterprises with the American way. On the contrary, other authorities on Indian letters, such as Amit Chaudhuri, resent this celebration of the English language having become the preferred language of Indian literature. Without denying the value of this literature, Chaudhuri criticizes the commercial drive he sees behind it. Instead, as the editor of *The Picador Book of Modern Indian Literature* (2001), Chaudhuri tries to bring to the attention of an international audience (in English translation) some names of Indian authors within languages other than English.

A similar view on Indian fiction in English is expressed by Graham Huggan, who sees in the phenomenon of the Golden Jubilee *New Yorker* issue one of those highly commercial 'mediated events'. Such events are, Huggan maintains, 'characteristic of the current appeal of India, and more specifically of Indian literature in English, as a literalised *consumer item*' (Huggan, 2001, p. 59). Huggan also criticizes Buford's rather patronizing attitude in assessing the situation: 'Buford, albeit facetiously, echoes the common view that Indian literature as a composite entity is largely a fiction of the Western press, a metropolitan media creation' (Huggan, 2001, pp. 59–60). Even though he notices that *The New Yorker* takes possession of all this Indian writing by tailoring it 'to the magazine's identifiable house style', Huggan does not have a problem with the English language as such (Huggan, 2001, p. 60). On the contrary, Amit Chaudhuri – himself an Indian novelist – problematizes the use of English in a more radical way.

In the introduction to the Sunetra Gupta entry in the anthology, Chaudhuri describes the young Indian woman author as 'one of the few genuinely talented writers to have emerged from that aggressively marketed group of practitioners called "Indian writers in English"' (Chaudhuri, 2002, p. 582). Moreover, in the final paragraph of the 'Modernity and the Vernacular' section of his introduction to the anthology, he challenges the comparison between the beginnings of postcolonial Indian literature in English and American literature. He also disproves the common tendency of current criticism to situate contemporary Indian literature reductively under the wide umbrella of postcolonial literatures and forget about its specificities. The English language is an important factor to take into account:

> The position of English, in India, is both inescapable and ambiguous, an ambiguity that is perhaps insufficiently mapped in its fiction and criticism. It is a unique ambiguity; for it is misleading to compare the way English is used in India, by a small but substantial group, not all of its members by any means well-to-do or privileged, with the space that the language occupies in, for instance, Africa or America. Moreover, to say that English is now an Indian language – while that may be true – requires all kinds of qualifications and a careful re-examination of that claim; for English is not an Indian language in the way it is an American language; nor is it an Indian language in the way that Bengali or Urdu, for instance, is one. The position and meaning of English in India is still on the verge of becoming clear; it is still part of a process that is far from being complete. But to understand, fully, the story of the English language and its most profound impact and extraordinary outcome in India in the past 150 years, one has to turn, paradoxically, from English and the issue of colonialism to the vernacular languages and indigenous history. (Chaudhuri, 2002, p. xxii)

The comparison with Bengali and Urdu is interesting to read against Rushdie's article in *The New Yorker*, as it is the example of Urdu (his mother tongue) that Rushdie uses to support precisely the opposite argument:

> But my own mother tongue, Urdu, which was the camp argot of the country's earlier Muslim conquerors, was also an immigrant language, forged from a combination of the conquerors' imported Farsi and the local languages they encountered. However, it became a naturalised subcontinental language long ago; and by now that has happened to English, too. English has become an Indian language. (Rushdie, 1997, p. 54)

In comparing the two examples of foreign languages grafted on to the Indian stock and bringing with them cultural diversity, Rushdie clearly means to celebrate the internationalism of contemporary Indian writing in English. This internationalism has certainly been possible because English is widely accessible to reading audiences across the world. Also, Rushdie defends the novel from his own position as a novelist, for whom the most important thing is that his writings are accessible to wide audiences, and thus should find a place in the literary canon.

Looking at the world through the Other's eyes

Taking the tradition that Rushdie has established further, Roy takes possession of the English language and challenges its established patterns in *The God of Small Things*. My aim here is to examine how her rhetoric of 'small things', by means of which she raises the need to look at the world through the Other's eyes, developed from her anti-establishment concerns as an author in post-independence India. Such an approach makes my work different from other critics who discuss and debate connections between Roy and Rushdie in terms of the narrative techniques and strategies that she imitated from him.[5] Just as Rushdie sprinkles his writing with Urdu words, Roy uses Malayalam. More than that, she uses babytalk and coins portmanteau words with a powerfully creative linguistic urge which reminds one, as John Updike noticed, of 'Salman Rushdie's jazzy riffs' (Updike, 1997, p. 156).

In the *The New Yorker* special issue, Updike discusses *The God of Small Things* at length in an article entitled 'Mother Tongues' (Updike, 1997, pp. 156–61). The article analyses Roy's novel within the wider context of contemporary Indian writing in English. Updike shows that the option for English may enlist these Indian authors 'in a foreign if not enemy camp, that of the colonizer' (Updike, 1997, p. 156). However, their use of the language is highly personal and creative. English, far from being just an adopted language whose global nature has to be acknowledged, is turned by Roy (as well as by her peers) against its grain. It is made to express meanings that are not of the colonizer, but of contemporary postcolonial culture:

> phrases and whole sentences of Malayalam, sometimes translated and sometimes not, seep into the book's English, whose mannerisms – compound and coined words, fragmentary sentences, paragraphs a word or a phrase long, whimsical capitalization – underline the eccentricity of the language in relation to the tale's emotional centre. Estha and Rahel, male and female dizygotic twins who serve as the central characters, remember how their great-aunt Navomi Ipe, incongruously called Baby Kochamma, inflicted English upon them, making them write 'I will always speak English' a hundred times and practice their pronunciation by singing, 'Rej-Oice in the Lo-Ord Or-Orlways/And again I say rej-oice.' The twins' sensibilities, uncannily conjoined, are expressed in a confidently unorthodox prose that owes something to Salman Rushdie's jazzy riffs:

> 'Their lives have a size and a shape now. Estha has his and Rahel hers. Edges, Borders, Boundaries, Brinks and Limits have appeared like a team of trolls on their separate horizons. Short creatures with long shadows, patrolling the Blurry End. Gentle half-moons have gathered under their eyes and they are as old as Ammu [their mother] was when she died.

> Thirty-one.
> Not old.
> Not young.
> But a viable die-able age.' (Updike, 1997, p. 156)

Updike's aim here is to draw the readers' attention to one of Roy's most striking point-of-view devices. The world is seen through Estha's and Rahel's eyes as they grow up, with an emphasis on the changes triggered by the growing-up process. Concepts are made concrete by the animistic logic of childhood. Thus Roy reworks the classical convention of the fool who, under the assumption of madness, is the only character allowed to speak the truth (as happens in Shakespeare's plays). Here, it is the children who speak the truth and who, even though punished once in a while, get away with it in the end, under the assumption of their childishness. But it is in the undermining of the main story with their comments that Roy makes her actual points. To a great extent, this undermining comes from her use of language. The emphasis on small things, central to the novel, points to a sensitivity to detail that is meant to have primacy over the large and all-encompassing categories of various traditions.

The concept of small things is borrowed from Jawaharlal Nehru's self-contradictory nationalist rhetoric. In her essay 'The Greater Common Good' from *The Cost of Living*, in which she criticizes dam-building as a large-scale project that damages the lives of thousands of people in India, Roy quotes Nehru's main political line on the matter:

> In the fifty years since Independence, after Nehru's famous 'Dams are the Temples of Modern India' speech (one that he grew to regret in his own lifetime), his footsoldiers threw themselves into the business of building dams with unnatural fervour. Dam-building grew to be equated with Nation-building. (Roy, 1999, p. 15)

In Note 4 to 'The Greater Common Good', Roy mentions Nehru's later rephrasing of his own ideology:

> In a speech given before the 29th Annual Meeting of the Central Board of Irrigation and Power (17 November 1958) Nehru said, 'For some time past, however, I have been beginning to think that we are suffering from what we may call "the disease of gigantism". We want to show that we can build big dams and do big things. This is a dangerous outlook developing in India [...] the idea of big – having big undertakings and doing big things for the sake of showing that we can do big things – is not a good outlook at all.' And [...] It is...the small irrigation projects, the small industries and the small plants for electric power, which will change the face of the country far more than half a dozen projects in half a dozen places'. (Roy, 1999, p. 104)

Roy uses Nehru's correction to turn the rhetoric of Indian nationalism on its head and to denounce this 'disease of gigantism' as a highly flawed concept, based on a false assumption of Indian unity. While India only defined itself as a nation state in contrast to the British occupation, the post-independence totalizing discourses of the nation have tended to sacrifice the interests of the common people to the allegedly greater cause of 'Mother India'. In her essays, Roy is hugely critical of this attitude displayed by the state authorities. Far from acknowledging it as a necessity imposed by the requirements of modernization, she reads in this sacrifice of individuals for the 'greater common good' a reflection of the institutionalized prejudice represented by the caste and subcaste system:

> A huge percentage of the displaced are Adivasis (57.6 per cent in the case of the Sardar Sarovar dam). Include Dalits and the figure becomes obscene. According to the Commissioner for Scheduled Castes and Tribes[6] it's about 60 per cent. If you consider that Adivasis account for only 8 per cent and Dalits another 15 per cent of India's population, it opens up a whole other dimension to the story. The ethnic 'otherness' of their victims takes some of the pressure off the Nation Builders. It's like having an expense account. Someone else pays the bills. People from another country. Another world. India's poorest people are subsidising the lifestyles of her richest. (Roy, 1999, p. 21)

The metaphor of small things thus becomes for Roy a way of addressing marginalization. If caste is one important issue which falls under this category in India, then gender is another. When asked whether she has a feminist agenda, Roy is usually faithful to her general rejection of big categories. However, while getting around direct questions about her treatment of female characters in *The God of Small Things*, Roy says that her reason for not wanting to talk about it is that the book is finished and out there: 'My book is my case, I have no further pleas to make' (Abraham, 1998, p. 92). It will therefore be up to the book to make her point. As I shall show, the book seems to make it. Through Ammu's stifled revolt and Baby Kochamma's and Mammachi's resigned oppression, Roy suggests that the structures of Keralan society will grant women no insider position. Therefore, one must assume one's outsider role as a vantage point (in the way Roy herself does) and speak from there. What I will do next is to show how Roy voices her criticism of various forms of exclusion in Indian society through the structural changes in her novel. Together with her rhetoric of 'small things', she manages to turn fiction writing into a polemically subversive act that anticipates the engaged language of her essays.

The small things

The God of Small Things is a novel about Kerala in that it is, as its title shows, a novel about the small things (or the prevalence of detail over big words, categories or systems). Behind the forced stratification and inequality maintained primarily by caste and similar substantive views on being in Indian society for centuries, Arundhati Roy looks at a complex web of exclusions. She brings them to light and analyses them in her treatment of this tropical Romeo and Juliet story. She shows that they are equivalent in their reduction of human beings to the simplified features of their guilt (Chanda, 1997, p. 38). Exclusion, of one kind or another, affects most of the characters in the novel. Ammu – the 'divorced daughter from an intercommunity love marriage' – steps from one guilt into another, and, finally, trespasses caste boundaries in her affair with Velutha (Roy, 1997, p. 45).

Her twins, Estha and Rahel, defined by Baby Kochamma from the very beginning as 'doomed, fatherless waifs', separated after 'the Terror', never find their place anywhere and become 'Quietness and Emptiness' (Roy, 1997, pp. 45, 236). Their incestuous reunion at the end of the novel, twenty-three years later, their sharing of 'hideous grief' in breaking the Love Laws of which they are victims, is (as death is ultimately shown to be in the novel), a form of resistance to barren conformity. But it is also a desperate attempt at coming back to life, of finding wholeness (Roy, 1997, p. 328). A good example is Baby Kochamma who tries to hide her own sense of guilt for not being able to overcome her old passion for Father Mulligan by punishing other people. Being the embodiment of barren conformity, she converts for his sake to Roman Catholicism. As a result she becomes a bitter old lady. Mammachi and Papachi, in turn, are an unhappy couple. Papachi's repeated beatings of Mammachi, which she accepts with submission, are emblematic of the cruelty of traditional patriarchal power relations, where violence remains the only form of communication. Thus both the excluded and their excluders share some form of marginality, being victims of prejudice.

Arundhati Roy has a lot to say about religion and its power to separate rather than unite people as they are engaged in a worldly competition for power. It is not by chance that she places Marxism – the secular, materialist ideology *par excellence* – among religions. Roy seems to want to suggest in her novel that Marxism, through the effects it has on people, often operates as a religion to those who have embraced it:

A lot of the atmosphere of *A God of Small Things* is based on my experiences of what it was like to grow up in Kerala. Most interestingly, it was the only place in the world where religions coincide, there's Christianity, Hinduism, Marxism and Islam and they all live together and rub each other down. When I grew up it was the Marxism that was very strong, it was like the revolution was coming next week. I was aware of the different cultures when I was growing up and I'm still aware of them now. When you see all the competing beliefs against the same background you realise how they all wear each other down. I couldn't think of a better location for a book about human beings. (Simmons, 2002a)

In her novel, Roy questions these totalizing discourses, which she rebukes equally for the damaging effects they have on excluded categories of people. This corruption of the spiritual by political agendas results in a collapse of the primary purpose of both religion and politics. In siding with these excluded categories (namely, with untouchables and women, represented by Velutha and Ammu), Roy, in a sense, challenges the cliché of the allegory of individual biography as national history. In writing about small things, Roy refuses to fall into the cliché of representing the nation as a duty of the postcolonial author. The strength of her criticism lies in the way she analyses the impact these big categories have on the lives of individuals. The novel certainly makes a point of exposing the denial of any rights to women and untouchables in Kerala. However, this particular point is made through the emotional impact that Ammu and Velutha's story has on the reader. It is, again, the microscopic level of individual lives, of small things, that is given more weight than the bigger picture. The bigger picture is, in fact, made up of such small things.

In her novel, Roy discusses caste extensively around the character of Vellya Paapen, Velutha's father. In a world with a Hindu background, where Christianity and communism are supposed to be instruments of freedom, their supposedly freeing effect is lost on Paravans. Roy shows the castelessness of Christianity to bring nothing more than a reformulation of caste separation:

> They were made to have separate churches, with separate services and separate priests. As a special favour they were even given their own separate Pariah Bishop. After Independence they found they were not entitled to any Government benefits like job reservations or bank loans at low interest rates, because officially, on paper, they were Christians, and therefore casteless. It was a little like having to sweep away your footprints without a broom. Or worse, not being *allowed* to leave footprints at all. (Roy, 1997, p. 74)

Exclusion is deeply internalized, which results in excessive feelings of gratitude and obligation for the smallest attention coming from higher castes. It distorts the most natural emotions of human beings. Vellya Paapen considers himself so undeserving of attention and kindness that Mammachi's gesture of buying him a glass eye triggers in him enormous gratitude. His resulting devotion goes so far that he tells Mammachi he has seen Ammu and Velutha making love and thus condemns his son to death. It is for similar convictions, but from a different position, that Comrade Pillai (the local communist leader) does the same, and Baby Kochamma asks Estha to lie in order to protect her own lies.

Caste, the epitome of exclusion, originates in the culturally constructed pure/polluted opposition, and so does gender. This opposition affects not just certain categories of people but, even more widely, women. The Ammu/Velutha couple stands for this double gender – caste exclusion, which Roy shows to operate so strongly in Indian society. But, at the same time, the thwarted Anglophilia exhibited by Chacko (Ammu's brother) demonstrates a deeply misunderstood dependence of the Syrian Christian aristocracy on the approval of the former centre of the colonial empire. This leads to a partly unconscious, but very present self-exclusion of the postcolonial culture from power, which comes as a result of a similarly internalized inferiority complex, projected on a wider scale. It is a denial of the Other within oneself, and thus of whoever does not conform to the established artificial categories, which, in conditions of crisis, govern the self. An illustration of this could be Baby Kochamma's programmatically 'backwards-lived' life, following her killing of hope in any potential or real form of revolt. It is not an accident that Velutha, the excluded Untouchable, also identified in Ammu's dreams with the God of loss, is seen marching in the Marxist demonstration with a red flag in his hand. Excessive revolt runs the risk of becoming a form of loss, since its cause is doomed to failure by the system from the very beginning. It is this proud acceptance of marginalization that underlies Ammu's and Velutha's love. Despite their end in death, their union is victorious. It is, as the end of the novel indicates, not a sign of the loss of the past, but a symbol of the living power of tomorrow. So is the twins' act of love a sublime recovery of the lost blissful oneness they used to share in their mother's womb.

In Roy's Kerala, Christianity and Hinduism come face to face. Paradoxically, the mind/body conflict between them is reformulated in such terms that they become mutually supportive with respect to the categories of both caste and gender. As previously shown, the castelessness of Christianity only deepens the exclusion of the outcastes. Moreover, the union between Ammu (a *brahmin* woman, symbolically corresponding to the mind of the primeval being Purusha) and Velutha (an outcaste, originating from Purusha's feet, therefore the lowest part of the body) is perceived as wrong from both a Hindu and Christian perspective. But in Roy's writing it transcends them both. The sublime consummation of their love is celebrated in the final chapter (consecrated by the projection into a kind of eternal future expressed by the last word, 'tomorrow') which, though subsequent to the two characters' deaths, draws the book to a close.

As well as its privileged position as the last (therefore conclusive) chapter, the love scene is also written somewhat differently from the rest of the novel.

It gives up the ironic tones that underlie Roy's text throughout the novel, especially the fragments told in the children's language, which heavily rely on double-meaning. Roy's choice here is to use adult, even poetic, language. This also gives away her authorial intention: of urging us to take the side she takes, namely in favour of the individual rather than the communal. This is achieved by means of an intricate structure based on her celebrated architectural skills, which she describes as follows:

> The only way I can explain how I wrote it was the way an architect designs a building. You know, it wasn't as if I started at the beginning and ended at the end. I would start somewhere and I'd color in a bit and then I would deeply stretch back and then stretch forward. It was like designing an intricately balanced structure and when it was finished it was finished. There were no drafts. But that doesn't mean I just sat and spouted it out. It took a long time.
>
> When I write, I never re-write a sentence because for me my thought and my writing are one thing. It's like breathing, I don't re-breathe a breath . . . Arranging the bones of the story took time, but it was never painful. (Simmons, 2002b)

As such, Roy's writing displays a disregard for chronological order; circularity as opposed to linearity; poetic, non-rational logic; and the rhythms of the body inscribed in the text. This is particularly obvious in two chapters, which break the reality of the novel and propose an alternative dimension to it, possible only in the order of dreams. These are Chapter 11, 'The God of Small Things' (which, for good reasons, gives its title to the book as well); and Chapter 21, 'The Cost of Living' (the novel's coda). These two chapters are supplemented by a kind of appendix to Chapter 20, 'The Madras Mail', which narrates the story of Estha's 'Return' to his stranger father. This appendix, starting on a new page, also records a bodily experience – that of the twins' belated re-encounter in incestuous lovemaking – which, like all the others, breaks the 'Love Laws. That lay down who should be loved. And how. And how much' (Roy, 1997, p. 328).

Ammu's dream of the God of Small Things, also called the God of Loss, is a dream of lack and sorrow as they affect her own life. It boldly conceives of an alternative version of divinity that would not be accepted by Christianity (but who, in Ammu's world, is the only god of her love). This allegorical figure seems to be modelled on the Hindu idea that each small thing in the world has its own god, even though this god may be no more than one of the many manifestations of a supreme deity. This god is one-armed, therefore marked by a lack. This lack points to a similarity between outcastes and women with respect to the Law. He leaves no footprints on the shore (a clear reference to Velutha). He stands for the only chance, albeit a short-lived one, left for Ammu after she is placed outside the law and, therefore, outside any promise of forgiveness. This dream makes her aware of her body which, never discovered before, now emerges as her only hope, all she has left. This is soon followed by her moment of recognition, in the bathroom mirror. Instead of her own image, 'the spectre of her future appeared in it to mock her. Pickled. Grey. Rhumy-eyed. Cross-stitch roses on a slack, sunken cheek' (Roy, 1997, p. 222). What Ammu sees in the mirror, instead of her beautiful body, is a spectre of 'Age and Death', as well as the hard path ahead of her. In the chronological, logic-driven succession of events that make the story of the novel, this is indeed the faithful representation of her future. In the plot, as the circular structure of Roy's writing will have it, this moment of recognition triggers the fulfilment which in the novel comes last. It is during this careful examination of her body, of its youth and of the madness of wasting it (rather than the madness befalling Syrian Christians for inbreeding), of the 'cold feeling on a hot afternoon that Life had been Lived', that the final scene is made possible (Roy, 1997, p. 222).

The scene of the union between the twins in Chapter 20, 'The Madras Mail', prefigures the ending of the novel, or, rather, its coda. The scene of Ammu's and Velutha's defiance of law and time is projected into an eternal tomorrow through love. The structural and symbolic similarities of the two episodes integrate these two couples (the only accomplished ones in the novel) within a similar matrix of identification between people who are, fundamentally, the same, even though the world will not see them as such. Estha's and Rahel's encounter in the dark re-establishes their union in their mother's womb. This fulfils them in a way that the world denies them. Such fulfilment is expressed through a whole set of abstract concepts capitalized in Roy's ironic discourse against patriarchy and its 'Love Laws', which 'would separate Sex from Love. Or Needs from Feelings' (Roy, 1997, p. 328). The scene is depicted in allusive terms, based on repetition of obsessive babytalk patterns: 'Not old. Not young. But a viable die-able age' (Roy, 1997, p. 327). Lovemaking is alluded to poetically, with an emphasis on the symbolic meanings of the gesture rather than on what actually happened:

> But what was there to say?
> Only that there were tears. Only that Quietness and Emptiness fitted together like stacked spoons. Only that there was a snuffling in the hollows at the base of a lovely throat. Only that a hard honey-coloured shoulder had a semi-circle of teethmarks on it. Only that they held each other close, long after it was over. Only that what they shared that night was not happiness, but hideous grief. Only that once again they broke the Love Laws. That lay down who should be loved. And how. And how much. (Roy, 1997, p. 328)

The power of this passage is triggered by its constant denial of the expectations it creates. The sentence 'But what was there to say?' suggests the impossibility of articulating an experience that is not devoid of richness, but is impossible to account for in language. In depicting it in the following paragraph, Roy eludes conventional discourse. The sentences that follow start with the word 'only', the strength of which lies in the constant denial of its meaning. Far from emphasizing a lack of content, this stresses the overwhelming abundance of content in the scene depicted. In doing this, Roy attempts to describe a bodily experience – which can only make sense within a bodily logic, since it is ruled out by the Law. She writes the body, by using a language that breaks grammatical rules; thus also suggesting a break in the order of the Law. In this light, Roy's writing as a political gesture comes close functionally – even though in a different political context – to the French *écriture feminine* project that Hélène Cixous defined as writing through the body; as an approach to discourse that eludes the linear logic of the patriarchal system and transcends the Western separation between mind and body (Cixous, 1991, p. 351). Roy comes to transcend that separation from a different perspective, namely that of her Indian background, where such a separation does not exist in the same way. But, in her case, this elusion of linear logic supplements her subversion of the patriarchal order on the level of content. This kind of writing represents a very effective political tool for Roy to voice her concerns as a female postcolonial author.

Chapter 21, 'The Cost of Living', bears the same title as Roy's 1999 volume of essays. This suggests that, when writing it, the author would have had in mind a broader set of political concerns, which she then expressed more directly in her essays. But, in the novel, one cannot fail to notice the sharp criticism hidden behind the poetic language of the last chapter. This chapter launches Ammu's and Velutha's sublimely fulfilled love into a kind of eternally optimistic future, expressed through an unspecified Malayalam *naaley* (tomorrow). Like the lovemaking scene between the twins (which interrupts the continuity of Chapter 20 through a paragraph break standing in for the lack of any title), the scene depicted in Chapter 21, 'The Cost of Living', is also placed outside the historical time of Kerala, with its rigid rules of exclusion.

Like Estha's and Rahel's union, Ammu's and Velutha's is an acknowledgment of an unspeakable similarity. Though seen as fundamentally different by society, because they belong to different castes, Ammu and Velutha identify through sharing a similar marginality. In Ammu's union with Velutha, Roy literally uses a bodily discourse to express Ammu's denial of Velutha's attempt to prevent, through words, what in the order of the Law would be their undoing. If Velutha asks for an explanation in language, Roy has Ammu reply through her body:

Ammukutty . . . what is it?
She went to him and laid the length of her body against his. He just stood there. He didn't touch her. He was shivering. Partly with cold. Partly

terror. Partly aching desire. Despite his fear his body was prepared to take the bait. It wanted her. Urgently. His wetness wet her. She put her arms around him.
He tried to be rational: *What's the worst thing that can happen?*
I could lose everything. My job. My family. My livelihood. Everything.
She could hear the wild hammering of his heart.
She held him till it calmed down. Somewhat.
She unbuttoned her shirt. They stood there. Skin to skin. Her brownness against his blackness. Her softness against his hardness. Her nut-brown breasts (that wouldn't support a toothbrush) against his smooth ebony chest. She smelled the river on him. His Particular Paravan smell that so disgusted Baby Kochamma. (Roy, 1997, pp. 334–5)

This obvious opposition of two different discursive orders states nothing new. In fact, it alludes to previous recognizable points already made in the novel. Velutha's tender diminutive, meant for Ammu the child, offers (through language) a protection he was not allowed to offer by touching: the taboo over the Paravans' untouchability and Baby Kochamma's racist comment on the Paravans' smell. As the awareness of all of these is recalled to the reader's mind, the same story is retold, through bodily rhythms emerging in sheer poetry.

> They lay under the mangosteen tree, where only recently a grey old boatplant with boatflowers and boatfruit had been uprooted by a Mobile Republic. A wasp. A flag. A surprised puff. A Fountain in a Love-in-Tokyo.
> The scurrying, hurrying, boatworld was already gone.
> The White termites on their way to work.
> The White ladybirds on their way home.
> The White beetles burrowing away from the light.
> The White grasshoppers with whitewood violins.
> The sad white music.
> All gone.
> Leaving a boat-shaped patch of bare dry earth, cleared and ready for love. As though Estha and Rahel had prepared the ground for them. Willed this to happen. The twin midwives of Ammu's dream.
> . . .
> Once he was inside her, fear was derailed and biology took over. The cost of living climbed to unaffordable heights; though later, Baby Kochamma would say it was a Small Price to Pay.
> Was it?
> Two lives. Two children's childhoods.
> And a history lesson for future offenders. (Roy, 1997, pp. 335–6)

Through this different perspective, we come to realize that the finality of what we know has actually happened. It is destabilized by the change in the temporal order. By its ending, the novel appears to claim the inevitability of death, whilst Roy's two essays – as expected from such pieces of social activism – plead for ways of fighting against it. But the novel, by ending the way it does (with the word 'tomorrow'), proposes an optimistic interpretation. Roy, in fact, states this plainly:

> I think that one of the most important things about the structure is that in some way the structure of the book ambushes the story. You know, it tells a different story from the story the book is telling. In the first chapter I more or less tell you the story, but the novel ends in the middle of the story, and it ends with Ammu and Velutha making love and it ends on the word 'tomorrow'. And though you know that what tomorrow brings is terrible, the fact that the book ends there is to say that even though it's terrible it's wonderful that it happened at all. (Simmons, 2002b)

Thus Roy's novel consciously proposes two different plots: the one developed by the story and the one developed by the structure. While the former is a sad, dejected narrative of death and defeat, the latter – the story told through the ambushed structure – is a powerful critique of this and an uninhibited celebration of love and freedom. By looking at things from a different position in the development of events, Roy chooses to give precedence to individual revolt. She proposes an alternative discourse to the prevalent tendencies in contemporary postcolonial literature.

It is thus mainly through the emphasis on the political importance of individual revolt that Roy's act of decentralizing authorship is manifested. In proposing a politics of small things, she uses fiction as a strategy for destabilizing prejudiced systems of thinking. Attention to detail is contrasted to big and all-encompassing categories, such as the dichotomous position of much 'traditional' postcolonial writing (operating on the impulse of 'writing back to the centre'), or the hard and fast discourse of Indian nationalism (intent on sacrificing people's individual interests to an allegedly 'greater common good'). Roy chooses freedom from such binding conditioning. In doing so, she also states her belief in the political duty of authorship, which is to always question established political agendas.

Part IV
Authorship and Criticism

10
The Decline of the Critic

Terry Eagleton[1]

The idea of the author should not be confined to so-called creative writers. Critics are authors, too. As I shall argue in this essay, they have suffered a decline, which is in some ways akin to the celebrated 'death of the author'. The critic, it is true, has dwindled rather than died; his or her role has shrunk in both scope and significance in the later modern period. But this can be seen as one particular aspect of a more general 'decentring' of authorship. I intend here to offer a few comments on how exactly this decline has come about.

One could define an intellectual, roughly speaking, as the opposite of an academic. There are a great many distinguished academics around, but few of them are what one would want to call intellectuals. This is not to say that they are all hopelessly dim. Actually some of them *are* pretty dim, but saying they are not intellectuals is not a polite way of saying that because being an intellectual is not a matter of how devastatingly bright you are. It helps, if you are, of course, but it is not part of the job description. Not all intellectuals are intelligent, and not all the intelligent are intellectuals. The word 'intellectual' is a job description, like hairdresser or chief executive, rather than a personal predicate like reckless or dishevelled. There are some dumb intellectuals just as there are some erudite hairdressers. People who do not like intellectuals, but who also mistakenly imagine that 'intellectual' is a laudatory term, tend to talk scathingly about 'so-called' or 'soi-disant' intellectuals, for fear of paying an unwitting compliment to those they are criticizing; that is, for fear of implying that they are frightfully bright. But to call someone an intellectual is no more to imply that they are full of insight than to call someone a vicar is to imply that they enjoy the beatific vision.

Intellectuals differ from academics in at least three ways. For one thing, whereas academics tend to be politically middle-of-the-road or conservative, many intellectuals tend to be politically dissident. Since they have less investment in power than bankers or politicians, they can occasionally speak the truth to it. On the other hand, precisely because of their privileged remoteness from the centres of power, their speech tends for the most part to be fairly ineffectual; which is why intellectuals are pathetic as well as intimidating figures, faintly ridiculous as well as unnerving. (As for the latter, think of the spooky music of *Mastermind*.) Second, intellectuals tend to be conceptually promiscuous, roaming from one theoretical patch to another, unconstrained by the bounds of a specific discipline. Academics, on the other hand, tend to be specialists, as I discovered years ago in Cambridge when I used to spend my time reading lists of exotic, unintelligible thesis titles, of which the most intriguing was: 'Some Aspects of the Vaginal System of the Flea'. If one thinks, by contrast, of some of the more glamorous intellectual names of our age – Said, Chomsky, Williams, Arendt, Kristeva, Bourdieu, Rorty, Sontag, Habermas, Derrida, Spivak, Žižek, Anderson – it would be hard to categorize them in the sort of terms familiar to university departments. Intellectuals are a bookseller's nightmare, plunging their categories into disarray as surely as did the pious Catholic study of St. Theresa, 'the Little Flower' some years ago, which found itself catalogued under horticulture. On the other hand, this lack of definitive discipline can turn intellectuals into bungling amateurs or homespun visionaries, all the way from Matthew Arnold to D. H. Lawrence. Not all transgressions, including the transgressions of disciplinary boundaries, are by any mean to be euphorically endorsed, whatever the more dogmatic postmodernists may believe.

The third important difference, related to the above, is that intellectuals are concerned with the bearing of ideas on society as a whole, whereas academics typically are not. Indeed, Jean-Paul Sartre considered a physicist to be an intellectual only if he or she had signed a petition against nuclear weapons. This does not mean, of course, that intellectuals are only of the political left, though it is true, as I have just suggested, that they have been typically so. This is partly because some conservative thinkers are uninterested in or hostile to the social implications of ideas, but also because the category of 'society as a whole', something amenable to rational analysis, has by and large profited the left more than the right: Tom Paine rather than Edmund Burke. One way of denying the need for radical change is to deny that there is any coherent object called 'society' to be changed; and this has sometimes been a right-wing tactic. At the moment, however, it is a left-wing one too: radical postmodernism considers the idea of social totality to be an illusion, and therefore, logically, considers the classical intellectual, who somehow spoke to, from and on behalf of such a totality, to be outmoded too. An omniscient knowledge, it would seem, can only be politically oppressive. Though there is an intriguing paradox here, since if there is no longer any overall viewpoint, if there is nothing but fragments, then *how do we know this?* Isn't this in itself a 'totalizing' proposition? At what Olympian vantage point must we be standing to be able to deny the existence of Olympian vantage points? Isn't 'there is no totality' a self-cancelling statement? If we are not a totality or grand narrative for ourselves, how come we seem to be for Al Quaeda?

Anyway, in the shift from Jean-Paul Sartre to Michel Foucault, Bertrand Russell to Donald Davidson, the very idea of the classical intellectual has for some sunk without trace. For others, there is a gender issue here, too: the classical intellectual, with his wizened phallic, cerebrally anaemic, overbearing claim to some God's-eye form of knowledge, has now given way to a more humble, partial, pragmatic, bodily, feminine sort of wisdom. One thing, which helped above all to bring the classical intellectual into disrepute, was his or her apparent claim to disinterestedness – a category, may I remind the dehistoricizing postmodernists, that was revolutionary in its day. In the face of revolutionary rationalist disinterestedness, the custodians of the virulently partisan *ancien régime* could be seen to tremble. But an alternative current of modernity was deeply suspicious of all such lofty claims and, in its typically demystifying way, sought to unmask them as bogus. It sought to expose the unlovely subtexts of our thought, anchored as they were in power, desire, interests, practice, rivalry, repression and dominion. So, we are left with an apparent dilemma: the intellectual is either disinterested in a phoney way (the view from nowhere), or our thinking is purely situational and nothing but the reflex of our interests and desires, and so lacks all capacity to place them under critique.

In fact, there was always a kind of answer to this conundrum, and it lay exactly with the classical intellectual. For the odd thing about such intellectuals was that they claimed an overall viewpoint, yet they were often ferociously partisan. As such, whether they were right or wrong, they challenged the liberal assumption that the only valid view is the view from nowhere. They urged instead, or some of them did, the startling anti-Hegelian proposition that the truth itself is one-sided, partisan, and that you will only grasp it by standing at a certain angle to the work. You have, in the homely phrase, to be 'in a position to know'. Specific interests could thus be a mode of access to truth, not an obstacle to it. It was thus that 'intellectual' could come to mean, for its more redneck critics, both someone pathetically out of touch and someone hot-headedly *engagé*.

Intellectuals, as I have said, are concerned with the bearing of ideas on society, but also, very often, conversely, with the social roots of ideas themselves. This, paradoxically, has often led them to a scepticism about ideas. Indeed, it is possible to read the history of modern thought as a series of subversive strikes at the Cartesian *cogito*, or the belief in the sovereignty of reason. (Today, when the rational subject has become the consumerist one, one can perhaps rewrite Réné Descartes' famous saying as *Tesco ergo sum*.) But the rewriting has been going on for a long time: all the way from Arthur Schopenhauer (I think, therefore I am self-deceived), to Friedrich Nietzsche (I think, therefore I oversimplify), to Karl Marx (I think, therefore someone has been doing the work around here), to Jacques Lacan's flamboyant Freudian parody of Descartes (I am not where I think and I think where I am not); or, with Sigmund Freud himself (I think, therefore I have mercifully forgotten something absolutely vital to my making). There is also a whole philosophical tradition which wants to say, with G. W. F. Hegel,

'I think, therefore *you* are', or, with Martin Heidegger and Ludwig Wittgenstein, 'I think, therefore I must be always-already bound up with some practical form of life, some emotional attunement to the world, already pitched headlong to the midst of things'. For all these mighty figures of modernity, there is something that precedes and underpins our thought, something which thought itself therefore cannot quite turn round upon itself and encompass, whether you call it labour or *Geist*, the categories of power or the Will, forms of life or discursive formations. Thought for this tradition is always belated in respect to itself, can never quite catch up with itself, since we live forward but think backwards. The characteristic gesture of these thinkers, in anycase, is to chide and rebuke thought for its overweening hubris, its arrogant repression of its lowly material roots, its eagerness to claim a posher sort of parentage and pedigree for itself than the squalid, violent, self-interested one it actually has. It is from this *anti*-philosophical impulse, in a remarkable irony, that some of the finest, most strenuous philosophy of our epoch has sprung, all the way from Søren Kierkegaard and Friedrich Nietzsche to Theodor Adorno and Jacques Derrida.

What has all this to do with criticism? Well, 'critic' was just one traditional name for what I have been calling the intellectual, long before our current division of academic labour set in. This is because the role of the intellectual as I have described it – that concern for crossing academic boundaries in the service of social or cultural or political life – is one which, so to speak, revolves, passing from one academic discipline to another as the age demands. In medieval history, it was known as theology, queen of the sciences; in some regions, though not in the Anglo-Saxon world, the intellectual buck remained firmly with philosophy; there were great, doomed hopes in nineteenth-century Europe that it might lie with sociology or the natural sciences, so that the prototypically intellectualized were men like Auguste Comte and Herbert Spencer; and in our own neck of the woods, for about the last two centuries, more or less since Samuel Taylor Coleridge, it has taken up home, of all implausible locales, in literary criticism.

Now this, on any estimate, is alarming news. For whatever virtues may flourish among literary types, systematic thinking is hardly one of them. The phrase 'literary theory' has an oxymoronic ring to it, like 'sundrenched Mancunian' or 'Mormon intelligentsia'. You would not normally put a poet on the sanitation committee, or despatch specialists in the pastoral to report on the condition of the labouring masses. Indeed, from the Romantics onwards, or at least, should we say, somewhere between the later Percy Shelley and the early Alfred Tennyson, the 'literary' or 'poetic' in English culture has gradually been redefined to mean almost the opposite of thought and action – the very antithesis of the discursive prosaic, practical analytical, doctrinal, systematic. 'Political poetry' becomes a sort of oxymoron, and 'material culture' a contradiction in terms. Culture, literature, in its intuitive, affective, transcendental, sensuously particularized, ineffably individual way, is exactly what *resists* all that drearily utilitarian stuff – which is why materialist critiques of culture tend to attract more hostility than materialist critiques of politics or economics. It is not because culture is so important, but because it is thought to be intrinsically idealist. That is what it is there for. But this sense of the literary is, of course, historically very recent. It would no doubt have come as a mighty surprise to Dante, Chaucer, Milton, Pope, Swift, Voltaire, Goethe, Schiller, Stendhal, Heine, Tolstoy or Zola, to learn that the literary was sublimely remote from the doctrinal, practical, metaphysical or political.

Yet, no sooner has the literary been remodelled in this way than, in an astonishing double-think, it is called upon, all the way from Samuel Coleridge and Matthew Arnold to F. R. Leavis, George Orwell and I. A. Richards, to become the very custodian of our social values, moral integrity and cultural *sanitas*. This literary culture, which is now in fact constituted to its core by hostility to rational thought or practical reason, is to become a veritably foundational discipline, the new locus of intellectual life, the very paradigm of the ethical and cultural. It is now an ambitiously anthropological rather than a modestly aesthetic sort of affair, assuming responsibility for everything from dactyls to death, ethics to epistemology, metaphor to the Meaning of Life. How on earth could this have come about?

It happened, for one thing, because of the curiously low definition of literary studies – or to put the point rather less coyly, the fact that nobody since they were established had really been able to say what they were about. They were about literature, of course, but since nobody could define that either, this did not really help. But the fact that they seemed to be about nothing in particular – that they were, as Lenin remarked of theology, a subject without an object – meant that they could be about more or less anything you wanted. Their fuzziness was also their good fortune. Besides, if the critic was being increasingly forced into the role of sage, moralist and cultural commentator, it was partly because some rather more plausible candidates for this role had cravenly passed the buck or thrown in the towel. If you were landed with a narrowly analytic philosophy, an empiricist political science, a behaviourist psychology and a positivist sociology, all the embarrassingly large questions to which people still obstinately clamoured for answers, such as 'Why are we here? Are we alone? Why is there anything at all rather than just nothing?' – all these questions clearly were not going to get answered by the philosophers or sociologists; not least by philosophers like Gilbert Ryle, who once boasted that he had argued a nihilistically-minded undergraduate out of committing suicide by demonstrating to him that the grammar of 'nothing matters' differs from that of 'nothing chatters'.

So, the function of the intellectual circulated to literary criticism, which had the unenviable role of scooping up the big issues, jettisoned by its increasingly specialist, professionalized academic neighbours, and so became a sort of general humanist dumping ground. It was fortunate, to be sure, that it was areas such as ethics and psychology that literary studies muscled in on, rather than surgery or aeronautical engineering. But if we now have the mildly farcical spectacle of those trained to spot a para-rhyme or a pentameter holding forth on the unconscious, epistemological realism, the decentred subject and the Asiatic mode of production, this is partly, as I say, because those rather better equipped for such tasks have blandly passed the buck.

But there was a greater embarrassment still. For what criticism was really called upon to stand in for was not quite ethics or philosophy or psychology, but religion. From the mid nineteenth century onwards, it was 'culture' that had to perform the key ideological functions religion had performed so superbly in its day, but for which it was now less and less of a credible candidate. If you wanted a one-phrase reply to the question: 'Why the centrality of criticism?' you could do worse than reply: 'The failure of religion'. Not that the literary is an altogether implausible substitute for the divine. Both, after all, concern the mystery of creation. Indeed, Romantic aesthetics had been busy redefining art in precisely this way, so that, like religion, the literary was a matter of faith, intuition, sensuous immediacy, transcendence, inward experience and fundamental value, linking the personal to the universal, the elite (whether priestly or poetic) to the masses, esoteric ritual to popular sentiment – and all this, moreover, not just as set of theoretic ideas but as a set of actual, institutional practices. The only problem was that modernity never found, nor indeed is ever likely to, so finely effective a discourse as religion for linking the daily, exoteric experience of millions of ordinary people to the most sacred, esoteric of truths. The hope that the literary – an activity which involved no more than a tiny privileged handful of men and women – could substitute itself for this was bound to come badly unstuck. In its narrow, aesthetic sense of the arts and fine living, culture is too minority a pursuit to fulfil this role; in its broader, more anthropological sense of a whole way of life, it is too contentious and divided a domain to do so.

'Everything begins with mysticism and ends with politics', runs a celebrated French tag. With literary criticism, the opposite has really been true: what culminated with Matthew Arnold, F. R. Leavis, Benedetto Croce and the New Criticism as, if not exactly mysticism, then certainly a suitably secularized, comfortably undoctrinal version of religion, began as a form of discursive politics. When criticism first emerges in England, it does so as part of the bourgeois public sphere of the eighteenth century – as one discourse among several by which that newly emergent class is consolidating for itself a buoyant cultural identity. It belongs not to the universities but to the clubs, coffee houses, salons and periodical press. In the coffee houses of eighteenth-century England (and there were over 3,000 of them in London alone), men of letters rubbed shoulders with merchants, squires, noblemen, politicians, diplomats, lawyers, scientists, actors, theologians and the like. The business of criticism was cultural rather than, in the first place, literary: it was to form taste, codify norms, mould manners, reform conduct and shape new social intercourse. Criticism was a potent force in the construction of a new public opinion and cultural hegemony, a sort of free market in cultivated opinion. As such, it mixed together ethics, linguistics, psychology, literature, social commentary, political observations and the like, dealing with everything from how to run a government efficiently to how to cross a room elegantly.

Cultural studies, then, is no modish, new-fangled phenomenon. On the contrary, it is literary criticism, as we know it, in the sense of a narrowly textual or formal analysis, which is of fairly recent historical vintage. That came into its own only towards the end of the nineteenth century, as the public sphere, besieged from all sides by commercialism, professionalism, specialization and state intervention, became an increasingly impossible space to hold open. That general moral humanism, so characteristically English in tone and sensibility, was still just about possible at the time of Samuel Johnson; but Johnson himself can be found regretting the fact that knowledge and society are now so complex that they elude the synoptic view of any one individual. What undermines the public sphere, then, is the division of intellectual labour – but also the commercial market, since it is clearly this, and not the critic, who is now delivering the most authoritative literary judgements and determining the fate of both writers and readers. The critic as generalist survives for a time in Victorian England in the guise of the so-called 'man of letters', a jack-of-all trades or erudite hack who has to be able to review anything that comes to hand because he would starve if he tried to live by one specialism alone. But the rise of the universities is beginning to make him look embarrassingly amateurish, and the market is increasingly overriding his judgements. If the man of letters is a literary intellectual still grappling with material life – still down there in the intellectual market-place as public, activist, *engagé* – the Victorian *sage* is the literary intellectual who has withdrawn from the unseemly wranglings of social life, delivering his pontifical dictates of them from some Olympian vantage-point above the affray. The critic, in short, is now strung out between journalistic hack and aloof visionary, commercial profit and Old Testament prophet: George Henry Lewes and Thomas Carlyle.

In twentieth-century England, F. R. Leavis and his *Scrutiny* project tried, audaciously, if forlornly, to reinvent the classical public sphere, this time as a defensive coterie, though now from within academia. They also pose the question, which has always dogged criticism in England: is it an amateur or a professional pursuit? The dilemma would seem to be this: either criticism justifies its existence by its broad social and moral relevance, but in thus expanding its brief courts a disabling amateurism; or it justifies itself at the bar of professional, specialist, modernizing opinion, becoming a sort of hard-nosed technology of the text, but thereby renouncing any claim to more general cultural relevance. F. R. Leavis, I. A. Richards and the New Critics are perhaps the last point at which it seems you might still do both together, coupling the numinous with the hard-nosed. But, in general, one either assumes, immodestly, that one's ability to spot a parataxis gives one the right to pontificate about the Meaning of Life and the decentred subject, or one becomes a kind of Blairite of the literary realm.

The battle has fought itself out many times, not least in our own time in the guise of one between humanism and structuralism. I say humanism and structuralism, rather than, perhaps more predictably, humanism and 'theory', because there is a sense in which critical theory, understood in a certain way, offers to deconstruct this opposition. I mean simply that theory – which is itself no more than a provisional name covering a whole lot of very different ways of talking, which probably have little more in common than a shared protagonist – is neither quite amateur humanism or technocratic professionalism, but some strange, hard-to-categorize third thing beyond them both. On the one hand, it is clearly not an 'ordinary language' activity, since it believes quite properly in the need for jargon. I do not, of course, mean by jargon some wilfully obscurantist way of talking indulged in by cerebral young males out to prove how frightfully clever they are, but rather the kind of necessarily specialist talk that gardeners, model-aircraft makers and garage mechanics get up to; all of whom speak in ways often not immediately intelligible to outsiders because of the particularized nature of their trades. Nobody expects to pick up a biology textbook and understand it straight away, but some of those allergic to theory expect to pick up a work of criticism and do just that, which is even more arrogant than writing sentences that only five other people can understand. Indeed, what was wrong with some literary criticism in the past was that it was all too intelligible, assuming that a gentleman just *knows*, intuitively, that Anthony Trollope is a greater writer than Henry James in the same way that he can recognize a mature Riesling or a fine thoroughbred. There is an elitist cult of instant comprehension, just as there is a coterie cult of impenetrability.

Against such impenetrability, theorists tend to be democrats, claiming that the business of criticism is open not just to those with the right blood and breeding, which was certainly the case when I read English at Cambridge a long time ago, but open to anyone prepared to take the trouble to learn a certain sort of language. That language is necessarily a complex one; but the issues it engages – cultural, psychological, political – are of general, widespread, potentially popular concern. Theory, in short, by raising in a necessarily rigorous manner questions relevant to how to live more happily and peaceably, less miserably and unjustly, promises to dismantle the opposition between amateur and professional that has bedevilled criticism from the outset.

Radicals are always traditionalists; and it is cultural theory that is traditional, and criticism, in its more formalistic sense, that is the recent upstart. Indeed, all the major historical moments of criticism, from the neo-classical to the Romantic, from the Victorian man or woman of letters to the modern-day theorist, have been ones when criticism, just in order to answer certain questions raised by the arts, must ineluctably engage questions that reach far beyond the aesthetic, and do so moreover as a constitutive part of the act of criticism itself rather than as an agreeable appendage. If, as my title suggests, criticism is in decline today, it is because we have not yet been able to recover the ambitious reach of the traditional public critic in anything much more than theory, in both senses of the word. This is not, however, the fault of criticism, which cannot legislate a public sphere cavalierly into existence, as F. R. Leavis wistfully hoped it might. Whether the critic will again find a public role and relevance is a matter for the public – which is to say, of political and historical developments, which the critic as critic cannot pre-empt or determine. We do not know whether this will happen. What we can say for sure is that if it does not, criticism, caught up in its streamlined apparatus of conventions and publications, promotions and personalities, will continue to be as harmless a pursuit as clogdancing, and just about as pointlessly pleasant.

Notes

Introduction: Authorship and its Contexts

1. For a detailed analysis of the meanings as well as diversity of contexts for the study of literature, see Rylance and Simons, 2001, pp. xv–xxix.
2. For a valuable discussion of authorship as a mode of social production, a reading practice and a technique of the self, see Biriotti and Miller, 1993.
3. For general readers and overviews of book history, see Bell *et al.*, 2000; Johns, 1998; Finkelstein and McCleery, 2002.
4. For an overview of the developments of new media and related issues, see Lister *et al.*, 2003; and Fidler, 1999. More specifically for a discussion of the remediation, see Bolter and Grusin, 1999; and for how authorial subjectivity is remediated, see Kendrick, 2001, pp. 231–51.
5. For different perspectives on the public role of writers and intellectuals by other thinkers working in different fields from Eagleton, ranging from Edward Said and Bruce Robbins to Jacqueline Rose and Stefan Collini, see Small, 2002.

Part I   Nineteenth-Century Literary Market-Place

1   The Author, the Editor and the Fissured Text: Scott, Maturin and Hogg

1. See Sage, 1990 for a resume of the main battle-lines in the discussion, and some bibliography.
2. Trumpener explains the paradox, and how it is reversible, excellently:

> The historiographical structure of the Waverley novels depends on an important paradox or tension. Their central narratives (continuously, omnisciently, and for the most part unobtrusively narrated) represent the triumph of a single focus narrative history – and thus point towards the realist novel of the mid-century. At the same time, their elaborate documentary framework of footnotes and pseudo-editorial commentaries echo the footnoted debates between late-eighteenth-century antiquarians over editorial practices, the elaborate apparatus and ironic polyglossia of Gibbon's historiography, the growing narrative self-consciousness of the epistolary and Shandean novel at the end of the eighteenth century ... Such framing, of course, lends density to the historiographical survey of Scott's novels. Yet it also in some ways privileges the perspective of antiquarian narrators over that of historical participants, as the intellectual complexity of the act of historiographic assembly potentially exceeds the psychological complexity of historical experience itself. [Maturin and Owenson combat this editorial excess by] appropriating elements from two very different genres, the gothic novel and the annalistic history, which in some ways represent even more extreme forms of textualism than the historical novel itself. (Trumpener, 1993, p. 710)

3. See Scott's reviews of Ann Radcliffe, Charles Maturin, and Mary Shelley's *Franken-stein* in Scott, 1968, pp. 102–19, 273–97, 260–72.
4. For commentary on this relationship, see Sage's introduction to Maturin, 2000, pp. vii–xxxi. For background, see Scott, 1980; and there is a recent extended discussion in Robertson, 1994.
5. For Maturin, see Trumpener, who speaks of:

> the intense attention Maturin, Owenson, and Galt pay to the long-term effects of historical trauma, the deliberate or amnesiac repression of histor-ical memory, and the neurotic psycho-social mechanisms developed to contain its explosiveness. This difference in emphasis [that is, from Scott] expresses itself with particular clarity in the narrative organisation of their novels. (Trumpener, 1993, p. 710)

6. Ferris puts the point very succinctly: 'But to know an event historically, Arthur Danto has reminded us, is precisely to know it in a way that a witness cannot. It is to assume an enabling continuity – a different language, another knowledge' (Ferris, 1991, p. 194). Here is the precise point in the logic of representation at which the fissured text emerges.
7. See Jacques Derrida's remarks about the infinite regress of framing, in the intro-ductory section of *The Truth in Painting* (Derrida, 1987, pp. 1–13). But, apropos of the vertical and horizontal, see also Hasler's point about frame-breaking in narrative, which rests on a Marxist appropriation of Freud: 'The absence of narrative and syntactic hierarchy uncovers the workings of overdetermination' (Hasler, 1993, p. 65, nt. 36).
8. The notoriously complex relationship between Scott and Hogg is better docu-mented than that of Scott and Maturin. See Duncan, 1993; Hogg, 1983. See also the account of the background to the textual parodies given in the introduction to Hogg, 2001. For the point about feudalism, see MacLachlan, 1993; and Hasler, 1993, pp. 57–82.
9. Hasler draws our attention to the 'deeply disjunctive style' of Hogg and the way he disrupts the teleological relation established by Scott's rhetoric between the present and the past in the reading process itself. For a material and ideological translation of this teleology, see Duncan, 1992, pp. 61–2, 92. Describing *Waverley*, and paraphrasing the logic of Scott's representational procedure, Duncan says:

> historical being can only be rationally possessed, recognized, *as romance* – as a private aesthetic property, in the imagination, materially signified by the book we are holding. These are our stories because we have paid for them . . . Scott's narratives recount again and again that aesthetic property is the last and absolute theft: a sublimation that comprehends the violence of history, all the deaths that have produced us, now reading. (Duncan, 1992, pp. 61–2, 92)

Hasler's point is that it is the fissures in Hogg's text of *The Three Perils of Woman* (1823) which refuse this inexorable narrative teleology or sublimation.
10. From now on *The Private Memoirs and Confessions of a Justified Sinner* is abbreviated as *Confessions*.
11. The most recent overview is Garside's introduction to the *Confessions*. The row between Scott and Hogg over *The Tale of Old Mortality* (1816) and Hogg's novel *The Brownie of Bodsbeck* (1818) is obviously an important element of the background to the parody of Scott in *Confessions*. See Mack, 1999, pp. 1–26.

12. As with Maturin's representation of the seventeenth-century history of division between two brothers in a family, leading up to post-Union Ireland in 1816, Hogg's historical back-story of the divided origins of the two brothers (or half-brothers, depending on how one reads it) includes a parliamentary session of 1703, which played an important part in the events leading up to the Union of Scotland and England in 1707. The split in the house of Dalcastle represents a split in the Scottish nation. See Mack, 1999, p. 3.

13. Mack makes the crucial point in his discussion of the narrative presentation of the Brocken Spectre incident on Arthur's Seat. The Editor's language is notoriously full of Enlightenment scientific jargon and he opposes this to 'uninitiated and sordid man'. Mack's comments about this process of mutual discrediting in the relationship between the two narratives at this point are revealing about the reader's position in general:

> There are perhaps hidden dangers in interpreting human history as a movement from the deluded darkness of superstition into the light of a modern, rational scientific, objective enquiry. Such a view tends to encourage an assumption that one is oneself one of the children of the light, while others – the 'uninitiated and sordid man', as the Editor puts it, or 'the lesser breeds without the law' as Kipling puts it – inhabit the barbarous darkness . . . Regarded in this way, aspects of the assumptions of the Enlightenment can suddenly seem surprisingly similar to aspects of Robert Wringhim's assumptions about himself, and his role as God's chosen and elect champion whose strong hand will bring the wicked under control. (Mack, 1999, pp. 13ff)

14. 'In Gaelic, *gille-martuinn* means "fox", and in Gaelic folk-tales, Gille-Martuinn the fox is a shape-changing trickster, devious and cunning' (Mack, 1999, p. 10).

15. There is, of course, evidence that Scott himself undergoes considerable development in the disruption of his own earlier linearity, precisely by a more radical cultivation of the vertical aspects of the text in his later work. Both Penny Fielding and Fiona Robertson have argued this, while Ian Duncan has shown how Scott, in the most Gothic set pieces in his fiction, appropriates the tale-telling methods of Hogg. See the discussion of 'Wandering Willie's Tale' in *Redgauntlet* in Duncan, 1993, pp. 12–25.

2   'George Eliot', the Literary Market-Place and Sympathy

1. For other scholarly work on George Eliot and sympathy from whose insight this study draws, see Argyros, 1999; Dentith, 1986, pp. 30–55; and Ermath, 1985.

2. Gordon S. Haight (1968) played an important role in recasting Eliot as a novelist of ideas rather than feeling.

3. I distinguish between the Review as a format of periodical publication (for example, *Westminster Review*) and review as a genre of writing through the use of initial capitals.

4. For a similar view about the abundance of 'ill-trained' authors (women and children), see Lewes, 1847, p. 285.

5. Women who belonged to Eliot's category of 'cultured women' were, among others, Barbara Bodichon, the Brontës, Elizabeth Barrett Browning, Isa Craig, Emily Davies, Margaret Fuller, Sara Sophia Hennell, Anna Jameson, Geraldine

Jewsbury, Elizabeth Stuart Phelps, Mme de Sablé, George Sand and Harriet Beecher Stowe. Other women who were dismissed because of their tendency to exaggeration, sentimentalism and dogmatism that characterized 'lady novelists' were Mary Elizabeth Braddon, Frederika Bremer, Mme de Longueville and Bessie Rayner Parkes.

6. Despite Eliot's critique of Newman's work, she was sympathetic to all religious denominations (Eliot, 1954–78, vol. 4, p. 64). Although she was not an active member of the feminist movement, she helped to develop tolerance towards feminist reforms with her work and actions; for example, in 1854 she signed and passed on to Sara Hennell a copy of Barbara Bodichon's petition to support the Married Women's Property Bill (Eliot, 1954–78, vol. 2, p. 227).

7. It is in the context of her desire for voice that her signed publication of her translation of the German Higher Critic Ludwig Feuerbach's *Das Wesen Christenthums* (1841) (*The Essence of Christianity*) with her real name, Marian Evans, becomes intelligible. Whereas authors acquired recognition through their writing, translators were obscured under somebody else's authorial signature. Marian Evans as a signature signifies the lack of vocal resonance in translation whose affluence, in the case of literary writing, overrides the need for naming. For the challenges that nineteenth-century women translators, including Eliot, faced within the Anglo-German context, see Stark, 1999.

8. Eliot's cognitive aesthetic of feeling was based on William Wordsworth's idea that feelings were modes of cognition, ways of understanding the world.

9. For a more spiteful critique of Eliot's submission to Lewes' patronage, see Linton, 1899, p. 102; 1897, p. 88.

10. Similarly to Linton, Alice James (1981, p. 25), W. E. Gladstone (Eliot, 1954–78, vol. 1, p. 1, p. xiv), William Hale (1885) and Edmund Gosse (quoted in Woolf, 1971, p. 197) criticized the lifelessness of Cross' posthumous biographical portrait of Eliot.

11. For a discussion of the technique of suspending narrative in relation to Eliot's realism, see Levine, 2003, pp. 101–60.

3 Liberal Editing in the *Fortnightly Review* and the *Nineteenth Century*

1. The content of this chapter first appeared in *Publishing History*, vol. 53 (2003) pp. 75–96. My thanks to Simon Eliot and Peter Cockton for their close editorial scrutiny; also to Michael Bott, for guiding me through the holdings of the Reading University Library Archive.

2. For the figure of £8,000 see Trollope to Herman Merivale, 30 March 1865, in Trollope, 1983, vol. 1, p. 298. Trollope's *Autobiography* gives the figure as around £9,000, as does Everett, 1939, p. 17. Merivale may have contributed another £1,000 in response to Trollope's plea in the letter quoted. For the sum of £1,250 per individual, see Hirst, 1927, vol. 2, p. 64.

3. Various attempts were made to change the title, but no sufficiently appealing alternative was found; Meredith to Morley, 29 July 1875, in Meredith, 1970, vol. 1, p. 504.

4. According to one of Meredith's biographers, the upshot was a meeting between Meredith and Swinburne, at which Swinburne slapped Meredith's face. In spite of continuing strains between the two, Morley persuaded Swinburne to view writing

for the *Fortnightly* as an act of solidarity with himself as its editor against a financially grasping proprietorship. See Stevenson, 1954, pp. 166–7; and Swinburne to William Michael Rossetti, 18 March 1868, in Swinburne, 1959–62, vol. 1, p. 298. Two years later Meredith was himself receiving a paltry £5 for his 150-line poem *Phaedra* and bearing with the insult out of loyalty to Morley.

5. See Curwen, 1873; Hunnisett, 1980; entries for George Virtue and James Sprent Virtue in Boase, 1892–1921, reprinted 1965, vol. 3, p. 1105; and the *Dictionary of National Biography*, 1908–9, vol. 20, pp. 374–5.

6. See also Srebrnik, 1986, p. 89. The Chapman & Hall Minute Books at Reading University Library Archive appear to offer support but are not conclusive.

7. See also Meredith to William Hardman, 22 April 1862, in Meredith, 1970, vol. 1, p. 141; and Bicknell and Cline, 1973, pp. 28–31.

8. The *Contemporary Review, Fraser's* and *Blackwood's*, all published monthly, cost 2*s*.6*d*. in the 1860s and early 1870s and offered more pages than the *Fortnightly* for that sum.

9. Morley to William Abram, 24 June 1868, quoted in Hirst, 1927, vol. 1, p. 133; Morley to John Russell, Viscount Amberley, 22 January 1871, quoted in Russell and Russell, 1966, vol. 2, pp. 444–7.

10. Minute Books for Chapman & Hall, Reading University Library Archive Manuscript, Bk 2, 26 March 1884, MS OC/1/4/2, p. 206. Thereafter, abbreviated as RULA in the text.

11. Developed from Hamer, 1968, p. 119; see also p. 205.

12. Everett does note that there was a 'quarrel' with the proprietors of the *Fortnightly*, but gives no details (Everett, 1939, p. 317).

13. Copies of Strahan's pamphlets are included in the Gladstone Papers at the British Library. See BL Add. MS 44453, ff. 73–6 and 204–7.

Part II   Twentieth-Century Mythologies of Authorship

4   F. R. Leavis: The Writer, Language, History

1. Leavis' remarks on the 'realization' of the imagery in lines from *Macbeth* are from Leavis, 1940–41, pp. 314–15.

2. See also the recorded comparison with Charles Dickens and T. S. Eliot in Leavis, 1995, p. 88.

3. See in particular the contributions by L. C. Knights, Eve Mason, Felicity Rosslyn, Leo Salingar and John Worthen in *The Cambridge Quarterly*, 1996, pp. 357–60, 361–4, 395–9, 399–404 and 420–1.

5   Mind that Crowd: Flann O'Brien's Authors

1. I have discussed some of those joint productions elsewhere: see Brooker, 2003, pp. 74–98.

2. The name Hackett was to make a return in the last Flann O'Brien novel, *The Dalkey Archive* (1964).

3. For a first-hand account of the transition from letters page to *Cruiskeen Lawn*, see Gray, 1997, pp. 110–11.

4. For a political reading of this change, see Kiberd, 1995, p. 499. Among the best general accounts of the column is Young, 1997, pp. 111–18. See also ch. 6 in Brooker, 2005.

5. A full reading of the link between Dublin and the Wild West in this section of the book still waits to be made. In the meantime, see Kiberd, 2000, pp. 512–14; and on the Irish imagination of the American West, O'Toole, 1997, pp. 18–45.
6. This echoes the idea of cursing, in which words have power to wound: indeed, Sweeny's plight is the result of such an act (O'Brien, 1967, p. 65).
7. It is presumably the same Editor who adds a Foreword, dated 'The Day of Doom, 1964', two pages and twenty-three years later.
8. On O'Nolan's relation to Joyce, see also Cronin, 1989, pp. ix–x, 49–52, 247; and Brooker, 2004, pp. 198–202.
9. Mick asks to become Joyce's literary agent: he is as concerned with uncollected royalties as with an unearned reputation. This is another trace of O'Nolan's residually mercenary attitude to writing – with the twist that the case promises cash for work not done.
10. On *The Poor Mouth*'s debt to its predecessors, see Farnon, 1997, pp. 89–109. For an overview of the Blasket writers themselves, see ch. 29 in Kiberd, 2000.
11. A notable example of this is his satirical treatment of feminism: see, for example, O'Brien, 1988a, pp. 99–103.
12. For a sceptical discussion, see Burke, 1998, pp. 20–7.
13. It must be admitted that Wilde seems a lot more self-evidently Irish now than he did even fifteen or twenty years ago. Terry Eagleton's *Saint Oscar and Other Plays* (1997) is a notable signal of the change: see his discussion of the play in ch. 2 of this volume. See also McCormack, 1998; and Kiberd, 1995, pp. 33–50.
14. On the complexity of Wilde's thought here, see ch. 8 in Eagleton, 1995.
15. For a brief but stimulating discussion of this, see Deane, 1997, pp. 157–63. See also ch. 28 in Kiberd, 2000, esp. pp. 500–1, 515–17.
16. For O'Nolan on Eliot, see the depiction of Lionel Prune in O'Brien, 1988b, pp. 29–33; and O'Brien, 1968, pp. 238–9. The closest Brian O'Nolan comes to articulating a case for the autonomy of art is in a *Cruiskeen Lawn* column which declares that a painting must be considered in competition with, rather than as an imitation of, life: as 'a sort of legendary organism which is to be appreciated and can only be judged in terms of itself' (O'Brien, 1968, p. 260). But this defence of abstraction, while noteworthy in O'Nolan's *oeuvre* for its apparent seriousness, does not explain his relationship to notions of authorial absence and presence. It is the ludic practice of O'Nolan's writing which does that.
17. On O'Nolan's relationship to notions of art and artisanship, see ch. 6 in Brooker, 2005.
18. For a photograph, see Costello and van de Kamp, 1987, p. 122.

6 Authorship in the Writings and Films of William S. Burroughs

1. For more on Burroughs and postmodern theory, see Lydenberg (1987) which was the first major study of the author to explore this connection extensively. See also Murphy (1997), which examines the author in light of the philosophies of Gilles Deleuze and Félix Guattari, arguing successfully that Burroughs'

imagined communities of junkies and wild boys are nomadic and systematically decentred, forming an alternative to the binaries of normative/radical, surrender/revolution, and indeed to modernism/postmodernism.

2. For an analysis of the socio-political climate responsible for the emergence of the Hays Code and other forms of censorship in America, see Black, 1994, pp. 21–49.

3. In the week of the September 11 attacks, *Towers Open Fire* was scheduled to be shown in the Arts Centre of the New York Trade Centre. This is an ironic coincidence, given the story in the film (a guerrilla attack led by Burroughs dressed in military gear wearing a gas mask) and the guerrilla-style resistance to government, authority and conformity that his writings and films advocate. For a recent account of the film in the light of terrorism, see Russell, 2004, pp. 161–74.

4. An obvious expression of this is the graphic novel. David Punter's essay in this collection provides more detailed links between the graphic novel, postmodernism and postmodern culture. Also see Rapatzikou, 2001, pp. 73–86.

5. See Shaw, 2000, pp. 78, 162, 271, 346–54, 415–17.

6. Of course, this is a simplified view of medieval authorship, one that Burroughs would probably have been familiar with. For more on the complex relationship between Man and God, *auctor* (author) and *auctoritas* (authority), see Minnis, 1984, pp. 73–159.

7. Eliot's 'Hurry up, please. It's time' appears in *The Waste Land* (1922) several times. See, for example, lines 141, 152, 165, 168 and 169.

Part III   Postmodern Culture

7   Postmodernism, Criticism and the Graphic Novel

1. In a fuller account, this would necessarily have to be further related to the delay involved in the serialization of the 'original' issues.

2. This appears on the back cover. There is no pagination in the text. Therefore, all quotations from Rowson's *The Waste Land* do not include page numbers.

3. Such comments are, naturally, not fully attributed.

4. The outstanding contributions here are from Briggs, 1989, pp. 221–50; Hunt, 2001; and Hunt, 1992.

8   Authorial Identity in the Era of Electronic Technologies

1. 'In the world of literary production, the cyberpunk phenomenon marked the emergence of a new style and narrative technique, which can be characterized as a genre collage . . . as a blending of codes' (Rapatzikou, 2004, p. 5).

2. Bret Easton Ellis' *Less Than Zero* (1985) and Jay McInerney's *Bright Lights, Big City* (1984) constitute examples of a kind of writing depicting the consumer capitalism and 'mass hypnosis', as Malcolm Bradbury puts it, that characterized American society in the 1980s. For more information, see Annesley, 1998, pp. 84–107; and Bradbury, 1992, pp. 261–84.

9   Towards a Politics of the Small Things: Arundhati Roy and the Decentralization of Authorship

1. Graham Huggan's *The Postcolonial Exotic: Marketing the Margins* (2001) discusses Roy, Rushdie and Vikram Seth in terms of a 'strategic exoticism' employed by

contemporary Indian fiction in English in order to make its voice heard by a worldwide audience (Huggan, 2001, p. vii).

2. In the history of the Booker, since 1969 when it was founded, Roy has been preceded chronologically by other outstanding Indian authors (such as V. S. Naipaul in 1971 and Salman Rushdie in 1981). But, as Marta Dvorak points out, she 'has arguably been said to be the first Indian woman to do so, since Ruth Prawer Jhabvala, awarded the Booker Prize in 1975 for her novel *Heat and Dust*, is technically not a native, but Indian by marriage' (Dvorak, 2002, p. 41).

3. The phrase belongs to Shashi Tharoor (1989), who traces a mythical history of Indian fiction back to the *Ramayana* and the *Mahabharata*, with a view to showing the origin of the epic proportions of many modern Indian novelists.

4. In their introduction to the collective volume *Reading Arundhati Roy's The God of Small Things* (2002), editors Carole and Jean-Pierre Durix note the 'extraordinary publishing success' of the book, as well as the criticism it received in India from 'people who objected to the implicit criticism of local political practices and to what was considered as offensive sex scenes'. They relate this criticism to India's 'uneasy relationship with some of its novelists writing in English as the "Rushdie affair" shows' (Durix and Durix, 2002, p. 5). The 'Rushdie affair' they mention is the *fatwa*, the death sentence pronounced by the Ayatollah Khomeini of Iran against Salman Rushdie's novel *The Satanic Verses* (1988), widely considered by Muslim audiences (including Indian ones) as a blasphemy against the Quran and the prophet Mohammed.

5. For a summary of these debates, see Dvorak, 2002, p. 45.

6. Scheduled castes and tribes, that is, former untouchables according to the official terminology used by the Government of India (GOI). In endnote 19 to 'The Greater Common Good' (Roy, 1999, p. 106), Roy refers to GOI (1988–89) 28th and 29th *Report of the Commissioner for Scheduled Castes and Scheduled Tribes*, New Delhi.

Part IV   Authorship and Criticism

10   The Decline of the Critic

1. This chapter was originally delivered as a plenary address at the conference 'New Visions: The Writer in Literature and Criticism' (February 2002) at the University of East Anglia, upon the idea of which this book is based.

Works Cited

Aarseth, E. J. (1997) *Cybertext: Perspectives on Ergodic Literature* (Baltimore, Md./London: Johns Hopkins University Press).

Abraham, T. (1998) 'An Interview with Arundhati Roy', *ARIEL*, vol. 29, no. 1 (January), pp. 89–92.

Acker, K. (1986) *Don Quixote which Was a Dream* (London: Paladin Grafton Books).

Anderson, N. F. (1987) *Woman against Women in Victorian England: A Life of Eliza Lynn Linton* (Bloomington, Ind.: Indiana University Press).

Annesley, J. (1998) *Blank Fictions: Consumerism, Culture and the Contemporary American Novel* (London: Pluto Press).

Argyros, E. (1999) *'Without Any Check of Proud Reserve'. Sympathy and its Limits in George Eliot's Novels* (New York: Peter Lang).

Ariès, P. (1981) *The Hour of Our Death*, trans. Helen Weaver (London: Allen Lane).

Arnold, M. (1960–77) *The Complete Prose Work of Matthew Arnold*, ed. R. H. Super, 11 vols (Ann Arbor, Mich.: University of Michigan Press).

Asbee, S. (1991) *Flann O'Brien* (Boston, Mass.: Twayne Publishers).

Ashton, R. (2004) 'Marian Evans [George Eliot]', *Oxford Dictionary of National Biography*, accessed on 25 May 2006 on http://www.oxforddnb.com/view/article/6794.

Bakhtin, M. (1984) *Problems of Dostoevsky's Poetics*, ed. and trans. Caryl Emerson (Minneapolis: Minnesota University Press).

Bakhtin, M. (1988) 'From the Prehistory of Novelistic Discourse', in David Lodge (ed.) *Modern Criticism and Theory: A Reader* (London: Longman), pp. 124–56.

Baldwin, D. G. (2002) 'Word Begets Image and Image Is Virus: Undermining Language and Film in the Works of William S. Burroughs', in Kostas Myrsiades (ed.) *The Beat Generation: Critical Essays* (New York: Peter Lang), pp. 155–78.

Barthelme, D. (1969) 'See the Moon?', *Unspeakable Practices, Unnatural Acts* (London: Cape), pp. 153–70.

Barthes R. (1977a) 'The Death of the Author', *Image, Music, Text*, trans. Stephen Heath (London: Fontana), pp. 142–8.

Barthes, R. (1977b) *Image, Music, Text*, trans. Stephen Heath (London: Fontana).

Beer, G. (1986) *George Eliot* (Brighton: Harvester).

Bell, B., P. Bennett and J. Bevan (eds) (2000) *Across Boundaries: The Book in Culture and Commerce* (Winchester: St Paul's Bibliographies/New Castle, DE: Oak Knoll Press).

Bell, M. (1988) *F. R. Leavis* (London: Routledge).

Bell, M. (2000) 'Victorian Sentimentality and Truth of Feeling', *Sentimentalism, Ethics and the Culture of Feeling* (London: Palgrave), pp. 119–49.

Bicknell, J. W. and C. L. Cline (1973) 'Who was Lady Morley?', *Victorian Newsletter*, vol. 40, pp. 28–31.

Biriotti, M. and N. Miller (eds) (1993) *What Is an Author?* (Manchester: Manchester University Press).

Black, G. D. (1994) *Hollywood Censored: Morality Codes, Catholics, and the Movies* (Cambridge: Cambridge University Press).

Boase, F. (1965) *Modern English Biography: Containing Many Thousands Concise Persons Who Have Died during the Years 1851–1900, with an Index of the Most Interesting Matter*, 6 vols (London: F. Gass).

Bolter, J. D. (1996) 'Ekphrasis, Virtual Reality, and the Future of Writing', in Geoffrey Nunberg (ed.) *The Future of the Book* (Berkeley, Calif.: University of California Press), pp. 253–72.

Bolter, J. D. and R. Grusin (1999) *Remediation: Understanding New Media* (Cambridge, Mass. London: MIT Press).

Boucicault, D. (1860) *The Colleen Bawn: or, the Brides of Garryowen. A Domestic Drama in Three Acts* (New York: T. H. French).

Boumelha, P. (1987) 'George Eliot and the End of Realism', in Sue Roe (ed.) *Women Reading Women's Writing* (Brighton: Harvester), pp. 13–35.

Bradbury, M. (1992) *The Modern American Novel* (Oxford: Oxford University Press).

Briggs, J. (1989) 'Women Writers and Writing for Children: From Sarah Fielding to E. Nesbit', in Gillian Avery and Julia Briggs (eds) *Children and Their Books: A Celebration of the Work of Iona and Peter Opie* (Oxford: Clarendon Press), pp. 221–50.

Brooker, J. (2003) 'A Balloon Filled with Verbal Gas: Blather and the Irish Ready-Made School', *Precursors and Aftermaths: Literature in English, 1914–1945*, vol. 2, no. 1, pp. 74–98.

Brooker, J. (2004) *Joyce's Critics: Transitions in Reading and Culture* (Madison, Wisc.: University of Wisconsin Press).

Brooker, J. (2005) *Flann O'Brien* (Plymouth: Northcote House).

Buford, B. (1997) 'Declarations of Independence', *The New Yorker*, 23 & 30 June, pp. 6–8.

Bunting, M. (2002) 'Grassroots Gamine: Arundhati Roy Is a Thrilling Political Icon Who Represents the Coming of Age of Feminism', *Guardian*, 7 March, in *Guardian Unlimited*, accessed 15 August 2004 on http://books. guardian.co.uk/news/articles/0,6109,663274,00.html.

Burke, S. (1995) 'Introduction: Reconstructing the Author', in Séan Burke (ed.) *Authorship: From Plato to the Postmodern. A Reader* (Edinburgh: Edinburgh University Press), pp. xv–xxx.

Burke, S. (1998) *The Death and the Return of the Author: Criticism and Subjectivity in Barthes, Foucault and Derrida* (Edinburgh: Edinburgh University Press).

Burroughs, W. S. (1962) *The Ticket That Exploded* (Paris: Olympia Press).

Burroughs, W. S. (1964) *Nova Express* (New York: Grove Press).

Burroughs, W. S. (1969) *The Wild Boys: A Book of the Dead* (New York: Grove Press).

Burroughs, W.S. (1974) *The Book of Breething* (Essex: OU-editions).

Burroughs, W. S. (1976) *Cobble Stone Garden* (New York: Cherry Valley Editions).

Burroughs, W. S. (1979) 'Electronic Revolution', *Ah Pook Is Here and Other Texts* (London: John Calder), pp. 123–57.

Burroughs, W. S. (1982) *Cities of the Red Night* (London: Picador).

Burroughs, W. S. (1983) *The Place of Dead Roads* (London: Calder).

Burroughs, W. S. (1985) 'On Coincidence', *The Adding Machine: Collected Essays* (London: Calder), pp. 97–103.

Burroughs, W. S. (1986a) *Queer* (London: Picador).

Burroughs, W. S. (1986b) *The Soft Machine* (London: Paladin).

Burroughs, W. S. (1987) *The Western Lands* (London: Penguin).

Burroughs, W. S. (1991) 'Screenwriting and the Potentials of Cinema', in Keith Cohen (ed.) *Writing in a Film Age: Essays by Contemporary Novelists* (Niwot, Col.: University Press of Colorado), pp. 55–81.

Burroughs, W. S. (1992) *Painting and Guns* (Madras: Hanuman Books).

Burroughs, W. S. (1993) *Naked Lunch* (London: Flamingo).

Burroughs, W. S. (2001) *Burroughs Live: The Collected Interviews of William S. Burroughs 1960–1997*, ed. Sylvère Lotringer (Los Angeles: Semiotext(e) Double Agents Series).

Burroughs, W. S. et al. (1960) *Minutes to Go* (Paris: Two Cities Editions).

Burroughs, W. S. and A. Ginsberg (1963) *The Yage Letters* (San Francisco: City Lights Books).

Burroughs, W. S. and B. Gysin (1979) *The Third Mind* (London: Calder).

Cambridge Quarterly, The (1996) (Special Issue: F. R. Leavis), vol. 25, no. 4.

Carpenter, W. B. (1877) 'The Radiometer and its Lessons', *Nineteenth Century*, vol. 1 (April), pp. 242–56.

Caughie, J. (ed.) (1981) *Theories of Authorship: A Reader* (London/New York: Routledge).

Cavallaro, D. (2000) *Cyberpunk and Cyberculture: Science Fiction and the Work of William Gibson* (New Brunswick, NJ/London: Athlone Press).

Cervantes, M. (2003) *The History and Adventures of the Renowned Don Quixote*, trans. Tobias Smollett (Athens, Ga./London: University of Georgia Press).

Chanda, T. (1997) 'Sexual/Textual Strategies in *The God of Small Things*', *Commonwealth Essays and Studies*, vol. 20, no. 1 (Autumn), pp. 38–44.

Chapman & Hall Minute Books, Reading University Library Archive Manuscript OC/1/4/2.

Chaudhuri Amit (ed.) (2002 [2001]) *The Picador Book of Modern Indian Literature* (London: Picador).

Cixous, H. (1991) 'The Laugh of the Medusa', in Robyn P. Warhol and Diane Price Herndl (eds) *Feminisms: An Anthology of Literary Theory and Criticism* (New Brunswick, NJ: Rutgers University Press), pp. 347–61.

Clissmann, A. (1975) *Flann O'Brien: A Critical Introduction to His Writings* (Dublin: Gill & Macmillan).

Cobley, P. (2001) *Narrative* (London: Routledge).

Connor, S. (2000) *Dumbstruck: A Cultural History of Ventriloquism* (Oxford: Oxford University Press).

Cook, P. (1981) 'The Point of Self-Expression in Avant-Garde Film', in John Coughie (ed.) *Theories of Authorship: A Reader* (London/New York: Routledge), pp. 271–81.

Cooper, D. (1994) *Closer* (London: Serpent's Tail).

Costello, P. and P. van de Kamp (1987) *Flann O'Brien: An Illustrated Biography* (London: Bloomsbury).

Cronin, A. (1989) *No Laughing Matter: The Life and Times of Flann O'Brien* (London: Grafton).

Cumming, T. (2004) 'In the Cut: William Burroughs's Radical Films Are Finally Released on DVD', *Guardian*, 23 August, section Review, p. 9.

Curwen, H. (1873) *A History of Booksellers: The Old and the New* (London: Chatto & Windus).

Darnton, R. (2002) 'What Is the History of Books?', in David Finkelstein and Alistair McCleery (eds) *The Book History Reader* (London: Routledge), pp. 9–26.

Deane, S. (1997) *Strange Country: Modernity and Nationhood in Irish Writing since 1790* (Oxford: Clarendon).

DeKoven, M. (2004) *Utopia Limited: The Sixties and the Emergence of the Postmodern* (Durham: Duke University Press).

DeLillo, D. (1989) *Americana* (New York: Penguin).

DeLillo, D. (1989) *Libra* (London: Penguin).

Denielewski, M. Z. (2000) *House of Leaves* (London: Anchor).

Dentith, S. (1986) ' "The Extension of Our Sympathies" ', *George Eliot* (Brighton: Harvester), pp. 30–55.

Derrida, J. (1978) 'Ellipsis', *Writing and Difference*, trans. Alan Bass (London/Chicago: Routledge & Kegan Paul/University of Chicago Press).

Derrida, J. (1987) *The Truth in Painting*, trans. Geoff Bennington and Ian McLeod (Chicago/London: University of Chicago Press).

Derrida, J. (1988) 'Signature, Event, Context', *Limited Inc.*, trans. Samuel Weber and Jeffrey Mehlman (Evanston, IL: Northwestern University Press), pp. 1–23.

Dictionary of National Biography (1908–09), 21 vols (London: Smith, Elder and Co.).

Dilthey, W. (1961) *Meaning in History. W. Dilthey's Thoughts on History and Society*, trans. H. P. Rickman (London: George Allen & Unwin).

Dilthey, W. (1988) *Introduction to the Human Sciences: An Attempt to Lay a Foundation for the Study of Society and History*, trans. Ramon J. Betanzos (Detroit: Wayne State University Press).

Dilthey, W. (1989–96) *Selected Works*, ed. Rudolf A. Makkreeel and Frithjof Rodi, 5 vols (Princeton, NJ: Princeton University Press).

Dilthey, W. (1992) *Der Aufbau der Geschichtlichen Welt in den Geisteswissenschaften, Gesammlte Schriften*, Vol. VIII (Stuttgart: Teubner).

Duncan, I. (1992) *Modern Romance and Transformations of the Novel: The Gothic, Scott, Dickens* (Cambridge: Cambridge University Press).

Duncan, I. (1993) 'Shadows of the Potentate: Scott in Hogg's Fiction', *Studies in Hogg and His World*, vol. 4, pp. 12–25.

Duncan, I. (1994) 'The Upright Corpse: Hogg, National Literature and the Uncanny', *Studies in Hogg and His World*, vol. 5, pp. 29–54.

Durix, C. and J. P. Durix (2002) 'Introduction', in Carole and Jean-Pierre Durix (eds) *Reading Arundhati Roy's The God of Small Things* (Dijon: Editions Universitaires de Dijon), pp. 1–5.

Dvorak, M. (2002)'Translating the Foreign into the Familiar: Arundhati Roy's Postmodern Sleight of Hand', in Carole and Jean-Pierre Durix (eds) *Reading Arundhati Roy's The God of Small Things* (Dijon: Editions Universitaires de Dijon), pp. 41–5.

Eagleton, T. (1976) *Marxism and Literary Criticism* (London: Methuen).

Eagleton, T. (1995) *Heathcliff and the Great Hunger: Studies in Irish Culture* (London: Verso).

Eagleton, T. (1997) *Saint Oscar and Other Plays* (Oxford: Blackwell).

Eagleton, T. (2003) *After Theory* (London: Penguin).

Easley, A. (2004) 'Gender and Representation: George Eliot in the 1850s and 1860s', *First Person Anonymous: Women Writers and Victorian Print Media, 1830–70* (Aldershot: Ashgate), pp. 117–52.

Eliot, G. (1885) *George Eliot's Life as Related in her Letters and Journals, Arranged and Edited by her Husband J. W. Cross*, 3 vols (Edinburgh/London: Blackwood).

Eliot, G. (1954–78) *The George Eliot Letters*, ed. Gordon S. Haight, 9 vols (New Haven, Conn.: Yale University Press).

Eliot, G. (1963a) 'Woman in France: Mme de Sablé', in Thomas Pinney (ed.) *Essays of George Eliot* (London: Routledge & Kegan Paul), pp. 52–81.

Eliot, G. (1963b) 'The Morality of Wilhelm Meister', in Thomas Pinney (ed.) *Essays of George Eliot* (London: Routledge & Kegan Paul), pp. 143–7.

Eliot, G. (1963c) 'Silly Novels by Lady Novelists', in Thomas Pinney (ed.) *Essays of George Eliot* (London: Routledge & Kegan Paul), pp. 300–24.

Eliot, G. (1990a) 'Review of John Ruskin's Modern Painters, Vol. III', in Antonia S. Byatt and Nicholas Warren (eds) *George Eliot: Selected Essays, Poems and Other Writings* (Harmondsworth: Penguin Classics), pp. 367–78.

Eliot, G. (1990b) 'The Natural History of German Life', in Antonia S. Byatt and Nicholas Warren (eds) *George Eliot: Selected Essays, Poems and Other Writings* (Harmondsworth: Penguin Classics), pp. 107–39.

Eliot, G. (1990c) 'Worldliness and Other-Worldliness: The Poet Young', in Antonia S. Byatt and Nicholas Warren (eds) *George Eliot: Selected Essays, Poems and Other Writings* (Harmondsworth: Penguin Classics), pp. 164–213.

Eliot, T. S. (1922) *The Waste Land* (New York: Boni & Liveright).

Eliot, T. S. (1932) 'Tradition and the Individual Talent', *Selected Essays* (London: Faber & Faber), pp. 13–22.

Eliot, T. S. (1944) *Four Quartets* (London: Faber).

Eliot, T. S. (1960) *The Sacred Wood* (London: Methuen).

Eliot, T. S. (1961) *Selected Essays* (London: Faber & Faber).

Eliot, T. S. (1974) *Collected Poems, 1909–1962* (London: Faber & Faber).

Eliot, T. S. (1975) *Selected Prose of T. S. Eliot*, ed. Frank Kermode (London: Faber & Faber).

Ellmann, R. (1961) *Yeats: The Man and the Masks* (London: Macmillan).

Ellis, B. E. (1985) *Less Than Zero* (New York: Simon & Schuster)

Ermath Deeds, E. (1985) *George Eliot* (Boston: Twayne Publishers).

Escher, M. C. (1972) *The Graphic Work of M. C. Escher. Introduced and Explained by the Artist*, trans. John E. Brigham (London: Pan Books/Ballantine).

Escott, T. H. S. Escott Papers 1079C. British Library Additional Manuscript 58787.

Everett, E. M. (1939) *The Party of Humanity: The 'Fortnightly Review' and its Contributors, 1865–1874* (Chapel Hill, NC: University of North Carolina Press).

Farnon, J. (1997) 'Motifs of Gaelic Lore and Literature in Anne Clune and Tess Hurson (eds) *An Beal Bocht'*, *Conjuring Complexities: Essays on Flann O'Brien* (Belfast: Institute of Irish Studies), pp. 89–109.

Ferris, I. (1991) *The Achievement of Literary Authority: Gender, History, and the Waverley Novels* (Ithaca, NY: Cornell University Press).

Ferris, I. (2002) *The Romantic National Tale and the Question of Ireland* (Cambridge: Cambridge University Press).

Fidler, R. (1999) *Mediamorphosis: Understanding New Media* (London: Sage).

Finkelstein, D. (2002) *The House of Blackwood: Author–Publisher Relations in the Victorian Era* (University Park, Penn.: Pennsylvania State University Press).

Finkelstein, D. and A. McCleery (eds) (2002) *The Book History Reader* (London: Routledge).

Flaubert, G. (1997) 'Letter to Mademoiselle Leroyer de Chantepie, 18 March 1857', *Selected Letters*, trans. Geoffrey Wall (London: Penguin), pp. 247–8.

Foucault, M. (1976) *The Archaeology of Knowledge*, trans. A. M. Sheridan Smith (New York: Harper Colophon).

Foucault, M. (1980) *Knowledge/Power: Selected Interviews and Other Writings 1972–1977*, trans. Colin Gordon *et al.* (New York: Harvester Wheatsheaf).

Foucault, M. (1988) 'What Is an Author?', in David Lodge (ed.) *Modern Criticism and Theory: A Reader* (London/New York: Longman), pp. 197–210.

Fraser, H., S. Green and J. Johnston (2003) *Gender and the Victorian Periodical* (Cambridge: Cambridge University Press).

Gaiman, N. *et al.* (1996) *The Sandman, Vol. IX, The Kindly Ones* (London: Titan).

Gerstner, D. A. and J. Staiger (eds) (2003) *Authorship and Film* (New York/London: Routledge).

Gibson, W. F. (1995) *Neuromancer* (London: HarperCollins).

Gibson, W. F. (2003) *Pattern Recognition* (London: Viking).

Gilbert, S. and S. Gubar (1979) *The Madwoman in the Attic: The Woman Writer and the Nineteenth-Century Imagination* (New Haven, Conn.: Yale University Press).

Ginsberg, A. (1959) *Howl and Other Poems* (San Francisco: City Lights).

Goffmann, E. (1975) *Frame Analysis: An Essay on the Organization of Experience* (Harmonsworth: Penguin).

Goodman, M. (1981) *Contemporary Literary Censorship: The Case of Burroughs' Naked Lunch* (Metuchen, NJ/London: The Scarecrow Press).

Gray, T. (1997) *The Lost Years: The Emergency in Ireland, 1939–45* (London: Little, Brown).

Griffin, G. (1829) *The Collegians*, 3 vols (London: Saunders & Otley).

Haight, Gordon S. (1968) *George Eliot: A Biography* (Oxford: Oxford University Press).

Hale, W. (1885) 'Note on J. W. Cross's Biography of George Eliot', *Athenaeum*, 28 November.

Hamer, D. A. (1968) *John Morley: Liberal Intellectual in Politics* (Oxford: Clarendon Press).

Hardy, B. (1985) 'George Eliot: Allegory and Analysis; Narrators, Actors and Readers', *Forms of Feeling in Victorian Fiction* (London: Peter Owen), pp. 131–57.

Hargreaves, G. D. (1971) ' "Correcting in the Slip": The Development of Galley Proofs', *The Library*, 5th series, vol. 26, no. 4, pp. 295–311.

Harris, O. (2003) *William Burroughs and the Secret of Fascination* (Carbondale, Ill.: Southern Illinois University Press).

Hasler, A. J. (1993) 'Reading the Land: James Hogg and the Highlands', *Studies in Hogg and His World*, vol. 4, pp. 57–82.

Hayles, N. K. (2002) 'Saving the Subject: Remediation in *House of Leaves*', *American Literature*, vol. 74, no. 4 (December), pp. 779–806.

Heath, S. (1989) 'Modern Literary Theory', *Critical Quarterly*, vol. 31, no. 2, pp. 35–49.

Heidegger, M. (1971a) *On the Way to Language*, trans. Peter D. Herz (New York: Harper & Row).

Heidegger, M. (1971b) *Poetry, Language, Thought*, trans. Albert Hofstadter (New York: Harper & Row).

Hill, N. (1937) *Think and Grow Rich* (New York: Ralston Book).

Hirsch, P. (2001) 'Ligginitis, Three Georges, Perie-zadeth and Spitting Critics, or "Will the Real Mr Eliot Please Stand Up?" ', Simon Avery and Andrew Maunder (eds) *Critical Survey* (Special Issue: Literature, Fame and Notoriety in the Nineteenth Century), vol. 13, no. 2, pp. 78–97.

Hirst, F. W. (1927) *Early Life and Letters of John Morley*, 2 vols (London: Macmillan).

Hogg, J. (1983) *Anecdotes of Sir Walter Scott*, ed. Douglas S. Mack (Edinburgh: Scottish Academic).

Hogg, J. (2001) *The Private Memoirs and Confessions of a Justified Sinner: Written by Himself: With a Detail of Curious Traditionary Facts and Other Evidence by the Editor*, ed. P. D. Garside (Edinburgh: Edinburgh University Press).

Hogg, J. (2003) *The Three Perils of Woman*, ed. David Groves, Antony J. Hasler and Douglas S. Mack (Edinburgh: Edinburgh University Press).

Houghton, W. E. *et al.* (ed.) (1966–89) *The Wellesley Index to Victorial Periodicals, 1824–1900. Tables of Contents and Identification of Contributors, with Bibliographies of Their Articles and Stories*, 5 vols (Toronto: University of Toronto Press).

Howe, E. (ed.) (1947) *The London Compositor: Documents Relating to Wages, Working Conditions and Customs of the London Printing Trade, 1785–1900*, (London: Bibliographical Society).

Huggan, G. (2001) *The Postcolonial Exotic: Marketing the Margins* (London: Routledge).

Hughes, T. (1970) *Crow: From the Life and Song of the Crow* (London: Faber & Faber).

Hunnisett, B. (1980) *Steel-Engraved Book Illustration in England* (London: Scolar Press).

Hunt, P. (ed.) (1992) *Literature for Children: Contemporary Criticism* (London: Routledge).

Hunt, P. (2001) *Children's Literature* (Oxford: Oxford University Press).

Huxley, T. H. (1869) 'On the Physical Basis of Life', *Fortnightly Review*, n.s. 5 (February), pp. 129–45.

James, A. (1981) *The Death and Letters of Alice James: Selected Correspondence*, ed. Ruth Bernard Yeazell (Berkeley, Calif./London: University of California Press).

Jameson, F. (2003) 'Fear and Loathing in Globalization', *New Left Review*, vol. 23 (September–October), pp. 105–14.

Jay, E. (1995) *Mrs Oliphant: 'A Fiction to Herself': A Literary Life* (Oxford:Clarendon Press).

Johns, A. (1998) *The Nature of the Book: Print and Knowledge in the Making* (Chicago/London: University of Chicago Press).

Jones, J. B. (1976) 'British Printers on Galley Proofs: A Chronological Reconsideration', *The Library*, 5th series, vol. 31, no. 2, pp. 105–17.

Joyce, J. (1992) *A Portrait of the Artist as a Young Man*, ed. Seamus Deane (Harmondsworth: Penguin).

Kamuf, P. (1988) *Signature Pieces: On the Institution of Authorship* (Ithaca: Cornell University Press).

Kendrick, M. (2001) 'Interactive Technology and the Remediation of the Subject of Writing', *Configurations: A Journal of Literature, Science and Technology*, vol. 9, no. 2, pp. 231–51.

Kenner, H. (1997) 'The Fourth Policeman', in Anne Clune and Tess Hurson (eds) *Conjuring Complexities: Essays on Flann O'Brien* (Belfast: Institute of Irish Studies), pp. 61–71.

Kiberd, D. (1995) *Inventing Ireland* (London: Jonathan Cape).

Kiberd, D. (2000) *Irish Classics* (London: Granta).

Knowles, J. (1877) 'Introduction to "Modern Symposium"', *Nineteenth Century*, vol. 1 (April), pp. 331.

Knowles, J. 'Letter from Knowles to Tennyson, 6 January 1877', Tennyson Research Centre, Lincoln Central Library.

Landow, G. (2001) 'Hypertext and Critical Theory', in David Trend (ed.) *Reading Digital Culture* (Malden, Mass/Oxford: Blackwell Publishers) pp. 98–108.

Laplanche, J. (1999) *Essays on Otherness*, trans. John Fletcher (London: Routledge).

'Last Words from Alexander Strahan about "The Contemporary Review" and Mr. J. T. Knowles', British Library Additional Manuscript 44453, f. 204.

Lawrence, D. H. (1924) *Studies in Classic American Literature* (London: Heinemann).

Lawrence, D. H. (1968) 'Introduction to *Memoirs of the Foreign Legion*', in Warren Roberts and Harry T. Moore (eds) *Phoenix II: Uncollected, Unpublished and Other Prose Works of D. H. Lawrence* (London: Heinemann), pp. 303–61.

Lawrence, D. H. (1981) *The Letters of D. H. Lawrence*, ed. George J. Zytaruk and James T. Boulton, Vol. II, June 1913–October 1916 (Cambridge: Cambridge University Press).

Lawrence, D. H. (1994) *Twilight in Italy and Other Essays*, ed. Paul Eggert (Cambridge: Cambridge University Press).

Leavis, F. R. (1930) *Mass Civilization and Minority Culture* (London: Folcroft).

Leavis, F. R. (1933) 'Under What King, Bezonian?', *Scrutiny*, vol. 1, no. 3, pp. 205–14.

Leavis, F. R. (1940–41) 'Education and the University', *Scrutiny*, vol. 9, pp. 314–15.

Leavis, F. R. (1948) *The Great Tradition: George Eliot, Henry James, Joseph Conrad* (London: Chatto & Windus).

Leavis, F. R. (1952) *The Common Pursuit* (London: Chatto and Windus).

Leavis, F. R. (1962) *Two Cultures? The Significance of C. P. Snow . . . Being the Richmond Lecture, 1962. With an Essay on Sir Charles Snow's Rede Lecture, by Michael Yudkin* (London: Chatto & Windus).

Leavis, F. R. (1969) *English Literature in Our Time and the University* (London: Chatto & Windus).

Leavis, F. R. (1975) *The Living Principle: 'English' as a Discipline of Thought* (London: Chatto & Windus).

Leavis, F. R. (1995) *F. R. Leavis: Essays and Documents*, ed. Ian McKillop and Richard Storer (Sheffield: Sheffield Academic Press).

Leavis, F. R. and Q. D. Leavis (1969) *Lectures in America* (London: Chatto and Windus).

Leavis, F. R. and Q. D. Leavis (1969) 'Yeats: The Problem and the Challenge', *Lectures in America by F. R. Leavis and Q. D. Leavis* (London: Chatto & Windus), pp. 59–81.

Leavis, Q. D. (1938) 'Caterpillars of the Commonwealth Unite!', *Scrutiny*, vol. 7, no. 2, pp. 203–14.

Lee, L. L. (1966) 'The Devil's Figure: James Hogg's *Justified Sinner*', *Studies in Scottish Literature*, vol. 3, no. 4, pp. 230–9.

Levine, C. (2003) *The Serious Pleasure of Suspense: Victorian Realism and Narrative Doubt* (London/Charlottesville, Va.: University of Virginia Press).

Lewes. G. H. (1847) 'The Condition of Authors in England, Germany, and France', *Fraser's Magazine* (March), pp. 285–95.

Linton Lynn, E. (1897) 'George Eliot', *Women Novelists of Queen Victoria's Reign: A Book of Appreciation by Mrs. Oliphant, Mrs. Linton, Mrs. Alexander, etc.* (London: Hurst & Blackett), pp. 61–115.

Linton Lynn, E. (1899) *My Literary Life* (London: Hodder & Stoughton).

Linton Lynn, E. (1979) '[Extract from] "Womanliness" (1883)', in Patricia Hollis (ed.) *Women in Public* (London: Allen & Unwin), pp. 20–1.

Lister, M. *et al.* (eds) (2003) *New Media: A Critical Introduction* (London/New York: Routledge).

Lodge, D. (1981) *Working with Structuralism: Essays and Reviews on Nineteenth- and Twentieth-Century Literature* (Boston, Mass./London: Routledge & Kegan Paul).

Love, H. (2002) *Attributing Authorship: An Introduction* (Cambridge: Cambridge University Press).

Lydenberg, R. (1987) *Word Cultures: Radical Theory and Practice in William S. Burroughs' Fiction* (Urbana, Ill.: University of Illinois Press).

Mack, D. S. (1999) 'Revisiting *The Private Memoirs and Confessions of a Justified Sinner*', *Studies in Hogg and His World*, vol. 10, pp. 1–26.

MacLachlan, R. W. (1983) 'Scott and Hogg: Friendship and Literary Influence', in J. H. Alexander and David Hewitt (eds) *Scott and His Influence: The Papers of the Aberdeen Scott Conference, 1982* (Aberdeen: Association for Scottish Literary Studies), pp. 331–40.

Makkreel, R. A. (1975) *Dilthey: Philosopher of the Human Studies* (Pinceton, NJ: Princeton University Press).

Marx, K. (1996) 'Uneven Character of Historical Development and Questions of Art (from *Grundrisse*)', in Terry Eagleton and Drew Milne (eds) *Marxist Literary Theory: A Reader* (Oxford: Basil Blackwell), pp. 34–5.

Maturin, C. R. (2000) *Melmoth the Wanderer*, ed. Victor Sage (London: Penguin).

McCormack, J. H. (ed.) (1998) *Wilde: The Irishman* (New Haven, Conn./London: Yale University Press).

McHale, B. (1987) *Postmodernist Fiction* (New York/London: Methuen).

McInerney, J. (1984) *Bright Lights, Big City* (New York: Vintage)

Meredith, G. (1970) *The Letters of George Meredith*, ed. Clarence L. Cline, 3 vols (Oxford: Clarendon Press).

Metcalf, P. (1980) *James Knowles: Victorian Editor and Architect* (Oxford: Clarendon Press).

Miles, R. (2002) 'Europhobia: The Catholic Other in Horace Walpole and Charles Maturin', in Avril Horner (ed.) *European Gothic: A Spirited Exchange, 1760–1960* (Manchester: Manchester University Press), pp. 84–103.

Miller, N. (1988) *Subject to Change: Reading Feminist Writing* (Ithaca, NY: Cornell University Press).

Minnis, A. (1984) *Medieval Theories of Authorship: Scholastic Literary Attitudes in the Later Middle Ages* (London: Scolar Press).

Minute Books for Chapman & Hall, Reading University Library Archive Manuscript DC/1/4/2.

Morley, J. (1874) 'On Frederic Harrison's Essay on German Church Law', *Fortnightly Review*, n.s.15 (February), pp. 293–4.

Morley, J. (1875) 'Diderot. Part I', *Fortnightly Review*, n.s. 17 (February), pp. 151–68.

Morley, J. (1878) 'Memorials of a Man of Letters', *Fortnightly Review*, n.s. 23 (April), pp. 596–610.

Morley, J. 'Letter to Henry Crompton, 27 Apr. 1869', British Library Additional Manuscript 71701, f. 5.

Morley, J. (1917) *Recollections*, 2 vols (London: Macmillan).

Morrison, G. *et al.* (1999) *The Invisibles: Counting to None* (New York: Vertigo, DC Comics).

Mozley, A. (1971) 'Review of *Adam Bede*', in David Caroll (ed.) *George Eliot: The Critical Heritage* (London: Routledge & Kegan Paul), pp. 86–103.

Mukherjee, M. (1971) *The Twice Born Fiction: Themes and Techniques of the Indian Novel in English* (New Delhi/London: Heinemann).

Murphy, P. J. (1992) 'Impersonation and Authorship in Romantic Britain', *English Literary History*, vol. 59, pp. 625–49.

Murphy, T. S. (1997) *Wising up the Marks: The Amodern William Burroughs* (Berkeley, Calif./London: University of California Press).

Nietzsche, F. W. (1997) *Untimely Meditations*, ed. Daniel Breazeale, trans. R. J. Hollingdale (Cambridge: Cambridge University Press).

O' Brien, F. (1967) *At Swim-Two-Birds* (London: Penguin).

O' Brien, F. (1968) *The Best of Myles: A Selection from 'Cruiskeen Lawn'*, ed. Kevin O'Nolan (New York: Walker & Company).

O' Brien, F. (1983) *The Hard Life: An Exegesis of Squalor* (London: Abacus).

O' Brien, F. (1988a) *Further Cuttings from Cruiskeen Lawn* (London: Grafton).

O' Brien, F. (1988b) *Myles before Myles: A Selection of the Earlier Writings of Brian O'Nolan*, ed. John Wyse Jackson (London: Grafton).

O' Brien, F. (1988c) *The Third Policeman* (London: Paladin).

O' Brien, F. (1991) *Stories and Plays* (London: Grafton).

O' Brien, F. (1993a) *The Dalkey Archive* (London: HarperCollins).

O' Brien, F. (1993b) *The Poor Mouth* (London: HarperCollins).

Oliphant. M. (1885) 'George Eliot's Obituary', *Edinburgh Review*, vol. 161, p. 540.

Oliphant M. (1990) *The Autobiography of Margaret Oliphant: The Complete Text*, ed. Elisabeth Jay (Oxford: Oxford University Press).

Onslow, B. (2000) *Women of the Press in Nineteenth-Century Britain* (New York: St. Martin's Press).

O'Toole, F. (1997) *The Lie of the Land: Irish Identities* (London: Verso).

Palgrave, F. (1869) 'On the Scientific Study of Poetry', *Fortnightly Review*, n.s. 6 (August), pp. 163–78.

Petrie, D. (1992) 'The Sinner and the Scholar', *Studies in Hogg and His World*, vol. 3, pp. 57–67.

Porush, D. (1987) 'Cybernauts in Cyberspace: William Gibson's *Neuromancer*', in George E. Slusser and Eric S. Rabkin (eds) *Aliens: The Anthropology of Science Fiction* (Carbondale/Edwardsville, Ill.: Southern Illinois University Press), pp. 168–78.

Punter, D. and E. Bronfen (2001) 'Gothic: Violence, Trauma and the Ethical', in Fred Botting (ed.) *The Gothic* (Woodbridge: D. S. Brewer), pp. 7–21.

Pyle, F. (1995) 'Sympathy, or the Imagination of Community', *The Ideology of Imagination: Subject and Society in the Discourse of Romanticism* (Stanford, Calif.: Stanford University Press), pp. 147–71.

Pynchon, T. (1967) *The Crying Lot of 49* (London: Cape).

Pynchon, T. (1991) *Vineland* (U.S.A.: Minerva).

Rapatzikou, T. G. (2001) 'Visualizations of Cyber-Gothic Bodies in William Gibson's Trilogy and the Art of the Graphic Novel', *Foundation: The International Review of Science Fiction*, vol. 30, no. 83, pp. 73–86.

Rapatzikou, T. G. (2004) *Gothic Motifs in the Fiction of William Gibson* (Amsterdam/New York: Rodopi Editions).

Robertson, F. (1994) *Legitimate Histories: Scott, Gothic and the Authorities of Fiction* (Oxford: Clarendon Press).

Robinson, J. *et al.* (1996) *Witchcraft* (London: Titan).

Rousseau, J. (1825), *Julie, ou la nouvelle Heloise* (Paris: De Bure).

Rowson, M. (1990) *The Waste Land* (Harmondsworth: Penguin).

Roy, A. (1997) *The God of Small Things* (London: Flamingo, 1997).

Roy, A. (1999) *The Cost of Living: 'The Greater Common Good' and 'The End of Imagination'* (London: Flamingo).

Rubinstein, J. (1993) 'Varieties of Explanation in *The Shepherd's Calendar*', *Studies in Hogg and His World*, vol. 4, pp. 1–11.

Rushdie, S. (1988) *The Satanic Verses* (London: Viking).

Rushdie, S. (1991) 'Imaginary Homelands', *Imaginary Homelands: Essays and Criticism 1981–1991* (London: Granta & Penguin), pp. 9–21.

Rushdie, S. (1995) *Midnight's Children* (London: Everyman's Library).

Rushdie, S. (1997) 'Damme, This Is the Oriental Scene for You!', *The New Yorker*, 23 & 30 June, pp. 50–61.

Rushdie, S. (2002) *Step Across This Line: Collected Non-Fiction 1992–2002* (London: Vintage).

Russell, P. and B. Russell (eds) (1966) *The Amberley Papers: Bertrand Russell's Family Background*, 2 vols (London: Allen & Unwin).

Russell, J. (2004) 'Guerrilla Conditions: Burroughs, Gysin, Balch Go to the Movies', in Davis Schneiderman and Philip Walsh (eds) *Retaking the Universe: William S. Burroughs in the Age of Globalization* (London: Pluto), pp. 161–74.

Rylance, R. and J. Simons (2001) 'Introduction: Why Study the Contexts of Literature?', in Rick Rylance and Judy Simons (eds) *Literature in Context* (London: Palgrave), pp. xv–xxix.

Sade, M. (1990) 'The Fruit of Revolutionary Tremors', in Victor Sage (ed.) *The Gothic Novel: A Casebook* (London: Macmillan), pp. 48–9.

Sage, V. (ed.) (1990) *The Gothic Novel: A Casebook* (London: Macmillan).

Sarris, A. (1962–63) 'Notes on the Auteur Theory in 1962', *Film Culture*, vol. 27 (Winter), pp. 1–8.

Scott, W. (1968) *Sir Walter Scott on Novelists and Fiction*, ed. Ioan Williams (London: Routledge & Kegan Paul).

Scott, W. (1980) *The Correspondence of Sir Walter Scott and Charles Robert Maturin*, ed. William McCarthy and Fanny E. Ratchford (London/New York: Garland Publishing).

Scott, W. (1986) *Waverley, or 'Tis Sixty Years Since'*, ed. Claire Lamont (Oxford: Oxford University Press).

Selby, H. (1966) *Last Exit to Brooklyn* (London: Calder & Boyars).

Shattock, J. (1989) *Politics and Reviewers: The Edinburgh and the Quarterly in the Early Victorian Age* (London/Leceister/New York: Leceister University Press).

Sheridan, N. (1985) 'Brian, Flann and Myles', in Rüdiger Imhof (ed.) *Alive-Alive O!: Flann O'Brien's 'At Swim-Two-Birds'*, (Dublin: Wolfhound Press), p. 72–81.

Showalter, E. (1977) *A Literature of Their Own: British Women Novelists from Brontë to Lessing* (Princeton, NJ/Guildford: Princeton University Press).

Silverman, K. (2001) 'The Author as Receiver', *October*, vol. 96 (Spring), pp. 17–34.

Simmons, J. (2002a) *The Arundhati Roy Web*: 'Childhood', accessed 15 August 2004 on http://website.lineone.net/~jon.simmons/roy/tgost2.htm.

Simmons, J. (2002b) *The Arundhati Roy Web*: 'On Writing', accessed 15 August 2004 on http://website.lineone.net/~jon.simmons/roy/tgost4.htm.

Small, H. (ed.) (2002) *The Public Intellectual* (Oxford: Basil Blackwell).

Shaw, I. (ed.) (2000) *The Oxford History of Ancient Egypt* (Oxford: Oxford University Press).

Spottiswoode & Co. Out-Letters Book of Spottiswoode & Co. 28 Dec. 1867 to May 1897, Essex Record Office Manuscript D/F 182/4/1/1.

Srebrnik, P. T. (1986) *Alexander Strahan: Victorian Publisher* (Ann Arbor, Mich.: University of Michigan Press).

Stark, S. (1999) *'Behind Inverted Commas': Translation and Anglo-German Cultural Relations in the Nineteenth-Century* (Clevedon: Multilingual).

Starobinskin, J. (1988) *Jean-Jacques Rousseau: Transparency and Obstruction*, trans. Arthur Goldhammer (Chicago/London: University of Chicago Press).

Sterne, L. (1988) *Tristram Shandy* (Milton Keynes: Open University).

Stevenson, A. L. (1954) *The Ordeal of George Meredith. A Biography* (London: Peter Owen).

Sutherland, J. (1978) *Victorian Novelists and Publishers* (Chicago: University of Chicago Press).

Swinburne, A. C. (1959–62) *The Swinburne Letters*, ed. Cecil Y. Lang, 6 vols (London: Yale University Press).

Tabbi, J. (2002) *Cognitive Fictions* (Minneapolis/London: Minnesota University Press).

Tharoor, S. (1989) *The Great Indian Novel* (London/New York: Viking).

Thieme, J. (2003) *Post-Colonial Studies: The Essential Glossary* (London: Arnold).

Tollemache, L. A. (1868) 'Historical Prediction', *Fortnightly Review*, n.s. 3 (March), pp. 295–310.

Toschi, L. (1996) 'Hypertext and Authorship', in Geoffrey Nunberg (ed.) *The Future of the Book* (Berkeley, Calif.: University of California Press), pp. 169–208.

Tracy, R. (1994) 'Introduction to Flann O'Brien (Myles na gCopaleen)', in Robert Tracy (ed.) *Rhapsody in Stephen's Green: The Insect Play* (Dublin: Lilliput Press), pp. 1–17.

Trollope, A. (1983) *The Letters of Anthony Trollope*, ed. John N. Hall, 2 vols (Stanford, Calif.: Stanford University Press).

Trollope, A. Manuscript Letters. Bodleian MS. Don. c. 10*, ff. 7–10.

Truffaut, F. (1976) 'A Certain Tendency of the French Cinema', in Bill Nichols (ed.) *Movies and Methods: An Anthology* (Berkeley, Calif./London: University of California Press), pp. 224–37.

Trumpener, K. (1993) 'National Character, Nationalist Plots: National Tale and Historical Novel in the Age of Waverley, 1806–1830', *English Literary History*, vol. 60, no. 2, pp. 685–731.

Turkle, S. (1996) 'Constructions and Reconstructions of the Self in Virtual Reality', in Timothy Druckrey (ed.) *Electronic Culture: Technology and Visual Representation* (New York: Aperture), pp. 354–65.

Tyndall, J. (1870) 'Climbing in Search of the Sky', *Fortnightly Review*, n.s. 7 (June), pp. 1–15.

Updike, J. (1997) 'Mother Tongues: Subduing the Language of the Colonizer', *The New Yorker*, 23 & 30 June, pp. 156–61.

Volney, C. F. (2000) *The Ruins, or, a Survey of the Revolutions of Empires*, trans. James Marshall (Otley: Woodstock Books).

Watson, T. (1877) 'The Abolition of Zymotic Disease', *Nineteenth Century*, vol. 1 (May), pp. 380–96.

Wiener, J. H. (ed.) (1985) *Innovators and Preachers: The Role of the Editor in England* (Westport, Conn.: Greenwood Press).

Wilde, O. (1992) 'The Critic as Artist', in Joseph Bristow (ed.) *The Importance of Being Earnest and Related Writings* (London: Routledge), pp. 95–163.

Willett, J. (1991) 'UGH . . .', in Jennie Skerl and Robin Lydenberg (eds) *William S. Burroughs at the Front: Critical Reception, 1959–1989* (Carbondale, Ill.: Southern Illinois University Press), pp. 41–4.

Woolf, V. (1971) 'George Eliot', *Collected Essays* (London: Hogarth Press), pp. 196–204.

Wordsworth, W. (1895) *The Poetical Works*, ed. Thomas Hutchinson (London: Henry Frowde).

Young, E. and G. Caveney (eds) (1992) *Shopping in Space: Essays in American 'Blank Generation' Fiction* (London: Serpent's Tail).

Young, S. (1997) 'Fact/Fiction: Cruiskeen Lawn, 1945–1966', in Anne Clune and Tess Hurson (eds) *Conjuring Complexities: Essays on Flann O'Brien* (Belfast: The Institute of Irish Studies), pp. 111–18.

Further Reading

These publications, which vary from author-orientated to interdisciplinary studies of authorship within and across particular periods, are supplementary to the works cited. Many of them have extensive bibliographies of primary sources that can be used for further reading. The aim of this bibliography is to offer further insight into the issues that this collection raises in relation to the different modes of authorship, as well as to cover other material or scholarly approaches that exceed its scope but are still related to its subject matter.

Agger, B. (1990) *The Decline of Discourse: Reading, Writing and Resistance in Postmodern Capitalism* (London: Falmer).

Andrzejczak, K. (1998) *The Writer in the Writing: Author as Hero in Postwar American Fiction* (San Francisco: International Scholars Publications).

Atwood, M. E. (2002) *Negotiating with the Dead: A Writer on Writing* (Cambridge: Cambridge University Press).

Bakutman, S. (1993) *Terminal Identity: The Virtual Subject in Postmodern Science Fiction* (Durham, NC: Duke University Press).

Batten, G. (1998) *The Orphaned Imagination: Melancholy and Commodity Culture in English Romanticism* (Durham, NC/London: Duke University Press).

Behar, R. and D. A. Gordon (eds) (1995) *Women Writing Culture* (Berkeley, Calif./London: University of California Press).

Bell, M. D. (2000) *Culture, Genre, and Literary Vocation: Selected Essays on American Literature* (Chicago: University of Chicago Press).

Benesch, K. (2002) *Romantic Cyborgs: Authorship and Technology in the American Renaissance* (Amherst, Mass.: University of Massachusetts Press/London: Eurospan).

Brake, L. (1994) *Subjugated Knowledges: Journalism, Gender and Literature in the Nineteenth Century* (London: Macmillan).

Brake, L. (ed.) (2001) *Print in Transition, 1850–1910: Studies in Media and Book History* (Basingstoke: Palgrave).

Brake, L. and J. F. Codell (eds) (2005) *Encounters in the Victorian Press: Editors, Authors, Readers* (Basingstoke: Palgrave).

Brake, L., A. Jones and L. Madden (eds) (1990) *Investigating Victorian Journalism* (London: Macmillan).

Brake, L., B. Bell and D. Finkelstein (eds) (2000) *Nineteenth-Century Media and the Construction of Identities* (Basingstoke: Palgrave).

Brown, A. L. (1995) *Fear, Truth, Writing: From Paper Village to Electronic Community* (Albany, NY: State University of New York Press).

Carringer, R. L. (2001) 'Collaboration and Concepts of Authorship', *PMLA*, vol. 116, no. 2 (March), pp. 370–9.

Chartier, R. (1994) *The Order of Books*, trans. Lydia Cochrane (Cambridge: Polity Press).

Clery, E. J., C. Franklin and P. Garside (eds) (2002) *Authorship, Commerce, and the Public: Scenes of Writing, 1750–1850* (Basingstoke: Palgrave).

Cognard-Black, J. (2004) *Narrative in the Professional Age: Transatlantic Readings of Harriet Beecher Stowe, George Eliot, and Elizabeth Stuart Phelps* (New York/London: Routledge).

Colby, R. (1990) 'Harnessing Pegasus: Walter Besant, *The Author*, and the Profession of Authorship', *Victorian Periodical Review*, vol. 23, p. 3, pp. 111–20.

Cook, P. and M. Bernink (eds) (1985) *The Cinema Book* (London: British Film Institute).

Coultrap-McQuin, S. (1990) *Doing Literary Business: American Women Writers in the Nineteenth Century* (Chapel Hill, NC: University of North Carolina Press).

Cross, N. (1985) *The Common Writer: Life in Nineteenth-Century Grub Street* (Cambridge: Cambridge University Press).

Dauber, K. (1990) *The Idea of Authorship in America* (Madison, Wisc./London: University of Wisconsin Press).

Dauber, K. (1999) 'Realistically Speaking: Authorship in the Late Nineteenth Century and Beyond', *American Literary History*, vol. 11, no. 2, pp. 378–90.

Deane, B. (2003) *The Making of the Victorian Novelist: Anxieties of Authorship in the Mass Market* (New York/London: Routledge).

Demoor, M. (ed.) (2004) *Marketing the Author: Authorial Personae, Narrative Selves and Self-Fashioning, 1880–1930* (Basingstoke: Palgrave).

Desroches, V. and G. Turnovsky (eds) (1995) *Authorship, Authority/Auteur, Autorite* (New York: Columbia University Press).

Dettmar K. J. H. and S. Watt (eds) (1996) *Marketing Modernisms: Self-Promotion, Canonization, Rereading* (Ann Arbor, Mich.: University of Michigan Press).

Donoghue, F. (1996) *The Fame Machine: Book Reviewing and Eighteenth-Century Literary Careers* (Stanford, Calif.: Stanford University Press/Cambridge: Cambridge University Press).

Easley, A. (2004) *First Person Anonymous: Women Writers and Victorian Print Media, 1830–1870* (Burlington, VT: Ashgate).

Eggert, P. and M. Sankey (eds) (1998) *The Editorial Gaze: Mediating Texts in Literature and the Arts* (New York/London: Garland Publications).

Ericson, L. (1996) *The Economy of Literary Form: English Literature and the Industrialization of Publishing, 1800–1850* (Baltimore, Md./London: Johns Hopkins University Press).

Feltes, N. N. (1993) *Literary Capital and the Late Victorian Novel* (Madison, Wisc./London: University of Wisconsin Press).

Ferguson, S. L. (2001) 'Dickens's Public Readings and the Victorian Author', *SEL: Studies in English Literature, 1500–1900*, vol. 41, pp. 729–49.

Fink, S. and S.S. Williams (eds) (1999) *Reciprocal Influences: Literary Production, Distribution and Consumption in America* (Columbus, Ohio: Ohio State University Press).

Fisher, J. L. (2002) *Thackeray's Skeptical Narrative and the 'Perilous Trade' of Authorship* (Aldershot: Ashgate).

Flint, K. (1993) *The Woman Reader 1837–1914* (Oxford: Clarendon Press).

Franklin, C. and P. Garside (eds) (2002), *Authorship, Commerce, and the Public: Scenes of Writing, 1750–1850* (Basingstoke: Palgrave).

Freedman, J. (1990) *Professions of Taste: Henry James, British Aestheticism and Commodity Culture* (Stanford, Calif.: Stanford University Press).

Freiburg, R. and J. Schnitker (eds) (2000) *'Do You Consider Yourself a Postmodern Author?': Interviews with Contemporary English Writers* (Munster: Lit Verlag).

Gagnier, R. (1991) *Subjectivities: A History of Self-Representation in Britain, 1832–1920* (New York/Oxford: Oxford University Press).

Gardiner, J. (2000) 'Recuperating the Author: Consuming Fictions of the 1990s', *Papers of the Bibliographical Society of America*, vol. 94, no. 2, pp. 255–74.

Gottdiener, M. (1995) *Postmodern Semiotics: Material Culture and the Forms of Postmodern Life* (Oxford: Basil Blackwell).

Griffin, R. J. (1999) 'Anonymity and Authorship', *New Literary History: A Journal of Theory and Interpretation*, vol. 30, pp. 877–95.

Griffin, R. J. (ed.) (2000) *The Faces of Anonymity: Anonymous and Pseudonymous Publication from the Sixteenth to the Twentieth Century* (Basingstoke: Palgrave).

Hadjiafxendi, K. and T. G. Rapatzikou (2005a) (eds) 'The American Culture-Industry of Image-Making; Part I', *European Journal of American Culture* (Special Issue), vol. 24, no. 1, pp. 3–45.

Hadjiafxendi, K. and T. G. Rapatzikou (2005b) (eds) 'The American Culture-Industry of Image-Making; Part II', *European Journal of American Culture* (Special Issue), vol. 24, no. 2, pp. 87–129.

Hadjiafxendi, K. and T. G. Rapatzikou (2005c) (eds) 'The American Culture-Industry of Image-Making; Part III', *European Journals of American Culture* (Special Issue), vol. 24, no. 3, pp. 173–203.

Haltof, M. (1994) ' "Producing" Auteur: The Concept of Authorship in Film Theory and Criticism', *S: European Journal for Semiotic Studies*, vol. 6, no. 1–2, pp. 349–69.

Hewitt, M. (1994) 'Postmodernism and the Graphic Arts: The Issues of Appropriation and Authorship', *Platte Valley Review*, vol. 22, no. 1, pp. 135–53.

Hix, H. L. (1990) *Morte d'Author: An Autopsy* (Philadelphia: Temple University Press).

Hogan, P. C. and L. Pandit (eds) (1995) *Literary India: Comparative Studies in Aesthetics, Colonialism, and Culture* (Albany, NY: State University of New York Press).

Howe, M. and S. A. Aguiar (eds) (2001) *He Said, She Says: An RSVP to the Male Text* (Madison, Wisc.: Fairleigh Dickinson University Press).

JanMohamed, A. R. (1985) 'The Economy of Manichean Allegory: The Function of Racial Difference in Colonialist Literature', *Critical Inquiry*, vol. 12 (Autumn), pp. 59–87.

Jarvis, R. (1976) *The Romantic Period: The Intellectual and Cultural Context of English Literature 1789–1830* (London: Longman).

Jones, A. (1996) *Powers of the Press: Newspapers, Power and the Public in Nineteenth-Century England* (Aldershot: Scolar Press).

Jones, S. W. (ed.) (1991) *Writing the Woman Artist: Essays on Poetics, Politics and Portraiture* (Philadelphia: University of Pennsylvania Press).

Jordan, J. O. and R. L. Patten (eds) (1995) *Literature in the Marketplace: Nineteenth-Century British Publishing and Reading Practices* (Cambridge: Cambridge University Press).

Joyce, M. (2000) *Othermindedness: The Emergence of Network Culture* (Ann Arbor, Mich.: University of Michigan Press).

Karell, L. K. (2002) *Writing Together/Writing Apart: Collaboration in Western American Literature* (Lincoln, Nebr.: University of Nebraska Press).

Kastely, J. L. (1997) *Rethinking the Rhetorical Tradition: From Plato to Postmodernism* (New Haven, Conn./London: Yale University Press).

Keen, P. (ed.) (2004) *Revolutions in Romantic Literature: An Anthology of Print Culture 1780–1832* (Ontario: Broadview).

King, A. and J. Plunkett (eds) (2004) *Popular Print Media 1820–1900*, 3 vols, (London: Routledge).

King, A. and J. Plunkett (eds) (2005) *Victorian Print Media: A Reader* (Oxford: Oxford University Press).

Kingery, D. (ed.) (1996) *Method and Theory of Material Culture Studies* (Washington, DC: Smithsonian).

Kittler, F. A. (1990) *Discourse Networks 1800/1900*, trans. Michael Metteer with Chris Cullens (Stanford, Calif.: Stanford University Press).

Koestenbaum, W. (1989) *Double Talk: The Erotics of Male Literary Collaboration* (New York/London: Routledge).

Kropf, D. G. (1994) *Authorship as Alchemy: Subversive Writing in Pushkin, Scott, Hoffmann* (Stanford, Calif.: Stanford University Press/Cambridge: Cambridge University Press).

Lang, A. S. (1992) 'Class and the Strategies of Sympathy', in Shirley Samuels (ed.) *The Culture of Sympathy: Race, Gender and Sentimentality in Nineteenth-Century America* (New York: Oxford University Press), pp. 128–42.

Leader, Z. (1996) *Revision and Romantic Authorship* (Oxford: Clarendon Press).

London, B. (1999) *Writing Double: Women's Literary Partnerships* (Ithaca, NY/London: Cornell University Press).

McGann, J. (2001) *Radiant Textuality: Literature after the World Wide Web* (New York: Palgrave).

Meyer M. J. (ed.) (2004) *Literature and the Writer* (Amsterdam/New York: Rodopi).

Michie, E. B. (1993) *Outside the Pale: Cultural Exclusion, Gender Difference, and the Victorian Woman Writer* (Ithaca, NY: Cornell University Press).

Regard, F. (ed.) (2003) *Mapping the Self: Space, Identity, Discourse in British Auto/Biography* (Saint-Étienne: Publications de l' Université de Saint-Étienne).

Newlyn, L. (2000) *Reading, Writing and Romanticism: The Anxiety of Reception* (Oxford: Oxford University Press).

Pastorino, G. (2000) 'The Death of the Author and the Power of Addiction in *Naked Lunch* and *Blade Runner*', in Karen Sayer and John Moore (eds) *Science Fiction, Critical Frontiers* (London: Macmillan/New York: St. Martin's, Press), pp. 100–15.

Perloff, M. (2002) *21st-Century Modernism: The 'New' Poetics, Blackwell Manifestos* (Oxford: Blackwell).

Pykett, L. (1995) *Engendering Fictions: The English Novel in the Early Twentieth Century* (London: E. Arnold).

Pyle, F. (1995) *The Ideology of Imagination: Subject and Society in the Discourse of Romanticism* (Stanford, Calif.: Stanford University Press).

Raven, J., H. Small and N. Tadmor (eds) (1996) *The Practice and Representation of Reading in England* (Cambridge: Cambridge University Press).

Riley, D. (2000) *The Words of Selves: Identification, Solidarity, Irony* (Stanford, Calif.: Stanford University Press).

Rowland, G. (1996) *Literature and the Marketplace: Romantic Writers and their Audiences in Great Britain and the United States* (Lincoln, Nebr./London: University of Nebraska Press).

Schatz, T. (ed.) (2004) *Hollywood: Critical Concepts in Media and Cultural Studies*, Vol. II, *Formal–Aesthetic Dimensions: Authorship, Genre and Stardom* (London: Routledge).

Schleifer, R. (2000) *Analogical Thinking: Post-Enlightenment Understanding in Language, Collaboration, and Interpretation* (Ann Arbor, Mich.: University of Michigan Press).

Sedgwick, E. (2000) 'Magazines and the Profession of Authorship in the United States, 1840–1900', *Papers of the Bibliographical Society of America*, vol. 94 (September), pp. 399–425.

Shiffer, M. B. (1999) *The Material Life of Human Beings: Artifacts, Behaviour and Communication* (London: Routledge).

Singley, C. J. and S. E. Sweeney, (eds) (1993) *Anxious Power: Reading, Writing, and Ambivalence in Narrative by Women* (Albany: State University of New York Press).

Sloane, S. (2000) *Digital Fictions: Storytelling in a Material World* (Stamford, Conn.: Ablex Pub).

Stillinger, J. (1991) *Multiple Authorship and the Myth of Solitary Genius* (New York/Oxford: Oxford University Press).

Suleiman, S. R. and I. Crossman (eds) (1980) *The Reader in the Text* (Princeton, NJ: Princeton University Press).

Trimbur, J. (2000) 'Agency and the Death of the Author: A Partial Defense of Modernism', *JAC: Journal of Composition Theory*, vol. 20, no. 2, vol. 283–98.

Vanderbilt, A. T. (1999) *The Making of a Bestseller: From Author to Reader* (Jefferson, N.C.; London: McFarland).

Walder, D. (ed.) (2001) *The Nineteenth-Century Novel: Identities* (London: Routledge).

Waldron, K. E. (2000) 'No Separations in the City: The Public–Private Novel and Private–Public Authorship', in Monika M. Elbert (ed.) *Separate Spheres No More: Gender Convergence in American Literature, 1830–1930* (Tuscaloosa, Ala.: University of Alabama Press) pp. 92–113.

Weber, R. (1997) *Hired Pens: Professional Writers in America's Golden Age of Print* (Athens, Ohio: Ohio University Press).

Wells, P. *Animation and America: Cartoons to Computers* (Keele: Keele University Press, 1999).

Wells, P. (2002) *Animation: Genre and Authorship* (London: Wallflower).

Willison, I., W. Gould and W. Chernaik (eds) (1996) *Modernist Writers and the Marketplace* (London: Macmillan).

Wirtén, E. H. (2004) *No Trespassing: Authorship, Intellectual Property Rights, and the Boundaries of Globalization* (Toronto, Ont./London: University of Toronto Press).

Yellowlees, D. J. (1999) *The End of Books – or Books Without End?: Reading Interactive Narratives* (Ann Arbor, Mich.: University of Michigan Press).

Zurbrugg, N. (1984) 'Burroughs, Barthes, and the Limits of Intertextuality', *The Review of Contemporary Fiction*, vol. 4, no. 1, pp. 86–107.

Index

Aarseth, Espen J. 148–9, 153
Abraham, Taisha 173
academia 11–12, 191; *see also* canon,
     criticism, politics, professionalism
accountability 110
Acker, Kathy 115, 126
addiction 113
advertising 58, 156
aesthetic(s): and authorship 4, 6, 51,
     114; and MUDs 153; art 199n;
     constraints 34, 54; discourse 33,
     35, 40; function 3, 47, 49;
     judgement 34, 55, 83, 199n;
     language 40; literary 148, 152;
     modernist 5–8, 109; of feeling 43,
     54, 197n; of sympathy 34–6, 40,
     47; postmodernist 9–12; Romantic
     190; *see also* art, authorship
affect 6, 33–5, 40, 42, 47; *see also*
     authorship, George Eliot, reader
agency 11–12, 43, 126, 136
allegory 21, 27, 175; allegorical
     figure 177
allusion 21, 42, 141, 143
ambiguity 84, 115; and language
     166, 170
Anderson, Benedict 49
Anderson, Fix Nancy 186
Annesley, James 121, 200n, 202n
anonymity 3, 33, 43, 45–7, 62, 95, 104,
     137, 148; of narrator 98; *see also*
     author, professionalism
Anti-philosophy 198
anxiety 34, 41, 43, 46, 48–9, 64, 67, 71,
     103; and personality 48; of
     influence 140, 166
Argosy, The 44
Argyros, Ellen 33, 197n
Ariès, Philippe 126
Arnold, Matthew 7, 56, 64, 68, 76,
     85–7, 186, 189–92; *see also* culture,
     tradition

art: 2, 6, 33, 35–7, 40–1, 43, 47, 52–3,
     79, 82–4, 88, 108–10, 125–6, 146–7,
     160–1, 190, 193, 199n; art criticism
     57; art work 77, 146, 160; artefact
     9, 110, 119, 123, 126, 148, 161;
     artist 3, 9, 40, 75–9, 81–3, 100,
     109, 111–12, 117, 120–1, 126, 132,
     143, 145; artistic achievement 83;
     artistic creation 127, 145; artistic
     expression 116, 128; artistic
     impersonality 82; artistic media
     145; artistic trends 5; artistic vision
     117; artistic will 76, 83; as product
     52; as religion 109; computer art
     project 158; contemporary art 53;
     digital art 10, 145, 150, 158–60;
     European art 87; literary artifice
     54; *see also* critic, culture, discourse,
     language
artificial Intelligence 155
Asbee, Sue 98
Athenaeum 50
auctor 126, 200n
auteur: 117–19, 123, 127; and *auctoritas*
     200n; and avant-garde film 118;
     and personality 118; auteur theory
     117; *see also* criticism, film, theory
author: absence of 3, 15; and
     anonymity 45, 95; and character
     49, 97, 99, 102; and control 116;
     and critics 185; and cut-up text
     114–15, 121; and digital
     technologies 145; and ego 75;
     and Enlightenment 16; and film
     121, 123, 128; and hypertext 150;
     and identity 8; and impersonality
     83, 107; and intention 84; and
     literary market-place 5; and
     modernism 4; and personality
     3–4, 7, 85; and postmodernism 4,
     128; and print culture 35; and
     reader 2, 44, 49, 76, 105, 112–13,
     147, 149, 152, 155, 158, 161–2, 191;